Post-Soviet Civil Society

I0127704

The development of civil society has varied greatly across the former Soviet Union. The Baltic states have achieved a high level of integration with the West and European Union membership, while some regions in Russia lag far behind.

Now, for the first time, there is a comparative study of civil society and democratization in different regions across post-Soviet national borders. *Post-Soviet Civil Society* offers unique data on developments in Russia, Estonia, Latvia and Lithuania. Applying an innovative analytical framework derived from theories of democratization, civil society, social movements and transnational relations, the researcher was able to formulate broader comparisons and generalizations without neglecting the specific post-Soviet context. Providing a systematic comparison across civil society sectors as well as regions, this book includes sections on NGOs, the relationship between state and civil society, and transnationalization. Quantitative survey data is combined with qualitative interviews and case study research to both confirm previous findings about the weakness of post-communist civil society and to qualify previous research in a number of ways.

Post-Soviet Civil Society will be of interest not only to scholars and students of Russian and East European politics, but also to those with a general interest in democratization and civil society.

Anders Uhlin is Associate Professor of Political Science at Lund University, Sweden. His main fields of research are democratization, civil society and transnational relations. Previous publications include *Indonesia and the 'Third Wave of Democratization'* (Curzon, 1997) and *Transnational Activism in Asia* (Routledge, 2004) (co-edited with Nicola Piper).

BASEES/Routledge Series on Russian and East European Studies

Series editor:

Richard Sakwa, Department of Politics and International Relations, University of Kent

Editorial Committee:

George Blazyca, Centre for Contemporary European Studies, University of Paisley

Terry Cox, Department of Government, University of Strathclyde

Rosalind Marsh, Department of European Studies and Modern Languages, University of Bath

David Moon, Department of History, University of Strathclyde

Hilary Pilkington, Centre for Russian and East European Studies, University of Birmingham

Stephen White, Department of Politics, University of Glasgow

This series is published on behalf of BASEES (the British Association for Slavonic and East European Studies). The series comprises original, high-quality, research-level work by both new and established scholars on all aspects of Russian, Soviet, post-Soviet and East European Studies in humanities and social science subjects.

Post-Soviet Civil Society

Democratization in Russia and the
Baltic States

Anders Uhlin

Routledge
Taylor & Francis Group

LONDON AND NEW YORK

First published 2006
by Routledge
2 Park Square, Milton Park, Abingdon, Oxon, OX14 4RN

Simultaneously published in the USA and Canada
by Routledge
270 Madison Ave, New York NY 10016

Routledge is an imprint of the Taylor & Francis Group

Transferred to Digital Printing 2007

© 2006 Anders Uhlin

Typeset in Perpetua by
Keystroke, Jacaranda Lodge, Wolverhampton

All rights reserved. No part of this book may be reprinted or reproduced
or utilised in any form or by any electronic, mechanical, or other means,
now known or hereafter invented, including photocopying and recording,
or in any information storage or retrieval system, without permission in
writing from the publishers.

British Library Cataloguing in Publication Data
A catalogue record for this book is available from the British Library

Library of Congress Cataloging in Publication Data
Uhlin, Anders.
Post-Soviet civil society : democratisation in Russia and the Baltic States /
Anders Uhlin.
p. cm. — (BASEES/Routledge series on Russian and East European
Studies ; 25)
Simultaneously published in the USA and Canada.
Includes bibliographical references and index.
1. Former Soviet republics–Politics and government. 2. Democratization–
Former Soviet republics. 3. Civil society–Former Soviet republics.
4. Post-communism–Former Soviet republics. I. Title. II. Series.
JN6531.U35 2005
300'.947—dc22   2005004827

ISBN10: 0–415–36804–9 (hbk)
ISBN10: 0–415–44405–5 (pbk)

ISBN13: 978–0–415–36804–9 (hbk)
ISBN13: 978–0–415–44405–7 (pbk)

To Ameli and Alva

Contents

Figures and tables

Figures

Tables

Acknowledgements

Research for this book was carried out within a research project funded by the Swedish Baltic Sea Foundation. I would like to express my sincere gratitude to the other project participants for excellent cooperation throughout the project. They include the project coordinator Professor Sten Berglund and PhD-candidates Jan Björklund, Per-Ola Nilsson and Linda Åström. I would also like to thank my colleagues at Södertörns högskola (University College), my professional home during most of the work with this book, as well as colleagues at my new (and old) home institution: the Department of Political Science at Lund University.

The surveys, which form a major part of my empirical material, could not have been carried out without the hard work of a number of local research partners in Russia and the Baltic states. They include Dr. Elena Belokurova and her team in St Petersburg, Dr Vasili Rudenko and his team in Sverdlovsk, Dmitri Ivanov and his team in Novgorod, Katya Tatarinova and her team in Pskov, Olga Grigoreva, Sveta Yakovleva, Andrey Efimov, Mikhail Orekhov, Katya Romas, and Tanya Sovenko in Kaliningrad, Anneli Tarkmeel and her team in Estonia, Madara Grinsteine and her team in Latvia and Vaidas Morkevicius and his team in Lithuania. Thanks also go to Per Sjapiro, Mattias Ågren and Fredrik Jörgensen for recruiting interviewers in Kaliningrad, Novgorod and Pskov respectively. The surveys were a cooperative undertaking within the project, but Linda Åström in particular made a fantastic job in all phases of the difficult work with the surveys. Johnny Rodin, who worked as a research assistant for the project, also made an excellent job in coordinating the interviews in the Russian regions and coding the huge material. Thank you very much for this!

When conducting qualitative interviews Dr Elena Belokurova in St Petersburg, Dmitri Ivanov in Novgorod and Dmitri Vishernyovin in Pskov were immensely helpful in arranging interviews and (when needed) acting as interpreters. I am very grateful for their very competent assistance.

During the early phases of the research project, discussions with a number of Russian researchers were very important for the elaboration of the research strategy. I would especially like to thank Dr Grigori Golosov, Dr Anna Temkina and Dr Elena

Zdravomyslova at the European University in St Petersburg, Professor Boris Grinchel at the Eurograd Institute in St Petersburg, Dr Alexander Duka at the Russian Academy of Sciences and Viktor Vorenkov and Elena Nikiforova at the Centre for Independent Social Research in St Petersburg.

A number of colleagues have read whole or parts of my manuscript and given me valuable comments and advice, for which I am very grateful. In addition to the already mentioned project participants they include Dr Caroline Boussard, Dr Michal Bron, Anna Jonsson, Tove Lindén, Associate Professor Bo Petersson, Johnny Rodin and Pelle Åberg. I am also grateful for very constructive comments from Routledge's anonymous reviewer.

Jan Björklund helped me with the transliteration of Russian names and words and worked very hard with the translation of some Russian texts. Thank you very much for this!

I would also like to thank Peter Sowden, editor at Routledge, for his professional assistance in the process of producing this book.

Last, but not least, my sincere gratitude goes to my beloved Ameli and Alva who mean everything to me and to whom this book is dedicated.

Anders Uhlin
Lund, December 2004

Abbreviations

AFL-CIO	American Federation of Labour – Congress for Industrial Organization
DPR	Democratic Party of Russia
DU	Democratic Union
FNPR	Federation of Independent Trade Unions of Russia
GONGO	governmentally organized non-governmental organization
GRINGO	governmentally regulated and initiated non-governmental organization
INGO	international non-governmental organization
IREX	International Research and Exchanges Board
KEDR	Constructive Ecological Movement of Russia
MANGO	manipulated non-governmental organization
NED	National Endowment for Democracy
NGO	non-governmental organization
RHhDD	Russian Christian Democratic Movement
RPR	Republic Party of Russia
SDPR	Social Democratic Party of Russia
SEU	Social-Ecological Union
Sida	Swedish International Development Cooperation
SM	social movement
SMO	social movement organization
SWC	Soviet Women's Committee
TACIS	Technical Assistance to the Commonwealth of Independent States
TSM	transnational social movement
TSMO	transnational social movement organization
URW	Union of Russia's Women
USAID	United States Agency for International Development
USSR	Union of Soviet Socialist Republics

Russian words have been transliterated using the British Standard system.

1 Introduction

Five years after his sudden rise to presidential power following Boris Yeltsin's New Year resignation, Vladimir Putin has taken a firm grip on Russian politics. A number of undemocratic measures – not least related to the brutal warfare in Chechnya and the 'war on terrorism' – make many observers of Russia warn that the country is heading towards a new form of authoritarian rule. Whatever the future path taken, it is clear that the process of democratization in Russia has experienced severe obstacles. In a state with increasing authoritarian tendencies, the role of civil society as a potential democratic corrective on the state becomes extremely important. Post-Soviet civil society in Russia, however, is generally described as weak (e.g. Howard 2003; White and McAllister 2004). It might rightly be questioned to what extent Russian civil society can function in a pro-democratic way.

Meanwhile, Estonia, Latvia and Lithuania have experienced a more profound process of democratization and are, since May 2004, members of the European Union. However, there have been problems in the process of democratization in these countries too, not least related to the treatment of Russian-speaking minorities in Latvia and Estonia. Like Russia, the Baltic states suffer from a problematic Soviet heritage. Also in these countries the role of civil society in the post-transition context is unclear. By including the Baltic states in the study, we get interesting points of reference for an in-depth examination of post-Soviet civil society in Russia.

It is often argued that post-communist civil society is comparatively weak, but there is a lack of solid data on the specific problems of contemporary post-Soviet civil society. Acknowledging the enormous variation within the huge Russian federation (as well as within the much smaller Baltic states), this book offers unique data on civil society developments in different regions in Russia, Estonia, Latvia and Lithuania. It presents a systematic cross-regional comparative analysis of the relationship between civil society and the state in the post-Soviet context. Furthermore, the book distinguishes between developments within different civil society sectors and pays special attention to the transnationalization of parts of post-Soviet civil society. Through this analysis, it is hoped, we can get a better base for understanding democratic prospects in Russia as well as in the Baltic states.

This introductory chapter provides a brief overview of previous research in this field, presents the research problem and elaborates the research design of the study, and ends with a brief outline of the book.

Previous research on post-Soviet civil society

The unexpected collapse of communist regimes in Eastern Europe and the USSR stimulated extensive and intensive research. Area specialists as well as comparativists have offered us a multitude of data and interpretations of these processes of regime transition and democratization. However, whereas a large amount of research on democratization on the national level has given us a good understanding of such processes, comparatively little is known about democratization on the local level. Even less has been done on the role of transnational relations in the process of democratization. And the impact of transnational relations on local democratization is certainly an under-researched problem area. This is true not only for the post-communist context, but also in general.

Much research on democratization investigates the role of civil society. Despite the growing interest in this field, there is still a lack of solid data on contemporary civil societies in the post-communist countries. Too often civil society is conceived as independent from and opposed to the state in a zero-sum way. The complex relationships and unclear boundaries between civil society, the state and other social spheres do not always get sufficient attention. Furthermore, civil society is mostly conceptualized and analysed as a geographically limited entity in relation to the state. Until recently there has been a lack of transnational perspectives, which seems strange considering that '[u]nlike the state, civil society is not territorially bound. It is a field of action whose boundaries can shift to suit the requirements of new issues and changing circumstances.' (Camilleri and Falk 1992: 210).

The major actors in civil society – social movements and non-governmental organizations (NGOs) – may play an important role in promoting or resisting democratization. Increasingly these actors operate across state boundaries. The independent labour union and pro-democracy movement Solidarity, for instance, was the driving force behind the process of democratization in Poland. Part of its strength was the contacts and cooperation it had with actors in other countries. Popular Fronts in the Baltic states also benefited from transnational support. Since the breakdown of communist regimes, new civil society groups have emerged, often supported from abroad. Their transnational relations and their impact on local democracy remain comparatively unresearched.

Previous research on post-communist (and more specifically post-Soviet)[1] civil society has mainly been country-specific. There are several case studies on civil society in Russia (e.g. Devlin 1995; Fish 1995; Gill and Markwick 2000; Marsh 2000a; Weigle 2000; Caiazza 2002) including some valuable contributions from Russian researchers (e.g. Temkina 1997; Kholodkovsky 1998; Volodin *et al.* 1998;

Golenkova 1999; Shineleva 2002)[2] whereas the Baltic states have received far less scholarly attention in this respect (but see Latvia Human Development Reports and several publications by the Baltic Data House for empirical data on civil society in Latvia, as well as Ostrowska 1997; Zepa 1999; Karklins and Zepa 2001). Comparative cross-country studies on post-communist civil society are also relatively rare, although Weigle and Butterfield (1992), Bernhard (1993); Berglund *et al.* (2001); Gill (2002); Howard (2003) and Kopecky and Mudde (2003) have made important contributions. A general conclusion from most of these studies is that post-communist civil societies – not least in the case of Russia – are weak and fragmented.

Most studies tend to focus on civil society at the national level. Research on post-Soviet civil society on local and regional levels indicates significant differences in civil society development within a single country (cf. Duncan 1992; Duka *et al.* 1995; Fish 1995).

Much research on post-Soviet civil society tends to be mainly descriptive, but there are also several theoretically informed studies, which apply theoretical frameworks constructed within general democratization, civil society and social movement theory. The best research combines theoretical sophistication with in-depth empirical research. For instance, Fish (1995) provides an insightful analysis of the new political movements that emerged under *perestroika* and *glasnost*, solidly grounded in comparative political theory. Sperling (1999) offers a thoroughly researched account of the Russian women's movement systematically analysed from a political opportunity perspective. Zdravomyslova (1996) also applies the political opportunity framework as well as other concepts from social movement theory to the case of the Russian pro-democracy movement.

Most research on post-Soviet civil society has a more narrow focus on one specific issue area – especially women (Essig and Mamonova 1991; Nechemias 1991; Racioppi and O'Sullivan See 1997; Temkina 1997; Berthusen Gottlick 1999; Sperling 1999; Dawn Hemment 2000; Henderson 2000, 2003; Ferree and Risman 2001; McIntosh Sundstrom 2002; Richter 2002), but also labour (Bova 1991; Sedaitis 1991; Aves 1992; Temkina 1997; Crowley 2002; Kubicek 2002), environmentalism (Ziegler 1991; Wolfson and Butenko 1992; Henry 2002; Powell 2002; Crotty 2003) and social welfare NGOs (White 1999). There are also a few studies of civil society as a whole (e.g. Evans Jr. 2002; Hale 2002), but systematic comparisons across sectors are rare.

More research has focused on the dramatic years of *glasnost* and *perestroika* when independent civil society groups emerged (Petro 1991; Rau 1991; Sedaitis and Butterfield 1991; Hosking *et al.* 1992; Miller 1992; Karklins 1994; Lieven 1994; Urban 1997; White 1999). So far there is much less research on civil society after the transition, especially in the case of the Baltic states (but see Ruutsoo 2002). Two special issues of the journal *Demokratizatsiya* have provided a much-needed account of the problems of Russian civil society at the turn of the century. There are also some useful Russian publications, including Shineleva (2002) and Kholodkovsky (1998), with a particularly interesting analysis of corporativist tendencies in state–civil society relations.

Most of this research focuses on domestic factors. The international – or transnational – dimension is often neglected (but see Patomäki and Pursiainen 1998; 1999) although foreign funding of NGOs has received considerable scholarly attention. These studies tend to stress negative consequences of foreign aid upon the development of civil society, pointing out the lack of grassroots connections of many foreign-funded NGOs (Henderson 2003; Henry 2001; McIntosh Sundstrom 2001; Mendelson and Glenn 2002; Sundstrom 2003). A few studies have also stressed the importance of transnational activism for the transformation of communist regimes (Cortright 1993; Chilton 1994; Evangelista 1999; Thomas 1999).

The research problem

This study aims at contributing to the field of democratization studies and civil society research in general and the specific problems of post-Soviet democratization in particular. Through an examination of local civil societies in Russia, Estonia, Latvia and Lithuania, with a particular focus on relationships to local state structures and other social spheres and the participation of local civil society groups in transnational networks, I hope to be able to help fill some significant gaps in previous research.

Hence, this book offers a broad analysis of post-Soviet civil societies on a local as well as a transnational level. The aim is not only to provide an empirical overview of the state of post-Soviet civil society in the beginning of the twenty-first century, but primarily to examine to what extent and in what way civil society contributes to different aspects of democratization in specific regions in post-communist Russia and the Baltic states. It differs from most previous research in this field in several respects. First, the study applies an innovative analytical framework derived from theories of democratization, civil society, social movements and transnational relations, thus allowing broader comparisons and generalizations, without neglecting the specific post-Soviet context. Second, instead of examining a particular sector of civil society, it provides a systematic comparison across sectors. Third, unlike most previous research, which has had a national focus, this study focuses on the local and regional levels, offering systematic cross-regional comparisons. Fourth, the book includes a thorough analysis of the transnationalization of parts of local civil society in post-Soviet Russia and the Baltic states. Fifth, the study combines quantitative survey data with qualitative interviews and case study research. The following research questions guide the analysis:

- How did civil society emerge as a relatively independent arena in the 1980s, and what role did it play in the fall of the communist regime? (Chapter 3)

- What are the characteristics of actors and activities in post-Soviet civil society in the early twenty-first century? (Chapter 4)
- How is civil society related to other arenas like the state, political society and economic society? (Chapter 5)
- To what extent do local civil society actors have transnational links, and what are the political implications of transnational civil society relations? (Chapter 6)
- To what extent and in what way does post-Soviet civil society contribute to different aspects of democratization? (Chapter 7)
- How does all this differ between regions, and how can regional variations be explained? (Chapters 3–7)
- How does all this differ between civil society sectors, and how can variations between sectors be explained? (Chapters 3–7)

Research design

The study has a particular focus on the selected Russian regions. Paying special attention to developments in regions within the core country of the Soviet empire seems natural in a study of the post-Soviet situation. In order to put the Russian regions in perspective, regions in Estonia, Latvia and Lithuania are also covered. In the latter countries the transition to, and consolidation of, democracy has been more smooth and successful than in Russia where the democratization process has been much more problematic. Hence, it is interesting to examine if civil society in Russia is weaker too, reflecting the more limited process of democratization there. Furthermore, the EU accession process contributes to the creation of a different context in the Baltic states compared to Russia. Making cross-country comparisons, however, is not the main purpose of the study. The comparative design is primarily intended to cast some light on two dimensions: regional variations[3] and variations between different types of civil society groups. These are neglected dimensions in previous research on post-Soviet civil society. Hence, systematic comparisons in these respects can help fill some gaps within this field of research. The main time period analysed is the post-transition period of the late 1990s until early 2000.[4] As a historical background, the pre-transition and actual transition phases (approximately 1985–1991) are also briefly covered.

Given the relative lack of previous research in this specific field, the research design is explorative. Deductive and inductive approaches are combined. The broad theoretical framework, derived from a reading of literature covering problems of democratization and civil society, as outlined in the following chapter, is a point of departure for the empirical analysis. Based on this framework, questions for a survey are formulated and initial material gathered. Initial analysis of this material and previous research findings help to specify the theoretical framework. With sharper analytical tools we can then continue with a second round of empirical analysis –

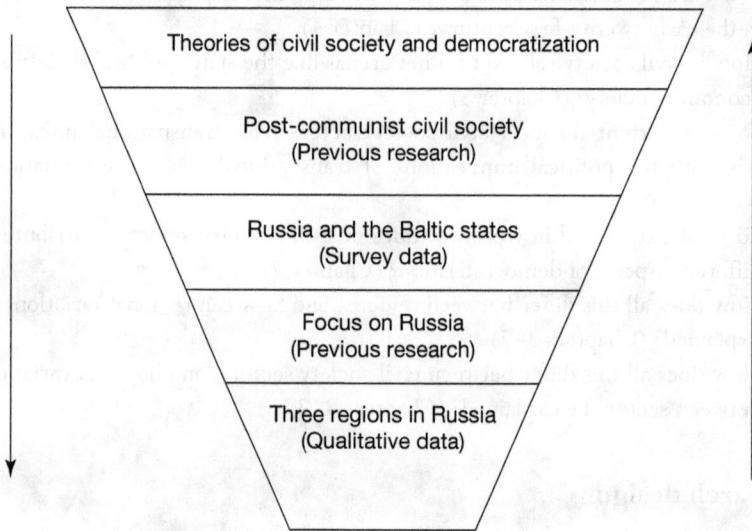

```
Theories of civil society and democratization

Post-communist civil society
(Previous research)

Russia and the Baltic states
(Survey data)

Focus on Russia
(Previous research)

Three regions in Russia
(Qualitative data)
```

Figure 1.1 Research design

now based mainly on qualitative data gathered from three Russian regions. The present research design is thus based on a conviction that a combination of deductive and inductive approaches, combined with quantitative and qualitative methods is most fruitful for researching this highly complex problem area.

The research design of this study can be summarized in Figure 1.1. Starting on the theoretical level, the formulation of the research problem and the construction of an analytical framework are based on a reading of general theories of civil society, as well as more specific empirical findings about post-communist and post-Soviet civil societies. Drawing on unique survey data, a comparison between several regions in Russia and the Baltic states is provided. A tighter focus on Russia is offered. This is partly because of the centrality of Russia in the post-Soviet context, and partly due to the fact that there is more previous research on civil society in Russia than in the Baltic states to relate to. The focus on Russia is further narrowed down to three regions: Novgorod, Pskov and St Petersburg. This allows more in-depth qualitative research. Finally, going up again in the figure, I try to offer some theoretical reflections based on the empirical findings.

Conducting interviews in post-communist societies poses several problems, including difficulties in the selection of respondents due to incomplete information, problems in locating and contacting respondents, negative attitudes towards foreigners and/or interviews, an aversion to advance scheduling, and suspicions against standard demographic questions (Werning Rivera *et al.* 2002: 683). I will in the following sections discuss how I have dealt with such problems.

Selection of regions

Data collection in all regions in the four countries, while scientifically the optimal solution, is not possible without a huge research organization and almost unlimited funds. Neither is it possible to select a few regions that are fully representative of the whole country and thus enable us to make solid generalizations about the Russian Federation, Estonia, Latvia and Lithuania respectively. Given the main aim of the project and the limited research resources, a comparative design with a selection of regions in each country is most suitable. Each region is selected because of its specific features that are thought to be important for our research problem – not because it is representative of the country as a whole.

The Russian Federation has 89 administrative areas.[5] Based on a database of regions in Russia containing a variety of political, social and economic variables and our understanding of previous research, discussions with various informants and other available information, we selected the four regions of Kaliningrad, Novgorod, Pskov and Sverdlovsk, and the city of St Petersburg.[6] Kaliningrad, Novgorod and Pskov are similar in size and in a range of social and economic factors. They are all located in Western Russia. Thus the logic of 'most similar cases' has influenced the selection of these regions. St Petersburg, representing a large metropolitan area, was included because of its obvious political significance in North-Western Russia. A decision not to limit the study to just Western Russia made us select Sverdlovsk, situated on the eastern slope of the Central and Northern Urals.

In the Baltic states the range of selection is more limited. In Estonia there are 15 regions (or counties). We selected the Harju region (with the capital Tallinn), Ida-Viru (with the administrative centre Jõhvi and a large Russian-speaking majority, especially in the city of Narva next to the Russian border), Tartu (known as an educational and cultural centre) and the more peripheral and rural region of Põlva. In Latvia (with 26 counties and 7 municipalities) and Lithuania (with 10 counties) respectively, we selected the capital (Riga and Vilnius) and one other major centre (Valmiera and Kaunas). In most regions, rural (or more peripheral) municipalities were selected in addition to the urban centres (see Table 1.1). However, it proved hard to find many relevant civil society groups in the peripheral municipalities. The number of respondents in municipalities outside of the regional capital is shown in Table 1.2. Only in Novgorod and Sverdlovsk did we find a substantial representation from the peripheral municipalities.

The survey[7]

Selection of respondents for survey interviews

It has not been possible to identify the 'universe' of civil society groups in order to select a representative sample. Data on civil society organizations in these countries

Table 1.1 Regions and municipalities included in the study

Region	Administrative centre	Peripheral municipalities
Kaliningrad	Kaliningrad	Svetlogorsk
Novgorod	Novgorod	Borovichy, Pestovo, Starya Russa, Valday
Pskov	Pskov	Ostrov, Pechory
St Petersburg	St Petersburg	
Sverdlovsk	Yekaterinburg	Alapayevsk, Artemovsky, Kamyshlov
Harju	Tallinn	
Ida-Viru	Jõhvi	Narva, Sillamäe, Toila
Põlva	Põlva	Laheda, Räpina
Tartu	Tartu	
Riga	Riga	Sigulda
Valmiera	Valmiera	
Kaunas	Kaunas	Various towns and villages
Vilnius	Vilnius	Various towns and villages

tend to be outdated and inaccurate, or even non-existent.[8] On the one hand, many registered NGOs are not active. On the other hand, there are many civil society groups that (for different reasons) do not register with the authorities. In order to identify civil society groups for the survey, local partners in each of the regions included in the study carried out fieldwork and provided me with lists of civil society groups.[9] The local researchers consisted of senior researchers in political science (St Petersburg and Sverdlovsk), master degree students in political science (the three Baltic states), university students in a Swedish organization (Novgorod), graduates from a teachers college (Pskov), and university students (Kaliningrad).

Civil society groups in the fields of democracy and human rights, women, labour, environment, and nationalism and ethnicity were identified in each of the local communities selected for the project. In this way civil society groups which could be assumed to have a political agenda were prioritized whereas less politically oriented groups, such as charity foundations and other social welfare organizations, were included only if more openly political NGOs did not exist to a sufficient extent in a particular region. Non-political groups like sports clubs and other recreational organizations were not included at all. (For a more elaborate theoretical motivation to the categorization and selection of civil society groups, see Chapter 2.)

Naturally, these lists provided by local research partners did not include all civil society groups in the respective regions and municipalities. Lacking a clear picture of the total universe of civil society groups in each region we have to be very careful with our interpretation of data. There is no guarantee that those groups included in the study are fully representative of the civil society in the region. We should therefore avoid making too firm general conclusions about regional differences. However, the combination of survey data and data gathered through more intensive qualitative research in three of the Russian regions provides a sufficient base for regional comparisons. (On the qualitative aspects of the research design, please see below.)

The distribution of respondents in different regions and categories of civil society groups is shown in Table 1.2. Human rights and democracy-oriented groups work for the acceptance of universal human rights rather than the protection of group-specific rights. In this category we also find organizations which aim to improve local or national democracy, such as citizen watch groups. Women's groups work with women's issues, but (as will be shown in Chapter 4), there is a great division between traditional antifeminist groups and politically radical feminists. The category 'trade unions and labour' includes both old traditional unions and some newer organizations for the protection of labour rights. Environmental groups may be anything from traditional nature-protection societies to radical green movement organizations. The 'ethnic and nationalist' category includes both organizations for the protection of the rights of ethnic minorities and nationalist, exclusivist and even xenophobic organizations. Social welfare organizations support disabled and other disadvantaged groups. They are often – but not always – charity organizations with no clear political objectives. The 'other' category includes civil society resource centres and umbrella organizations, NGOs working with consumer rights, local development, youth, culture, education and international exchange. Working in diverse fields, they still tend to share a less political and oppositional approach to local authorities, especially compared to most human rights and environmental groups.

Seventy-five per cent of respondents are heads/directors of their organizations (and often also the founder of the organization). The other respondents also have influential positions within their organizations as vice-president, secretary, board member or head of department (in bigger organizations). Hence, the respondents constitute a civil society elite, although the actual political influence of most of these actors (as will be shown in the following analysis) is very limited.[10]

The interviews

Given the aim of the study and the relatively large number of respondents, data collection had to be through structured interviews. In order to get as high a response rate as possible and increase reliability, face-to-face interviews were the best option. A questionnaire – containing attitudinal questions on political values and perceptions of the political system, as well as more specific questions on the activities of civil society groups – was constructed. The questionnaire was translated into Russian, Estonian, Latvian and Lithuanian respectively.[11] Our local research partners in each region tested it. Interviewers received written and oral instructions by me or a research assistant working for the project. Each face-to-face interview lasted approximately one hour. Respondents were promised full anonymity. The interviews in Russia were carried out between November 1999 and February 2000.

Table 1.2 Distribution of respondents per region and category of civil society group (absolute numbers)

	Human rights and democracy	Women	Trade unions and labour	Environment	Ethnic and nationalist	Social welfare	Other	Total	In peripheral municipalities
Kaliningrad	3	1	0	1	3	2	3	13	1
Novgorod	6	6	0	5	1	18	11	47	25
Pskov	4	2	11	5	2	8	8	40	3
St.Petersburg	9	9	9	10	7	3	4	51	–
Sverdlovsk	13	2	11	2	5	6	1	40	14
Harju	3	3	5	3	4	1	4	23	–
Ida-Viru	1	3	5	0	8	0	1	18	7
Põlva	0	1	2	1	0	3	6	13	4
Tartu	1	4	1	6	3	2	6	23	–
Riga	2	7	8	3	4	0	2	26	1
Valmiera	0	1	5	0	1	3	0	10	–
Kaunas	7	3	9	2	3	1	6	31	4
Vilnius	7	5	7	5	6	0	6	36	6
Total	**56**	**47**	**73**	**43**	**47**	**47**	**58**	**371**	**65**

Source: Democratization: Local and Transnational Perspectives Survey (DLTPS) 1999–2000.

The most important political events that took place during the time when the interviews were undertaken were the parliamentary elections in December 1999 and the resignation of President Boris Yeltsin on 31 December 1999. These events made it a time of more intense political activity. Many civil society activists were active in election campaigns, and the general political temperature was high following the change of president. As a consequence we could expect respondents to be somewhat more interested in political issues than under more normal circumstances. In Estonia and Latvia interviews were carried out between January and March 2000. Interviews in Lithuania were conducted between February and May 2000.

The aim of this survey was primarily to create a base for further qualitative inquiry into the general research questions. The survey was intended to provide at least preliminary answers to the following questions:

1   What is the character of local civil society? What is the number of groups in different fields? What are the activities and orientations of local civil society activists?
2   What is the relationship between civil society, the state, and political and economic society on the local level?
3   What is the pattern of transnational contacts of local civil society groups like?

Response rate

The total response rate of 77 per cent (see Table 1.3) must be considered satisfactory for this kind of survey. There are, however, some disturbing regional differences. The most obvious shortcoming is the very low response rate in Kaliningrad. This is most likely due to the failure of the local researchers to complete their tasks and should not be taken as an indicator of attitudes among civil society activists in this region. The number of interviews from Kaliningrad is so small that no conclusions can be drawn about this region. These interviews will, however, be included in the total analysis.

The researcher responsible for Lithuania provided me with very extensive lists, which allowed a serious selection. The response rate for Lithuania is, however, less impressive. From Estonia I received reasonably adequate lists and a reasonable response rate. The low number of organizations listed for peripheral municipalities (in all regions) is most likely a reflection of the low number of civil society groups there. Researchers in St Petersburg, Sverdlovsk and Latvia did not provide long lists of potential respondents, but they did follow my criteria of civil society groups relevant for the study and hence most of the organizations they listed were highly relevant. In Latvia the local researchers had problems identifying civil society groups (especially in Valmiera) because the updated NGO database provided by an NGO Centre in Riga was temporarily out of order so they had to rely on a list of NGOs

Table 1.3 Response rate

	Original list supplied by local researchers	Selection by author	Completed interviews	Response rate (%)
Kaliningrad	37	32	13	40
Novgorod	22	22+25*	47	
Pskov	23	23+17*	40	
St. Petersburg	71	53	51	96
Sverdlovsk	45	45	40	89
Harju	79	31	23	74
Ida-Viru	32	24	18	75
Pölva	19	17	13	76
Tartu	63	29	23	79
Riga	44	39	26	67
Valmiera	11	11	10	91
Kaunas	370	57	31	54
Vilnius	1211	54	36	67
Total	**2027**	**479**	**371**	**77**

Source: Democratization: Local and Transnational Perspectives Survey (DLTPS) 1999–2000.

Note: *Approved after the interviews had been completed.

from 1997. Response rates for St Petersburg and Sverdlovsk are very high, whereas the rate for Latvia (Riga) is somewhat less satisfactory, probably due to the above-mentioned problem.

In Novgorod and Pskov, local researchers failed to supply adequate lists of potential respondents before starting the interviews. Due to a misunderstanding of the instructions given, they set out to make interviews with a relatively large number of respondents who had not been selected by me. My criteria for selection of organizations were, however, followed rather closely and most of these interviews could be approved after they had been carried out. As the researcher responsible for the survey, it is very unsatisfactory to lose control of the vital selection process in this way. Nevertheless I am confident that all interviews included in the study are done with respondents that I would have selected before the interviews were carried out if I had had a chance to do it. The very high number of social welfare NGOs – a category that was to be included only if other types of organizations did not exist – in Novgorod (and to a lesser extent in Pskov), however, could to some extent be a result of this failure in the selection process. But after having personally carried out field research in Novgorod and Pskov, I have no indications that there are a large number of relevant NGOs, which were ignored by the local researchers. Hence, it is likely that the composition of respondents in these two regions does reflect the actual situation.

Reasons given for lack of response are mainly that the organization has ceased to exist. Variation in response rate across regions is probably mainly due to different ways of putting together lists of potential respondents. Those researchers who made careful research of which relevant organizations were available have achieved a high response rate, whereas those who provided lengthy list of all kinds of organizations have a somewhat lower response rate.[12] There is no reason to believe that the lack of response reflects any substantial difference between regional civil societies. Refusal to participate in the interview was very rare in all regions. Most civil society elites were very willing to participate (whereas political and economic elites tended to be somewhat more sceptical). Representatives of civil society organizations were often flattered by the attention they received (particularly in peripheral municipalities where foreign research was rare or non-existent).[13]

Honesty of respondents

The reliability of survey data is often problematic. There are however some measures that can be taken in order to improve reliability. We asked the interviewers to judge the reliability of the answers from each interview. Reliability was judged as satisfactory, not entirely satisfactory, or poor. If interviewers suspected that reliability was not satisfactory they were asked to explain why. Twenty interviews were considered not entirely satisfactory, but none was deemed to have poor reliability. This means that the reliability of 95 per cent of the interviews was judged as satisfactory by the interviewers. Reasons given for suspecting that the answers were not entirely satisfactory were that the respondent showed a lack of interest in or sceptical attitude towards the survey, that the respondent was in a hurry, or that the respondent tried to be 'politically correct'. The interviews that were judged by the interviewers as not entirely satisfactory have been closely examined. Answers seem to be consistent and reasonable, although some answers are missing. Hence I decided to keep these respondents in the study.

Through follow-up interviews with a selection of respondents, I had the opportunity to check the reliability of the survey answers. Before interviews for the survey started, all local partners were informed about the plans to make follow-up interviews with a selection of respondents, although they did not know which regions and which respondents would be selected. These follow-up interviews did not give any reason to suspect flaws in the survey data.

Presentation of results

Results from the survey are presented in tables. The explorative character of the study and the aim to carry out systematic comparisons across regions as well as civil society sectors have made it necessary to include a relatively large number of tables. In order not to overload the text with statistical data, I refer to some simple survey results without presenting them in table form, but in most cases I found it necessary to include tables in order to give the reader a chance to critically examine the reliability of data and not lose relevant information.

Qualitative interviews

The general overview provided by quantitative survey data is complemented with qualitative case studies of specific civil society groups in order to arrive at a better understanding of the conditions for civil society activities in contemporary post-Soviet societies. A methodological problem with the survey is that it is a snapshot of perceptions at a given time. We have not had enough resources to carry out a new survey at a later time. The analysis of a process like democratization should ideally be based on time series data, but due to limited research resources we have to be satisfied with one survey at one specific time. To some extent this problem is overcome through the collection of additional data – not least in the form of qualitative interviews – at more than one occasion. Thus, we will be able to say something about changes over time.

Interviews with activists and officials, direct observation and a review of existing published sources are the best material for the analysis of civil society (cf. Fish 1995: 139). Based on a preliminary analysis of the survey data, thirty respondents were selected for qualitative interviews. These respondents were selected among the civil society elites (including a few representatives of local authorities dealing with NGOs) in three of the Russian regions: St Petersburg, Novgorod and Pskov. The reason behind this selection was that the survey indicated that these regions represented very different forms of civil societies. (See further elaboration in Chapter 7.) Hence, it seemed fruitful to make a closer analysis of local state–civil society relations there. Furthermore, the geographical proximity of St Petersburg, Novgorod and Pskov was a logistical advantage when carrying out fieldwork. Respondents were selected in order to get representatives of NGOs within different fields of activity and with different relations to the local government. These respondents are in no way representative of civil society elites in general in the respective regions, but the interviews do provide important insights into the functioning of local state–civil society relations. Interviews were semi-structured. Questions focused on two main issues: 1) specific aspects of state–civil society relations in the respective region and municipality; and 2) foreign funding as well as other forms of transnational relations. As an interviewer, I made it clear that the respondent was the expert on the specific topic of the interview (cf. Leech 2002: 665).

The interviews, conducted in April and October 2001, typically lasted about one to one-and-a-half hours. A few lasted only half an hour, and a few lasted up to three hours. Most interviews were conducted in Russian through the assistance of an interpreter, but some were conducted in English. All interviews except one were tape-recorded. I also took rather comprehensive notes. A list of interviews in each of the three regions is provided in the reference section.[14] All respondents were offered anonymity, but denied the offer and allowed me to quote them by name.

Written material

During fieldwork I gathered additional written material in the form of publications and documents from some of the selected organizations. These were useful complements to the interviews, providing a clearer picture of the way different groups would like to present their activities and goals. A few NGOs also have websites with similar material.

Outline of the book

In Chapter 2 I examine theories of democratization and civil society in order to position myself on key theoretical and conceptual issues and arrive at an analytical framework for the study. Chapters 3–6 make up the main empirical analysis. They are structured according to the analytical framework outlined in Chapter 2. Chapter 3 examines the emergence of a civil society under *perestroika* and *glasnost* and its impact on the fall of the communist regime. Chapter 4 provides a largely descriptive analysis of actors and activities in contemporary post-Soviet civil societies. Here the focus is on NGOs per se, and the way they mobilize resources and engage in different forms of activities. Chapter 5 offers a theoretically informed analysis of civil society relations to the local state apparatus and other arenas. Here the focus shifts from specific NGOs to civil society as a social sphere or arena. Chapter 6 brings in the transnational dimension, with an analysis of the transnational funding and networking of local civil society groups. Each of these chapters begins with a review of previous research, then outlines my own empirical findings based on quantitative as well as qualitative data, and finally assesses my empirical results in relation to previous research and the analytical framework of the study. Chapter 7 aims at integrating the findings from the previous chapters in a multilevel analysis of civil society and democratization. Here the regional comparison is further elaborated, and three models of civil society and local democracy are outlined.

2 Democratization and civil society

A framework for analysis

This chapter outlines an analytical framework for the study. It starts with a brief discussion of democracy and democratization, continues with an elaboration of different aspects of civil society, and concludes with an overview of civil society's potential democracy-strengthening functions.

Democracy and democratization

Democracy and democratization are fundamental, yet commonly contested, concepts within the social sciences. This section briefly discusses key definitions and approaches in order to lay the ground for a more in-depth analysis of the relationship between civil society and democratization in a post-communist context.

Defining and measuring democracy

The theoretical (and practical) discourse on democracy is to a large extent characterized by the antagonism between two opposing positions concerning the definition of democracy. On one side we have proponents of narrow, formal, macro-level, institutionalist, and electoralist definitions. On the other side we have those favouring broad, substantive, micro-level, society-oriented, participatory, and equality-oriented definitions. The former are common within empirical democratic theory and typically draw on the minimalist definition used by Schumpeter (1976), which sees democracy simply as a process for electing leaders based on elite competition. The main argument for a narrow formal definition of democracy is that it provides the researcher with a useful tool for empirical research. Democracy becomes possible to 'measure' and there are plenty of real, existing democracies to study. If social and economic equality is included in the concept, there would be no real existing democracies, and it would also be impossible to examine how variation in social and economic dimensions is related to variations in formal political democracy (Diamond *et al.* 1990: 6).

The main disadvantage, as pointed out by proponents of a broader definition, is that a focus on form rather than substance devalues the concept of democracy by including political systems and processes which have many undemocratic features. There is also a risk that a narrow definition limits the research agenda, excluding many relevant problems of democracy. Proponents of a broader societal and more substantial conception of democracy argue that structural inequalities (especially those related to capitalism) make liberal democratic assumptions of pluralism invalid. In practice, formal democratic arrangements make little sense for people who lack social and economic power. Political equality is impossible without a basic level of social and economic equality, according to this argument. Hence, democracy is not only about elections and political parties. It also involves struggles to eliminate authoritarian social practices (Grugel 2002: 31). Societal conceptions of democracy find support in participatory democratic theory (Pateman 1970) and direct our attention to women's movements and other popular movements (e.g. Waylen 1994; Hippler 1995), which tend to be ignored by researchers using a narrow formal definition of democracy.

While I find narrow, formal conceptions of democracy inadequate, especially in a post-communist context characterized by deep inequality and political exclusion based on gender and ethnicity, I recognize the analytical problems associated with definitions of democracy, which include substantial socio-economic equality. As a middle-way, I use a definition of democracy which is procedural, but still far more substantial than most mainstream definitions. With David Beetham (1993: 55) I define democracy as 'a mode of decision-making about collectively binding rules and policies over which the people exercise control'. The most democratic arrangement is 'where all members of the collectivity enjoy effective equal rights to take part in such decision-making directly' (ibid.). The key components of this definition are popular control and political equality.

Most scholarship on democracy takes for granted that democracy requires a state. Some scholars even insist that political democracy is 'a form of authority creation *in a modern state*' (Linz and Stepan 1996: 17, note 3, emphasis added). If democracy is conceptualized as by definition related to a modern state there is no space for interesting and relevant questions of democratization on other societal levels, including democratization at the work place or within the family, or the possibility of global and transnational democracy. Most relevant for the present study, the democratization of civil society itself also falls outside the analysis. This would be a far too narrow approach. Beetham's definition of democracy is therefore very useful, as it is applicable to any collectivity, not only states. Using this definition as a base we should analyse broader societal and participatory dimensions of democracy as well as formal procedural aspects. When examining the potential democratic functions of civil society, I therefore distinguish between civil society's impact on formal democracy (FD) and societal democracy (SD).[1]

Another advantage with Beetham's definition of democracy is that it makes democracy a relative concept, which means that political systems can be more or less democratic. The unfruitful democracy–authoritarianism dichotomy is, thus, avoided. Furthermore, this principal definition of democracy avoids establishing certain institutional practices developed in Western countries as a norm against which other political systems should be measured. The definition is so generally formulated that it could not be said to be firmly rooted in a certain culture and completely alien to other cultures (Uhlin 1997: 12).

As this study partly draws on quantitative indicators of civil society it might be fruitful to match this data with quantitative measurements of democracy. However, common indicators of democracy used when constructing democracy indexes are all more or less problematic. Turnover in elections and competition per seat (Vanhanen 1997; Marsh 2000a; 2000b) are simple indicators, but they are hardly based on any firm theoretical understanding of democracy. It is unclear how electoral turnover or competition leads to a responsive government. Attitudinal indicators, like votes for reformers, are also biased. They capture citizens' attitudes, but not the practice of democratic rights. Expert judgements (from Freedom House, for example) are inherently subjective and depend on the values of individual evaluators as well as their knowledge about specific countries. Having these critical points in mind, we will still elaborate on some quantitative indicators of democracy in Chapter 7. A more qualitative evaluation of democratic aspects of civil society development will, however, make up the main part of the analysis. This analysis draws on the definition of democracy given above and the discussion of different aspects of democratization in the rest of this chapter.

Approaches to democratization

Whereas democracy has been one of the main topics within modern political science research, the process towards democracy, i.e. democratization, used to be far less studied. Transitions from authoritarian rule in Southern Europe in the 1970s and later in Latin America and to a lesser extent in Asia and Africa, however, made the examination of processes of democratization a prioritised area for political science research. The sudden and unexpected breakdown of communist regimes in Eastern Europe in the late 1980s and early 1990s further increased the interest in this field of research, and raised new questions and problems, which will be discussed below.

As most research on democratization uses a narrow definition of democracy, the main focus has been on the democratization of formal political institutions. If a broader definition of democracy is applied, the analysis of democratization processes becomes quite different. Democratization can be seen as *the creation, extension and practice of collective decision-making based on the principles of popular control and political equality*. This notion implies a power struggle about who is entitled to take part in decision-making. The main advantage of this definition is that it introduces a power perspective and a focus on social relationships. According to this view, the existence of formally democratic institutions, while necessary, is not enough for democracy to exist. Democracy also requires 'popular consent, popular participation, account-ability and a practice of rights, tolerance and pluralism' (Grugel 1999: 11–12).

In this study I focus on both formal institutional democratization, as analysed in most mainstream democratization studies and the form of societal democra-tization discussed above. These two aspects of the democratization process are treated as analytically distinct. Formal institutional democratization and societal social democratization may accompany and strengthen each other, but they may also conflict. A certain process of formal institutional democratization can, for instance, be an obstacle to societal democratization and the deepening of democracy that this implies.[2]

A wide variety of analytical perspectives has been applied to the study of (formal institutional) democratization. A modernization perspective, stressing the importance of economic development in combination with other socio-economic and cultural factors (Lipset 1959; Diamond *et al.* 1990; Hadenius 1992), has had a prominent position. Following Stein Rokkan, researchers have focused on cleavages in transitional societies (Berglund, Hellén and Aarebrot 1998). Other stucturalists have focused on the power relations between different social classes or other social forces (Moore 1966; Rueschemeyer *et al.* 1992). Rejecting what they consider to be deterministic tendencies in the structural perspectives, other researchers have focused on negotiations between different actors in the transition from authoritarian rule (O'Donell and Schmitter 1986).

While the focus on agency has brought new insights to the analysis of democ-ratization, a too strong emphasis on actors is not satisfactory. Actor and structure approaches must be integrated in an analysis of various actors that are both constrained by the structural context and try to change certain structures (cf. Karl 1990; Linz and Stepan 1996). A focus on actors in civil society and the structural constraints and opportunities they meet in relation to states and other social spheres as well as within civil society itself implies an integration of actor and structure perspectives. I assume that we deal with rational actors. This does not mean applying an individualistic rational choice model of behaviour. I see individual actors not as autonomous decision-makers, but as embedded in social networks and structures that influence their decision.

Linz and Stepan (1996) suggest five arenas that are relevant when analysing the consolidation of democracy, namely civil society, political society, rule of law, state bureaucracy, and economic society. Rather than applying such a comprehensive approach, I find it more fruitful to concentrate on the arena that is of obvious and immediate relevance for political participation, i.e. civil society, and analyse other arenas – such as the state, political and economic society – only in relation to civil society.

Most theorising on problems of democratization – both in the transition and consolidation phase – have been concerned with the national level. This is natural, as modern democracy has been closely related to the nation-state project.

Nevertheless, international factors were profound in the rapid breakdown of communist regimes in Eastern Europe. In a time when local and transnational actors increasingly challenge the authority of nation-states, the importance of local and transnational perspectives on democratization should be evident. A focus on external influences is, however, not enough. We need to seriously consider all levels of analysis and how they are interwoven with each other. The different levels include transnational (in which case we should distinguish between truly global and more geographically limited transnational relations), national, subnational region, and local. Not only do the different levels have an impact on democratization on the national level, democratization may also be a relevant problem on all levels. Without completely neglecting the nation-state level, I focus on local/regional and transnational processes related to democratization. In an effort to go beyond simple levels of analysis research, I aim at integrating the local and transnational dimensions.

Local democratization – like democratization on other levels – may have both an institutional and a societal aspect. It means the democratization of local political institutions. Local democratization also provides an opportunity for more participatory forms of democracy, as the community is smaller and the distance between voters and the elected is less than on the national level. However, local democracy is not necessarily more participatory and inclusive than democracy on the national level. Local strongmen may dominate the local political arena in a way that is seldom possible on the national level. The specific local context must therefore be taken into account when analysing local democratization. The transnational dimension of democratization (related to civil society) will be elaborated towards the end of this chapter. Next, a few notes on the concepts of transition and consolidation are required.

Transition and consolidation

Different phases in the process from authoritarianism to democracy can be identified. Scholars emphasising the role of agency in the process tend to concentrate on the actual regime transition, which is usually a short time period. A democratic transition is completed when there is sufficient agreement on political procedures to elect a government, a new government, which has *de facto* authority, is elected in free and fair general elections, and when the executive, legislative and judicial power do not have to share power with other bodies *de jure* (Linz and Stepan 1996: 3). The pre-transition phase – characterized by increasing popular pressure for democracy, conflicts within the ruling elite and a provisional tolerance of dissent, but no changes in the political rules in order to guarantee individual and collective rights (Uhlin 1997: 155–9) – has received less scholarly attention. Problems of the consolidation of democracy have received increasing interest as it has become evident that states that have experienced a regime transition hardly develop into stable democracies in a few years. A democracy can be said to be consolidated when democracy has become 'the only game in town' (Linz and Stepan 1996: 5). If no significant political groups seriously seek to overthrow the democratic regime, if the overwhelming majority of the people believe that political change must take place within the parameters of the democratic system, and if all major political actors accept the political rules for conflict resolution, then we have a consolidated democracy. It should be noted that the pace and form of democratic consolidation typically varies between different social spheres (Berglund *et al.* 2001: 10).

This study briefly examines civil society's relationship to the state and other social spheres and the local impact of transnational civil society groups in the pre-transition and transition phases (Chapter 3) and compares this to similar problems after the actual transition has taken place on the national level (Chapters 4–7). In the Baltic states this may rightly be described as a process of democratic consolidation, whereas it is more questionable to what extent Russia has yet completed a transition and entered a consolidation phase. (This will be further discussed in Chapter 7.)

The post-communist context

There has been a vivid scholarly debate on how different post-communist transitions are from other cases of democratic transitions (e.g. Bunce 2002; Nodia 2002). It is commonly pointed out that unlike Southern Europe and Latin America, the countries of Eastern Europe had no significant experience of democracy. Rather than going through a process of 'redemocratization', they had to 'build democracy from scratch' (Fish 1995). Furthermore, state socialism was a far more invasive system than the authoritarian regimes in other parts of the world. There was seldom any politically influential military in communist states and neither was there any bourgeoisie (Bunce 2002: 20). Most research has stressed mainly political and domestic factors in Southern Europe and Latin America, whereas mainly economic and international factors have been seen behind the post-communist transitions. Furthermore, the distinction between mass-mobilization and elite pacts – important in much research on Latin American transitions – breaks down in the post-communist cases (Bunce 2002: 21). Of even greater significance, unlike other transitions, national liberation was part of almost all post-communist transitions. Twenty-two of the twenty-seven states that make up the former Soviet Union and Eastern Europe are new (Bunce 2002: 22). It should, however, be noted that the transition from communism occurred before the break-up of the Soviet Union (Brown 2002: 209). In sum, the processes in Eastern Europe are not simply transitions to democracy. Rather they are revolutions including political, economic and social life. These different aspects of the process are often conflicting (Bunce 2002: 23). Hence, we need to consider the specific context of post-communist democratization. Unlike newly democratizing states in Southern Europe and Latin America, the former communist states have to manage a dual transition, from plan to market and from dictatorship to democracy, and in many cases a triple transition,

including in addition a new process of nation building and state formation
(Przeworski 1991; Linz and Stepan 1996). The complexities of these interrelated
processes must be taken into account in the analysis. We must also pay attention
to the fact that despite the collapse of communist rule, many elites managed to
keep their positions (Higley *et al.* 2002). There are also many more or less specific
challenges to post-communist democracy, such as party fragmentation, xenophobia
and nationalism, absence of legal and bureaucratic traditions sustaining human
rights, and weak civil society organizations (Berglund *et al.* 2001).

I do not argue that all these peculiarities of transitions from communism
necessarily make comparisons with other cases meaningless, but it seems fruitful to
limit the comparison to within the region of post-communist Eastern Europe.
Focusing the present study even more, I will concentrate on states which have been
parts of the Soviet Union, either as the dominant power (Russia) or as dominated
satellites (the Baltic states). The merit of this focused comparison is that we can hold
several factors more or less constant as the different cases have an intertwined
history and a common experience of communist rule (although from different
perspectives). It also allows us to make interregional comparisons within and across
countries.

Civil society

The present study applies a civil society approach to democratization research. This
section outlines the concepts, theoretical positions and approaches needed for the
empirical analysis, hence providing an analytical framework for the study.

Approaches to civil society

Civil society has become a key concept in the study of processes of democratization.
Scholars of very different ideological and scientific inclinations tend to focus on this
elusive concept. Many different definitions prevail in the literature on the subject,
and approaches to the analysis of civil society vary widely. The concept of civil
society is problematic as it tends to be 'an ideological rather than an analytical construct' (Beckman 1997: 1). There is a risk that (unintended) normative assumptions
are incorporated into the analysis if the concept is not used very carefully. Here
I will discuss different ways of using this concept and clarify my own position on a
number of significant issues related to civil society research.

The concept of civil society has a long history (see e.g. Keane 1988; Cohen
and Arato 1992, Kumar 1993, Hydén 1997a; Ehrenberg 1999) which we need
not discuss in any detail for the purpose of the present study. One of the major
sources of inspiration for contemporary liberal theory of civil society is de
Tocqueville and his writing on democracy in early nineteenth-century America.
De Tocqueville saw an active civil society made up of self-governing associations as

a bulwark against a too powerful state, but also against the 'tyranny of the majority'. According to this perspective civil society educates citizens and provides mechanisms for political participation (Hydén 1997b: 6–7). In a quite different theoretical tradition and writing at a time when communist movements were defeated in Central Europe in 1918–1921, Gramsci brought the concept of civil society into the twentieth century. He saw civil society as a political and ideological arena in which the bourgeoisie exercised indirect control, as opposed to the direct control within the state (Gibbon 1996: 22–4). Civil society was the arena outside the state where political culture was shaped. Gramsci's notion of civil society has had a great influence on contemporary post-Marxist political theorists (e.g. Cohen and Arato 1992). The concept of civil society, in yet a different understanding, was reinvented among East European intellectuals in the mid-1970s. Developing civil society became a strategy to overcome totalitarian regimes (Gibbon 1996: 24–6). The crisis of statist ideologies and political and economic systems (state socialism, Third World developmentalism as well as Western welfare states) in the 1980s led to a renewed worldwide interest in the concept of civil society.

Contemporary definitions of civil society range from 'minimalist' (only political, pro-democratic associations included) to 'maximalist' (anything outside the state realm included) (Hydén 1997a: 30–1). Some scholars reserve the concept of civil society for non-state *political* space or associations, whereas civic society is understood as a broader term also including non-political groups (Hewison and Rodan 1996: 41). According to this view, civil society does not include all relatively independent, voluntary social organizations. Only those that try to advance the interests of members through overt political action could be seen as part of civil society (Rodan 1997: 162). Hence, from this perspective, civil society is an inherently political sphere. (Post-)Marxists and critical theorists, following Gramsci, see civil society as a network of institutions between economic structures and the state through which groups in society represent themselves. State and civil society are interconnected. Civil society is a sphere of indirect domination, and democratization is needed not only of the state but also of civil society (cf. Cohen and Arato 1992; Macdonald 1997). In a related way of reasoning, civil society can be seen as political space, that is, 'avenues for contesting and shaping public policy' (Rodan 1997: 158). Civil society is the least restrictive form of political space (Rodan 1997: 162). It requires a public space independent from the exercise of state power, and the ability of organizations within it to influence the exercise of state power (Bernhard 1993: 308).

Following this line of reasoning, I would like to make a number of clarifications concerning the way the concept of civil society is used in this study. First, civil society should be seen as an arena or a social sphere (in addition to other arenas like the state, political society and economic society). Second, it should be stressed that state and civil society are highly connected and interdependent. Civil society can hardly be completely autonomous from the state. An analytical distinction between the state arena and the civil society arena is possible to make, but often it is the overlapping of, and connections between, the two spheres that are most fruitful to analyse. Third, civil society is a public sphere. Organizations concerned with inward-looking or private ends do not act in civil society (Boussard 2003: 81–2). Fourth, civil society actors are typically collectively organized around specific common interests, although it is also possible to conceive of individuals articulating interests of public concern on the civil society arena. Fifth, both political and apolitical actors may act within civil society, but it is important, especially when interested in the relationship between civil society and democracy, to distinguish between politically relevant and non-political sections of civil society. Politics may include struggles to influence decision-making on the distribution of resources as well as the construction of social meaning and identity (Clarke 1998: 6). Sixth, and related to the previous point, it is necessary to have a power perspective on civil society. In order to understand how civil society groups are engaged in struggles for social change we must understand how they fit into a larger picture of power structures. One way of introducing a power perspective is to focus on the functions, rather than the forms, of civil society groups (Van Rooy and Robinson 1998: 201). We should focus on power struggles and conflicts within civil society as well as between civil society and other arenas.

Finally, it should be stressed that civil society is not inherently 'good' or democratic. Many American scholars tend to see civil society as good, in and of itself. It is thought to be the realm of democratic norms. According to Diamond (1994: 6) a group has to strive for the 'public good' in order to qualify as part of civil society. Civil society, by definition, encompasses pluralism and diversity. By contrast, many European thinkers tend to have a more instrumentalist view of civil society. It is useful to the extent that it can reform the state (Hydén 1997a: 21). The rather romantic view of civil society in much (American) liberal theory is a problem. Empirically, it is obvious that there are a lot of inequalities based on class, gender, ethnicity, etc. within civil society. It should, however, be noted that not only liberal theories, but also post-structuralist and post-modernist studies of new social movements tend to see civil society as the morally good, whereas the state is considered to be repressive (Rodan 1997: 159–60). Civil society must be analytically separated from 'civic community' (Boussard 2003: 84–6). A civic community is characterized by mutual trust and cooperation. It includes only organizations that behave 'civilly'. But civil society is not inherently democratic.

Where does this elaboration of the concept take us? One possibility is to regard civil society as a residual category, including non-state organizations, institutions and activities or simply meaning 'associational life' (Beckman 1997: 1). I think we can be a bit more precise and, based on the above discussion, I suggest the following definition: *Civil society is a public sphere in which different kinds of actors – which have some degree of autonomy in relation to the state and other social spheres – develop identities and articulate interests.* Civil society groups are often political, but they should be distinguished from formal political institutions, such as political parties, parliaments and elections. Thus we are interested in one social sphere – civil society – that is the collectively organized but informal political part of society.

Based on this discussion it should be evident that I think the concept of civil society has some analytical power that can be useful in empirical research. However, we should not be too preoccupied with precise definitions of this theoretical construct. 'We need to analyse actual processes of incorporation, exclusion, creation of legitimacy and loyalty, expression of interests and identities without worrying too much about whether this or that piece of society conceptually should be considered to belong to civil society or not.' (Beckman and Sjögren 2001: 4) Hence, it is useful to focus on concrete actors that act within this social sphere.

Actors and activities in civil society

Civil society actors

I agree with Macdonald (1997: 141) that it is often misleading to discuss civil society in the abstract. It is a social sphere where many divergent views and conflicting interests meet. For the empirical analysis we need to identify specific actors within civil society. The two most important types of civil society actors are social movements and non-governmental organizations (NGOs). As should be clear from the above elaboration of the concept of civil society, civil society could not be reduced to simply designating NGOs and social movements. Individuals and loosely tied networks which could not be covered by the terms NGOs or social movements may also act within civil society. However, it is commonly accepted that NGOs and social movements are the most important civil society actors, and for the present study it is wise to focus on such collective actors.[3] Research on social movements on the one hand, and NGOs on the other hand, have to a large extent developed separately. It would be useful to unite these fields of research (cf. Fisher 1997: 451) and my aim here is to contribute to bridging the gap between social movement theory and NGO studies. First we need to define these actors in the civil society arena.

A social movement can be defined as 'an organized and sustained effort of a collectivity of inter-related individuals, groups and organizations to promote or to resist social change with the use of public protest activities' (Neidhardt and Rucht 1991: 450). Although a very large number of different definitions prevail in the literature, most include some core notions highlighted by the above definition. It is clear that a social movement is a form of collective action, it has some sustainability and it is oriented towards promoting or resisting social change. A social movement does not consist only of one single organization, but many different organizations and individuals more or less closely related to each other. Some kind of mass base is thus an essential characteristic of a social movement.

For the purpose of this study, there is not much use in categorising the research on social movements. What we are interested in here is why social movements striving for (or against) democratic change emerge, and with what outcomes. Research within the political process school seems to be most useful in this respect (cf. Pagnucco 1995). The concept of 'political opportunities' in particular may prove helpful. Before turning to this discussion we need to consider other types of actors within civil society.

Non-governmental organizations are formal, self-governing, voluntary, non-profit organizations (cf. Gordenker and Weiss 1996: 20). By self-governing we mean a relative autonomy in relation to states, capital and other organizations. In fact, the existence of what has been called GONGOs (governmentally organized non-governmental organizations), MANGOs (manipulated non-governmental organizations) and GRINGOs (governmentally regulated and initiated non-governmental organizations) is an indication of the complex relationship between state and non-state authorities (Higgott *et al.* 2000: 2). The extent to which NGOs are really voluntary is also an open empirical question. Civil society is not a sphere of unrestricted freedom of association (Warren 2001: 97). There are usually different types of actual exit costs when leaving an NGO. The term 'voluntary' is here applied in order to distinguish NGOs from other organizations in which membership is more or less compulsory for a certain group of people, e.g. states. By 'non-profit' we do not imply that an association must not have any income-generating activity to qualify as an NGO, only that (unlike private companies) its main purpose should not be to generate economic profit.

The distinction between NGOs and social movements is not clear-cut. Rather we can see NGOs and social movements as two end points on a continuum (see figure 2.1). NGOs can be distinguished from social movements by their more limited goals, more moderate means, more visible and institutionalized structures, and less popular participation. These characteristics mean that the political elite generally tolerates NGOs whereas people in power perceive many social movements, which mobilize large numbers of people and strive for social change, as a greater threat.

	NGOs		SMs
Goals	limited	_____	far reaching
Means	moderate	_____	confrontational
Structure	formal/institutionalized	_____	diffuse
Activists	few, professional	_____	mass base

Figure 2.1 Main differences between non-governmental organizations (NGOs) and social movements (SMs)

NGOs may be associated with social movements, but do not define or direct them. Social movement organizations (SMOs), with some NGO characteristics, often emerge from social movements because a more formalized organization may be necessary to sustain the movement. However, there is often a tension between NGOs and social movements. The weakening or disintegration of class-based and other social movements often go hand in hand with the proliferation of NGOs. This process might strengthen the state. As noted by Clarke (1998: 210), the 'sheer number of voluntary organizations [. . .] fragments interest articulation into a disparate range of issue-based demands that can easily be co-opted by the state on a selective basis.'

As will be argued in the following chapters, post-Soviet societies have experienced a development of civil society from a 'movement society' under *glasnost* and *perestroika* to an 'NGO-society' in the post-transition period. This is not a unique feature of the transition from communist regimes. Rather it is the typical development of civil society in most processes of democratization, although it has probably been more pronounced in the post-communist societies analysed here than in most other cases.

Civil society sectors

Some further clarifications concerning the types of civil society actors we are interested in are necessary. There are different sectors of civil society, including different categories of civil society groups, which have distinct goals and ways of acting. As we are interested in the function rather than the organizational form of civil society groups we do not include all kinds of NGOs and social movements in the study. We focus primarily on those groups that we can assume to have a political programme, including groups within the fields of human rights, women's rights, labour rights, the environment, ethnic or national identity and other political groups that do not run in elections and, thus, do not qualify as political parties. Charity organizations and other less political NGOs are included only in those regions where there are few outright political NGOs. Churches and other religious communities are excluded, despite the obvious importance of such actors in the struggle for independence in the Baltic states. Contemporary religious organizations in the post-Soviet context, however, organize around a common faith and do not give priority to articulating political interests. In this they differ from the politically oriented NGOs which are the focus of this study. Recreational and other non-political organizations are also excluded. The reason for this selection is that we are not interested in civil society in general, but certain political aspects of civil society – i.e. its impact on democratization. In this respect, politically oriented civil society groups – like interest organizations, advocacy groups and social movements – have more in common with political parties than with recreational, religious and charity organizations which also act within civil society. Hence, the important task for a researcher interested in democratization is not primarily to identify actors within civil society, but to identify politically relevant actors.

Civil society activists

The actor perspective does not only imply a focus on different civil society groups. Drawing heavily on interviews with individual civil society activists it is natural to pay attention to the activists too. We need to consider the basic characteristics of activists, such as sex, age, level of education, etc. Furthermore, the values and ideas of individual activists are important for the analysis.

Resource mobilization

Returning to the level of collective actors, an important aspect is the way civil society groups mobilize resources, including money, members and supporters. Resource mobilization theorists have focused on the critical role of resources in the rise of social movements (McAdam *et al.* 1996). This is equally important for NGOs and other types of civil society groups. Human and financial resources are necessary for any activity within civil society.

Activities

Activities of civil society groups (in addition to the mobilization of new human and economic resources) range from non-confrontational NGO activities like information gathering, public education and networking, via formal efforts to influence political decisions through lobbying and writing petitions, to more confrontational activities usually associated with social movements, such as demonstrations, boycotts, strikes and the occupation of buildings.

The definitions and arguments put forward in this section provide a framework for the empirical analysis in Chapter 4.

Civil society, the state and other arenas

As argued above, state, civil society, economic society and political society should be seen as arenas (Cohen and Arato 1992; Linz and Stepan 1996). A certain actor can act in several different arenas. It is useful to conceive of civil society, the state and other public arenas as 'multiple, overlapping and interpenetrated public spheres' (Braman 1996: 34). The boundary relationships between spheres are most fruitful to analyse. The spheres or arenas are often partly overlapping. As argued by Hydén (1997a: 19), civil society cannot be seen in isolation from either market or state. The emergence of the concept of 'civil society' is historically connected to the rise of capitalism and the development of a modern state.

Civil society and the state

Contemporary liberal theorists define civil society as the public space between the state and the individual citizen, comprised of voluntary associations autonomous of the state. Whereas the state is associated with repression, civil society is seen as the realm of freedom. Hence, a strong civil society fosters democracy, according to liberal theorists (cf. Diamond 1994; Hadenius and Uggla 1995). However, the state–civil society dichotomy can be seen as an attempt to delegitimize the state (Beckman 1998). While arguing against the 'simplistic antinomy between state and civil society, locked in a zero-sum struggle', Diamond (1994: 5) still portrays civil society mainly as a sphere controlling or reducing arbitrary state power. The same tendency is found among other liberal theorists.

One advantage of a post-Marxist, compared to a liberal, notion of civil society is that it allows for a more fruitful analysis of state–society relations. As stated by Beckman (1998: 56), '[c]ivil society does not exist independently of the state; it is situated in rules and transactions which connect state and society'. The state provides the legal framework for civil society. Civil society groups may seek democratization of civil society through the state. Civil society groups are also often incorporated or co-opted in the state structure (Rodan 1997: 161). Autonomy from the state should therefore not be part of the definition of civil society. Naturally, there has to be some degree of autonomy from the state otherwise the associations in question are by definition state institutions, but it is always a matter of relative autonomy and for some associations autonomy from capitalist institutions are more important than autonomy from the state. Classic Marxism would treat civil society as dominated by economic institutions but, under the influence of Gramsci, post-Marxists have tended to stress the non-economic dimension of civil society (Kumar 1993: 383). As argued by Cohen and Arato (1992: viii), 'the spontaneous forces of the capitalist market economy can represent as great a danger to social solidarity, social justice, and even autonomy as the administrative power of the modern state'.

A sphere outside state power and political governance is indeed a strange idea. Not even the market is free from state regulation. On the contrary, the whole institutional framework of the market economy is created and maintained by the state. Hence, close connections between state and civil society are not only more or less unavoidable – they may also be desirable, provided that the state has at least some democratic features. Walzer (1992) warns against the anti-political tendencies that often accompany the celebration of civil society. New social movements may not seek state power (as did the 'old social movements') but without some use of the state apparatus they will not reach their goals. The state 'both frames civil society and occupies space within it. It fixes the boundary conditions and the basic rules of all associational activity' (Walzer 1992: 103). '[C]ivil society left to itself, generates radically unequal power relationships, which only state power can challenge' (Walzer 1992: 104). Civil society is dependent on the state for its existence. '*Any* civil society can be created, supported, manipulated, or repressed by *any* state, and it is profoundly misleading to try to conceptualize it apart from political power' (Ehrenberg 1999: 238). The character of the state has a profound impact on civil society. For civil society to be consolidated, the autonomy of civil society must be legally institutionalized (Weigle 2000: 36) and this legal framework needs to be understood when analysing civil society. Furthermore, state authorities have a wide range of methods for controlling, co-opting or repressing civil society groups. The coercive agencies of the state (police, military and judiciary) can relate to civil society groups in three ways (Bermeo 2000: 242): by providing legal sanction, by outright repression, or by tolerating the group. Legal sanction is a mixed blessing as it also means state control.

Civil society groups are also part of the process of state formation (Beckman and Sjögren 2001: 4). They try to influence rules and practices of the state. However, civil society should not be seen as by definition in opposition to the state (Cohen and Arato 1992: x–xi). Cooperation with state authorities is perhaps more common than oppositional activities among civil society groups. The important question in this respect is how the process of political inclusion works. It is important to distinguish between inclusion in the state and inclusion in the polity more generally. Entry into the state may take the form of interest group lobbying activities, participation in policymaking through negotiations with state officials, participation in party and electoral politics, and the appointment of group leaders to government positions (Dryzek 1996: 475). According to Dryzek (1996), the inclusion of civil society groups in the state is good for democracy only if two conditions are met: 1) The main concerns of the group can be assimilated to an established or emerging state imperative. If this is not the case inclusion will result in cooption and the group will not gain any real influence. 2) Civil society is not weakened by the group's entry into the state. Pressure for democracy has almost always come from oppositional civil society. If pro-democracy actors leave civil society to enter the state, such pressures are likely to be weakened. Avoiding inclusion in the state does not mean that civil society groups have to remain powerless. Power can be exercised from and within civil society in several ways, including the changing of political discourse, the legitimation of particular forms of collective action, the establishment of policy-oriented institutions within civil society, and protest activities that leads to governmental responses (Dryzek 1996: 481). The strategic decision of civil society actors to opt for some form of inclusion in the state or to try to gain political influence from within civil society is dependent on regime type. Under an authoritarian regime the risk of co-optation is obvious, whereas prospects for mutually beneficial state–civil society relations are somewhat better under a more democratic regime.

Political opportunities

In order to further our understanding of how civil society is related to the state and political society we can borrow from sociological theorizing on social movements. Recent research on social movements has focused on political opportunities (e.g. McAdam *et al.* 1996; Tarrow 1998). Political opportunities (and constraints) external to the movement can help explain the emergence of social movements. The concept of political opportunities, however, can easily be used for almost any kind of contextual factors having an impact on social movements. Such a broad and vague conception is of little help. It is necessary to narrow the concept and give it a precise meaning. Drawing on McAdam (1996: 27) we can identify the following dimensions:

* The relative openness or closure of the formal political system.
* The presence or absence of elite allies.
* The state leadership's capacity for, and willingness to use, repression.

The concept is useful, as it links social movements (and other aspects of civil society) to these features of institutional politics. Political opportunities have often been analysed as opportunity structures, but, as Tarrow (1998: 77) points out, most opportunities and constraints are situational rather than structural. Social movements create new opportunities and constraints, both for themselves and their supporters and for their opponents (Tarrow 1998: 72). The relationship between political opportunities and social movements must therefore be seen as a dynamic interactive process. Most scholars have limited political opportunities to the national level, but, as pointed out by McAdam (1998) the concept can be used for a multi-level analysis. In the section on transnational civil society below, I try to formulate the implications of a transnational perspective for the conceptualization of political opportunities.

Civil society and political society

Some scholars make a distinction between formal and informal politics, where civil society represents the latter. Civil society is distinguished from political society which (in relation to democratization) means 'that arena in which the polity specifically arranges itself to contest the legitimate right to exercise control over public power and the state apparatus' (Linz and Stepan 1996: 8). Political society, thus, is made up of political parties, elections, legislatures, political leadership, etc. While distinguishing between civil society and political society, Cohen and Arato (1992: xvii) blur the distinction when they claim that the politics of civil society can also take 'normal institutional forms of political participation' (like voting or activity in political parties). It is more fruitful to think of actors operating in more than one arena (or in more than one sphere).

In the West, political society grow out of civil society. In Eastern Europe political society predated civil society, with the consequence that democracy had little societal grounding (Bunce 2000: 211). The ability of civil society groups to connect with political society is essential for the development of a pro-democratic civil society (Bermeo 2000: 244).

Civil society and economic society

In liberal theory there is sometimes a tendency to blur the distinction between civil society and the economy. Diamond (1994: 5) excludes 'the profit-making enterprise of individual business firms' from his definition of civil society, but a few lines later in the same text he seems to bring economic entities back into the concept of civil society by listing '*economic* (productive and commercial associations and networks)' (Diamond 1994: 6) as the first of seven different forms of civil society organizations. He also notes the 'market-oriented nature of civil society' (Diamond 1994: 7) in order to exclude religious fundamentalist and revolutionary movements from the definition.

I find it useful to distinguish between civil society and economic society, but the two arenas are often closely intertwined. Unlike actors in economic society, civil society groups are not first and foremost profit-seeking, but they are often dependent on financial support from actors in economic society, and market logics might have a strong impact also on civil society. A dominant economic society may be at least as dangerous for civil society as a dominant state. Even the influential capitalist George Soros, who has spent a lot of money supporting civil society against state power in post-communist Eastern Europe, warns against the negative impact of uncontrolled markets. According to him, the main enemy of the open society is no longer the communist, but the capitalist threat (*Atlantic Monthly*, February 1997: 45; quoted in Ehrenberg 1999: 250).

This section on civil society relations to the state, political society and economic society provides analytical tools for the empirical analysis in Chapter 5.

Transnational civil society

Approaches to transnational civil society

In contemporary discussions of civil society there is a trend away from state-centred approaches, both in the sense of a stronger emphasis on individual empowerment and personal autonomy and in the sense of territorial restructuring related to processes of globalization (Kaldor 2000: 108). This has given rise to a number of studies of 'global civil society' (e.g. Anheier *et al.* 2001; Kaldor 2003; Keane 2003). There are, however, many transnational civil society interactions that are not global but more geographically limited. It might therefore be more adequate to speak of transnational civil society and transnational activism (Piper and Uhlin 2004).

Transnational civil society is sometimes conceived as a political project rather than a descriptive or analytical term. According to Kaldor (1999: 195) transnational civil society constitutes a 'demand for a radical extension of democracy across national and social boundaries'. To be part of civil society implies a commitment to common human values and a global human rights culture (Kaldor 1999: 210). As argued in the previous section, I find it problematic and misleading to define civil society as something inherently good. In line with this reasoning and following O'Brien *et al.* (2000: 15) I see transnational civil society as 'an arena for conflict that interacts with both the interstate system and the global economy'. A purely descriptive definition would be 'the sphere of ideas, values, institutions, organizations, networks, and individuals located *between* the family, the state, and the market and operating *beyond* the confines of national societies, polities and economies' (Anheier *et al.* 2001: 17).

Despite many historical examples of transnational civil society activism (e.g. Keck and Sikkink 1998: ch. 2), it can be argued that civil society has mainly become transnational since the 1960s (Scholte 1999: 13). Globalization has a profound impact on activities within civil society. It makes events occurring far away relevant. It leads to the diffusion of forms of organization and strategies. Transnational political opportunities and constraints affect local activities. Local and national civil society groups become players in a 'multi-level game' (della Porta and Kriesi 1999: 6).

Transnational civil society actors

Actors operating within transnational civil society include local and national NGOs and social movements as well as their transnational varieties: international NGOs (INGOs) and transnational social movements (TSMs). Much research has focused on transnational social movement organizations (TSMOs) (e.g. Smith *et al.* 1997; Smith and Johnston 2002), although the actual organizations analysed are often better described as INGOs. The focus in this study is on how local post-Soviet civil society groups are linked to civil society groups based in other countries and to transnational civil society groups. A significant aspect of the transnational relations of post-Soviet civil society groups, however, is foreign funding, and this is an issue that we deal with first.

The problem of funding

Since the mid-1980s NGOs have been strongly supported by governments and multilateral institutions. Support for civil society (or rather some specific aspects of it) in the form of NGOs became part of neo-liberal politics (Pearce 2000: 19).

Funding is essential for many civil society activities. Within a framework stressing interests and resources the following actors in the funding context can be identified: donor states, developing states, multilateral donor organizations, international NGOs, national NGOs and grassroots organizations (Stiles 2000: 35). Instrumental in the transnational funding of civil society groups are also intermediary NGOs, which support local grassroots groups, membership-based NGOs, etc. and serve as a link between transnational NGOs and funding agencies on the one hand and local civil society groups on the other (Hudock 1999: 12). Intermediary NGOs play an especially important role in post-communist societies where real NGOs are a new phenomenon. Support for intermediary NGOs instead of local civil society groups, according to Hudock (1999: 13), means encouraging democracy by proxy rather than true democracy. Through foreign funding, NGOs become dependent on external actors. Thus, they may lose their capacity to contribute to the development of civil society. Instead of empowering local people, foreign-funded NGOs tend to focus on pleasing funding agencies in order to receive new grants (Hudock 1999).

Transnational networking

Networks are characterized by voluntary, reciprocal and horizontal exchanges of information and services (Keck and Sikkink 1998: 200), but they are not necessarily egalitarian. Interactions within transnational advocacy networks are often asymmetrical (Keck and Sikkink 1998: 207). Networks might be particularly good at transferring information, but for the collection and distribution of other types of resources they may be less reliable than other types of organizations. Access to information may be restricted to those who are already within the network (Ahrne 1998: 92).

The increase in transnational problems and the incapacity of governments to cope with these problems explain the emergence of transnational civil society networks. The development of communication and information technology is also helpful (Rucht 1999: 215–16). Other transnational political opportunities include potential allies within international organizations and the existence of international regimes and conventions (Uhlin 2002). Prospects for continued growth of transnational civil society networks, however, are perhaps not as good as often envisioned. There is an increasingly sharp competition for both funding and public attention. Problems of coordination when the number of groups grows, cases of misuse of funds, and a tendency for bureaucratization and deradicalization are other problems that may limit the growth of transnational civil society. There might also be a disappointment with transnational civil society groups due to unduly high expectations of what they can achieve (Rucht 1999: 217–19).

Transnational networking can take many different forms, including personal meetings at international conferences or through international education, contacts through surface mail, telephone, fax or e-mail. It can be a matter of simply exchanging information, but it may also involve cooperation in a coordinated transnational campaign. An important question is what effects transnational networking has on the activities of local civil society groups. Does it divert the focus from local problems and efforts at reaching out to the public in the local community or does it encourage new forms of more effective civil society activities and increase the political strength of local civil society groups?

This section provides a framework for the analysis in Chapter 6.

Civil society and democracy

Within this project we are not primarily interested in civil society as such, but its relation to democracy and democratization. Here it is important to remember what sort of democracy we are talking about (cf. Li 1999: 404). In the beginning of this chapter I made a distinction between formal institutional and societal democratization. Most research on civil society and democratization has used civil society as a variable explaining the democratization of formal political institutions. This perspective is of great interest for the present study, but we also need to consider the impact of civil society on the form of societal democratization discussed in the beginning of this chapter. Hence, when discussing potential democratic functions of civil society, we should differentiate between functions supporting formal democracy and functions supporting societal democracy. While most theorizing of the relationship between civil society and democracy implicitly deals with the national level we should remember that local politics is of utmost importance for civil society. As noted by Diamond (1994: 9), '[t]he democratization of local government [. . .] goes hand in hand with the development of civil society'. The local focus of this study is therefore particularly useful.

The literature is rich in hypotheses and more or less well grounded empirical findings about the relationship between civil society and formal political democracy. I will here briefly and critically discuss the main propositions in this field (see Figure 2.2). These include what has been termed the two main aspects of the 'civil society argument': 1) that associational life fosters 'patterns of civility' in the actions of citizens; and 2) that civil society is independent of the state and is thus capable of organizing resistance against an authoritarian regime (Foley and Edwards 1996: 39). In this context it is useful to distinguish between the role of civil society in a pre-transition context under an authoritarian regime, in the transition, and in a post-transition phase. Civil society organizations play different roles in the transition and post-transition phases. During a regime transition, civil society is mainly a countervailing force against an authoritarian state. After the transition, civil society has a mixture of state-supporting and countervailing functions (Boussard 2003: 97).

Under an authoritarian (or post-totalitarian) regime, those aspects of civil society that can exist may *form a parallel society* (cf. Benda *et al.* 1988), by setting up independent institutions that can perform functions otherwise claimed by a state with

---

Pre-transition:
Parallel society under an authoritarian regime (defensive) (SD)

Pre-transition/transition:
Countervailing force against an authoritarian regime (mobilizational) (FD)

Post-transition:
Producing political actors for new democracies (FD)
    But: Weakens civil society (SD)

Check against the abuse of state power (countervailing force) (FD)
    But: A strong state necessary for democracy

Aggregating, articulating and representing interests (influencing state policies)
(FD)
    But: Risk that powerful group interests take precedence over the
    common good

Assisting the sate (inclusion in the state) (FD)
    But: Inclusion may not lead to political influence (FD) and may weaken
    civil society (SD)

Increasing political participation (SD)
    But: Participation does not necessarily mean influence

Generating social capital (SD-FD)
    But: Also bad social capital

Figure 2.2 Democratic functions of civil society

Note: FD = Formal Democracy. SD = Societal Democracy.

totalitarian ambitions. This does not mean a direct confrontation with the state.
Rather it is a more defensive form of opposition in which citizens try to ignore and
bypass the powerful state, hence trying to establish elements of societal democracy,
despite the authoritarianism characterizing the formal political sphere.

In a pre-transition phase, as well as during the regime transition, *actors within civil
society mobilize to form a countervailing force against the authoritarian regime.* Pressure
from pro-democracy civil society actors has often been instrumental in regime
transitions. (This will be analysed in Chapter 3.) The role of civil society actors like
labour, women and environmental movements, human rights NGOs, etc. have been
widely acknowledged in the democratization literature (O'Donnell and Schmitter
1986; Rueschemeyer *et al.* 1992, ch. 5). The focus here is on formal democratization, but the widespread participation in pro-democracy movements may also
have a positive impact on societal democracy. Not all civil society actors, however,
struggle for democracy. Civil society may also contain anti-democratic forces.

After the actual transition, *civil society produces political actors for the new democracies.*
Actors within civil society take the step into political society by forming political
parties and other formal political institutions. Political leaders in new democracies

may be recruited from civil society groups. This is an important role that civil society plays in strengthening formal democracy after the transition, but we still need to differentiate between different actors within civil society. Civil society produces both pro-democratic and anti-democratic actors. Furthermore, when prominent civil society actors enter political society and/or the state, civil society is likely to be weakened, with potentially negative consequences for societal democracy.

A function of civil society that is commonly stressed is that of being a *check against the abuse of state power*. (This will be analysed in Chapter 5.) Within liberal theory, civil society is said to strengthen (formal) democracy because a strong civil society makes the state less dominant. The basic function of civil society is to control and limit state power (Diamond 1994: 7). The growth of civil society alters the balance of power between state and society. A strong civil society improves the accountability of the state. While this is an important function of civil society, two reservations are called for. First, it is far from clear that a strong civil society automatically decreases the power of the state. Civil society may sometimes strengthen the state (Clarke 1998). NGOs and other civil society groups may increase the effectiveness of state institutions, for instance in the case of a relatively democratic state plagued by corruption. Second, the weakening of the state might be good for democracy if the state is authoritarian, but it does not necessarily lead to democratization. Based on experiences of real, existing democracies, we may in fact conclude that a strong state is needed for democracy to work. The liberal distinction between an authoritarian state and a democratic civil society is simplistic.

Civil society creates channels for the *aggregation, articulation and representation of interests* (Diamond 1994: 8; Fish 1995: 53–4). (These aspects will be considered in Chapter 5.) A pluralist civil society balances different interests, and makes sure that power is not concentrated in one dominating group (Diamond 1994: 9). In this way, civil society groups complement political parties as channels that citizens can use to influence state policies. This is a major function of civil society in a formal democratic system. However, there is a risk that powerful group interests take precedence over the common good. Interest-group representation contains its own democratic problems.

Contrary to claims that civil society weakens the state, there is also the argument that civil society groups may *assist the state in the design and implementation of various public policies*, thus increasing the effectiveness and legitimacy of the state. (This is also a topic for Chapter 5.) Through various forms of service delivery, civil society may increase the capacity of people to improve their own welfare, thus lessening the demands on the state and increasing state stability. Civil society groups may also strengthen the efficacy and legitimacy of elected bodies by their participation in election campaigns and political institutions (Clarke 1998: 201). But the service delivery of civil society groups might be unprofessional and unreliable. In taking over responsibilities that are usually connected to state institutions, civil society groups may also undermine or even replace state institutions and undermine the legitimacy of the state with fatal consequences for democracy (Van Roy and Robinson 1998: 45). Furthermore, the form of inclusion that is implied in civil society assistance to the state may not mean any real political influence for civil society groups, and civil society itself may also be weakened by such co-optation.

Civil society supports democracy by providing avenues for *political participation* (Hydén 1995: 7). Post-Marxists typically argue that associational life in civil society stimulates political participation, thus deepening democracy. The distinction between participation and influence must, however, be problematized (Stubbergaard 1998: 11). Widespread popular participation in civil society organizations is not a guarantee of popular influence on political decision-making in the polity at large or even inside specific civil society organizations. A rich associational life may mean a more participatory and deeper form of democracy, but real power relations must be analysed. The actions of civil society groups are shaped and restricted by power relations connected to states and other entities. The existence of a large number of civil society groups does not automatically mean that all its members have political influence and power. There is a lack of power perspective in many studies of civil society. (These aspects are analysed in Chapter 5.)

Finally, an interesting hypothesis about civil society and democracy is that civil society strengthens democracy by *generating social capital*. Formal as well as societal democracy is strengthened by the collective trust and tolerance among citizens that develop within civil society (Putnam 1993; 2000). (This aspect is considered in Chapter 7.) Civil society may foster a democratic political culture, i.e. values of trust and cooperation, and a public sphere for discussion and debate (Hydén 1995: 7). However, civil society organizations need not be supportive of democracy. As pointed out by Levi (1996: 51), neighbourhoods and certain other networks of civic engagement promote trust among members, but distrust of outsiders. Hence, civil society may also generate 'bad social capital'.

The critical comments above indicate a need to abandon an overly romantic view of civil society as always supportive of democracy. Liberal theorists tend to define civil society as those associations that support liberal democracy. Groups that are not supportive of the liberal project are described as 'vested interests'. Defined in this way, it is obvious that civil society supports liberal democracy, but it is a circular reasoning (Beckman 1997: 2). Instead we should acknowledge that civil society groups become democratically relevant when they contest relations of domination within their own fields (Beckman 2001: 63). Furthermore, there is no reason why civil society should not be able to undermine a democratic regime just as well as an authoritarian one (Foley and Edwards 1996: 39). Elements of civil society may in fact take any position towards democracy, from support for authoritarianism, via passivity to active struggle for democracy of some variety (cf. White 1994: 380). It is easy to find examples of anti-democratic associations within civil society. An active civil society can therefore not be seen as by definition supportive of democracy, as civil society itself may have authoritarian tendencies. Patron–client relationships often characterize both the internal organization of civil society and the ties between civil society groups and state agencies (Clarke 1998: 198–9).

Finally, we should also consider democratic implications of transnational civil society. The emergence of a transnational civil society, and processes of globalization in general, raise new problems for democracy, which has historically been closely associated with the nation state. The basic problem is that structures of power and major issues of survival are firmly rooted in a global context, whereas participation, representation and legitimacy are fixed at the state level (O'Brien *et al.* 2000: 21–2). Some see a global civil society as the solution to this democratic problem, but many improvements in terms of representation and accountability etc. are needed if global civil society is to really enhance democracy in global governance (Scholte 2004).

Instead of focusing solely on the global or transnational level, we need to consider the complexities of multilevel systems (cf. Elofsson and Rindefjäll 1998). The local level cannot be fully understood if we do not analyse how it relates to not only regional and national levels, but also a transnational level. The contemporary world is a multilevel system where political decisions are made and implemented on local, regional, national, transnational, international and supranational levels. This must be our perspective – both when analysing existing democratic problems and when theorizing about a possible future democratic order.

In conclusion, civil society can be seen as a necessary but not sufficient condition for formal democracy. An emerging civil society may support democratization by forming a parallel society under an authoritarian regime, and by mobilizing as a countervailing force against the authoritarian regime. Following the transition, civil society may strengthen democracy by producing political actors for new democracies, by being a check against the abuse of state power, by aggregating, articulating and representing interests, by assisting the state in the design and implementation of various public policies, by increasing political participation, and by strengthening collective trust and tolerance among citizens. These conclusions, however, need some important qualifications. First, civil society actors are not the only democratizing forces. 'At best, civil society can destroy a non-democratic regime. However, a full democratic transition, and especially democratic consolidation, must involve political society' (Linz and Stepan 1996: 8). Second, the sharp distinction between state and civil society is misleading. Democratization must involve a transformation of both state and civil society, which in fact are often closely interrelated. Third, the inclusion of civil society actors in the state may weaken civil society, thus being negative for societal democracy. Fourth, civil society is not by definition supportive of democracy. It is a sphere of political struggle involving both pro- and antidemocratic forces. Fifth, power relations – both within civil society and between civil society groups and actors belonging to other social spheres – must be analysed. Sixth, we must differentiate between different actors within civil society. In order to be more precise about the impact of civil society on democracy we must focus on specific civil society actors. Finally, we should examine the relationship between civil society and democracy in a multilevel analysis. The emergence of transnational civil society has implications for local and national democracy as well as for a possible form of transnational democracy.

This theoretical analysis of civil society and democracy influences the whole study, but it is most explicitly applied in Chapter 7.

Conclusion

In this study, democracy is understood as a form of collective decision-making based on the principles of popular control and political equality. Democratization – the process towards democracy – may have both a formal institutional and a more substantive societal dimension. An actor-structure approach is applied, with a focus on actors within civil society and the structural constraints that shape their political space. The main focus is on problems of consolidation of democracy, but this is compared to dynamics in the pre-transition and transition phases. Unlike most studies of democratization that are mainly concerned with the national level, this study focuses on the local and transnational levels and links between them. The specific problems of post-Communist transitions as compared to processes of democratization in other contexts are emphasized.

Drawing on post-Marxist as well as liberal theories, civil society is defined as a public sphere in which different kinds of actors – which have some degree of autonomy in relation to the state and other social spheres – develop identities and articulate interests. Civil society groups are often political, but they should be distinguished from formal political institutions. Civil society is not by definition 'good' or democratic, but characterized by the same inequalities and power structures as the rest of society. A power perspective is necessary when analysing civil society. Power struggles and actual political influence are important – not the number of civil society groups and activists as such.

Social movements are typically the main civil society actors in the pre-transition and transition phases, but in post-transition civil societies more moderate and institutionalized NGOs tend to dominate. This study focuses primarily on openly political civil society sectors, like human rights, women, labour, the environment, and ethnic and nationalist issues. In addition to an examination of civil society groups it is useful to pay attention to the individual activists. Resource mobilization and other activities of civil society groups should be analysed. The application of a power perspective requires a solid analysis of civil society relations to other social spheres, including the state, political and economic society. The state provides the legal framework for civil society and state authorities have a wide range of methods for controlling, co-opting and repressing civil society groups. The process of inclusion of civil society groups into the state needs to be analysed. The concept of political opportunities provides another analytical tool for analysing state–civil society relations. The relative openness or closure of the political system, the state's capacity and propensity for repression and the existence of elite allies to a large extent condition the development of civil society. The ability of civil society groups to connect to political society, in the form of political parties, is essential for democratic development. Economic society may be an important source of financial support for civil society activities, but uncontrolled markets may also have a negative impact upon civil society.

Unlike the state, civil society has no clear territorial boundaries. Transnational civil society activities are becoming increasingly common. Transnational civil society actors interact with local civil societies through different forms of networking. Transnational funding provides vital resources for many local civil society groups, but it also creates dependencies and influences the character of local civil society activities. These aspects of civil society must be thoroughly analysed in order to understand how civil society is related to democratization.

Civil society may strengthen formal as well as societal democratization in a number of different ways, including by forming a parallel society under an authoritarian regime, by mobilizing a countervailing force against the authoritarian regime, by producing political actors for new democracies, by being a check against the abuse of state power, by aggregating, articulating and representing interests, by assisting the state in the design and implementation of various public policies, by increasing political participation, and by strengthening collective trust and tolerance among citizens. These arguments, however, need some important qualifications. First, civil society actors are not the only democratizing forces. Second, the sharp distinction between state and civil society is misleading. Democratization must involve a transformation of both state and civil society. Third, the inclusion of civil society actors in the state may weaken civil society, thus being negative for societal democracy. Fourth, civil society is not necessarily supportive of democracy. It is a sphere of political struggle involving both pro- and antidemocratic forces. Fifth, power relations and the actual political influence of civil society groups must be analysed. Finally, in order to be more precise about the impact of civil society on democracy we must focus on specific civil society actors.

3 Civil society and the fall of communist rule

This chapter provides an analysis of the emergence of civil society in the Soviet Union and the role played by civil society actors in the transition from communist rule. First, I briefly discuss to what extent there was a civil society before and under communist rule.

Civil society before and under communism?

The state in imperial Russia was indeed powerful and had strict control over most of society. Yet, the tsars could not rule entirely as they pleased. Even the intolerant Nicholas I (r. 1825–55) accepted philanthropic activities outside of the state sphere (Engelstein 2000: 24). Some researchers have traced the emergence of a civil society in Russia to the *zemstvo* institution, created by Tsar Alexander II as a bureaucratic apparatus for the management of local economic welfare and needs. It has been argued that this institution created political pluralism and ultimately led to the emergence of a civil society in late imperial Russia (Volodin *et al.* 1998: 45). Intended to serve the interests of central state power, the *zemstvo* institution increasingly came to reflect local interests, at least the interests of the local nobility. *Zemstvo* activities were supposed to be purely local, and efforts at forming interregional organizations for the coordination of relief and philanthropic activities were blocked by the state (Porter 1991). While the *zemstvo* institution did put some constraints on absolute state power, it was far from what we today understand as a civil society.

The revolution of 1905 and the subsequent implementation of certain aspects of rule of law laid the ground for the emergence of a more modern form of civil society in Russia, according to Wartenweiler (1999: 1). The development of modern political parties and a modern press as well as councils during the revolutions of 1905 and 1917, however, can be seen only as 'stirrings of the emergence of civil society' (Bernhard 1993: 311). The writings of liberal Russian academics between 1905 and 1914 reflect the ideas and values that we today link to the notion of civil society, but there was hardly any developed civil society in pre-revolution Russia.

By contrast, the Baltic states have a pre-communist historical legacy of relatively vivid civil societies. During the first period of independence (1920–1940) a civil society made up of organized peasants and labour as well as a secular intelligentsia in Estonia and Latvia and groups associated with the Catholic Church in Lithuania emerged. While civil society in Estonia and Latvia mainly had a liberal or social democratic orientation, civil society in Lithuania was more nationalist (anti-Russian) and more oriented towards the Catholic Church. Compared to the other Baltic states, civil society in Lithuania had more parochial features and was numerically weaker (Ruutsso 2002: ch. 3). The decline of democratic regimes and the imposition of authoritarian rule limited the space for civil society in the 1930s, especially in Lithuania and Latvia. The more fascist and militaristic form of authoritarian rule in Lithuania under Smetona gave little space for civil society outside the Catholic Church. In Latvia, the authoritarian-corporativist regime under the charismatic leadership of Karlis Ulmanis also put heavy restrictions on civil society activities. In Estonia, by contrast, the populist-authoritarian regime established by Konstantin Päts left the non-political part of civil society almost untouched (Ruutsoo 2002: 393).

Communist rule, and especially the terror under Stalin, destroyed what might have existed in the form of independent social activity. The Baltic republics suffered a particularly brutal process of Stalinization, and a large number of people were imprisoned or killed and all independent organization crushed (Gill 2002: 97).[1] Some scholars argue that some relatively autonomous organizations emerged in the post-Stalin Soviet Union. Skilling (1971), for instance, analyses 'interest groups' in the Soviet Union. These 'interest groups', however, were factions within the state, rather than civil society organizations. Ignoring their location within rather than outside the state leads to a conceptual stretching and the emphasis on elite conflicts makes these researchers neglect conflicts between state and society.[2]

Until the Gorbachev period, all non-state political activity was banned in the Soviet Union. Some independent organizations managed to exist – including the Orthodox Monarchist Union Order and dissident network People's Labour Union (with some transnational links), but they were forced to work underground, and had no capacity for regular public expression (Fish 1995: 31). Some oppositional voices were spread through unofficial *samizdat* publications. However, the independent organizations that developed in the Khrushchev period and re-emerged in the final years of Brezhnev's rule were too weak and isolated from the general public to form a social basis for the pro-democracy movement emerging during *glasnost* and *perestroika* (Weigle 2000: 88). There were three varieties of dissidence in the USSR, mainly represented by individuals. First, a traditional, religious and nationalist orientation (Aleksander Solzhenitsyn). Second, a liberal and civil libertarian tendency (Andrei Sakharov). Third, a Leninist tendency striving at internal reform (Roy Medvedev) (Bernhard 1993: 312). The roots of an ecological movement can also be traced back to the 1960s, and elements of a peace and human rights movement can be seen since the late 1970s (Patomäki and Pursiainen 1998: 46). Nationalist protests occurred in the Baltic republics, and some dissidents managed to survive Soviet repression (Lieven 1994: 103; Ruutsoo 2002: ch. 4). These emerging societal initiatives, however, were too weak and fragmented to make up anything resembling a civil society. The development of a genuine civil society was impossible under the totalitarian regime. Neither was there any developed form of 'parallel society' that emerged in some countries in Central and Eastern Europe (Benda *et al.* 1988).

I agree with Arato's (1991: 199) position in between the 'totalitarianism thesis' and the argument that there was a civil society in the USSR. Stalinism destroyed civil society and only some of its prerequisites were reconstituted during the post-Stalin era. Growing societal complexity and a somewhat less profound state control on the micro-level were not sufficient for the development of a civil society in the pre-Gorbachev period. There was a 'very low level of independent social organization even in the early Gorbachev period' (Arato 1991: 200). Hence, Russia's 'democratic entrepreneurs' had to 'build independent society – and democracy – from scratch' (Fish 1995: 172).

The emergence of civil society in Russia under Gorbachev

When Gorbachev announced *perestroika* in April 1985, the character of the Soviet political system began to change. There were signs that for the first time some public political opposition would be tolerated. One year later the first rallies in Moscow and Leningrad were held. The development of what would become a civil society in Russia can be divided into three phases. The first phase – from April 1985 to January 1989 – saw the birth of independent political groups in large cities and collective action in the form of rallies and manifestations. The second phase – from the election campaign of the First Congress of People's Deputies of the USSR until elections to the Russian and local soviets in 1990 – was the peak of the protest cycle. Mobilization was stimulated by electoral opportunities. The third phase included the removal of the sixth article of the Constitution ensuring the monopoly of the Soviet Communist Party in March 1990, the referenda on the Unity of the sovereignty of Russia in March 1991, and the presidential elections in May 1991. During this time there was an institutionalization of democratic social movements and a decline in protest actions (Zdravomyslova 1996: 123–4; Temkina 1997: 22–3).

The partial liberalization initiated by Gorbachev from 1985 aimed at a form of 'socialist pluralism' (Fish 1995: 32), not a fundamental transformation of the political, economic and social systems. The first independent associations that emerged were also rather moderate. They focused on the preservation of historical monuments, environmental protection or the struggle against alcoholism.

Groups with a clear political agenda began to emerge in 1987. Perestroika Club – a discussion group in Moscow – was formed in spring 1987. The human rights and democracy group Memorial was established in the summer of 1987. In August the same year, the human rights group Citizens' Dignity appeared. In August 1987 a conference for discussion groups from all over the Soviet Union was held. These new groups did not yet constitute a genuine opposition, but 'after six decades of ruinous existence in Russia, [the totalitarian regime] died quietly in 1987 in the apartments and small public conference rooms where the new political clubs convened' (Fish 1995: 33).

By 1987, more than 30,000 informal groups independent from the Communist Party had formed, and by 1989 the number had grown to 60,000. 'Popular fronts' had appeared in most republics (Weigle 2000: 79–80). Millions of Soviet citizens participated in informal groups, focusing on a broad range of issues and activities, ranging from recreation, to culture, social welfare and politics (Urban 1997: 95). Although most of these groups did not espouse liberal ideology, they opposed the hegemonic power of the Communist Party, and advocated rule of law and civil and political liberties.

Two stages of widening political opportunities can be identified (Butterfield and Sedaitis 1991: 3–6). First, *glasnost*, which made the political system more open and decreased the degree of state repression. When *glasnost* was proclaimed in 1988, there was an expansion in the number of non-state groups. More radical groups, not officially tolerated, emerged, and street demonstrations became increasingly common. The state reacted with everything from tolerance to repression, but *glasnost* meant that not even the most radical political groups, like the Democratic Union, suffered severe repression. Activists were sometimes detained for several hours or days, but they were not sent into prison camps as dissidents were before Gorbachev's rise to power (Butterfield and Sedaitis 1991: 4).

The second stage of widening political opportunities was the partly competitive elections. The elections to the USSR Congress of People's Deputies in March 1989 were the first partly open and competitive elections in the USSR, but rules still strongly favoured the Communist Party. Nevertheless, some democrats were elected. The most important impact of the elections, however, was that they stimulated popular mobilization (Fish 1995: 35–6). The year 1989 was the peak of mass mobilization. After the elections, the first umbrella group of democratic forces – the Moscow Union of Voters – was formed (Fish 1995: 37). In mid-1989 more coherent formal organizations and parties, including the Social Democratic Association, emerged from the now disbanded Moscow Popular Front and Democratic Perestroika.[3] Large national conferences of democratic movement organizations were held in the autumn of 1989 (Fish 1995: 38). The partly competitive elections, however, did not only make democratic social movement organizations consolidate and unite. National-patriotic and communist counter-movements also developed as a result of the elections (Zdravomyslova 1996: 131).

With the exception of the Democratic Union, founded in May 1988, most of the new groups did not yet challenge the Communist Party's monopoly on power (Fish 1995: 35). The Democratic Union presented itself as an all-union political party with branches in more than 30 cities. A marginal intelligentsia led it and many long-term dissidents participated. The group had 120 members in Leningrad. It advocated non-violent means to achieve radical change and was openly confrontational towards the Communist Party. It had its theoretical base in American political science conceptions of totalitarianism, and applied symbols from Western democracy, but it had vague ideas of civil society, the rule of law, and economic, political and ideological pluralism (Zdravomyslova 1996: 127–9). The organization never received any mass support, but as the first organization in Russia to confront the regime directly, the Democratic Union created political space in the initial phase of liberalization (Fish 1995: 107–9).

Parallel with the development of pro-democracy groups led by intellectuals, an independent labour movement emerged. Strikes in the coal mining industry in 1989 played an important role in the democratic mobilization (Fish 1995: 39). An independent labour movement had begun to develop in 1987–1988. It included both new labour organizations and reformed Soviet trade unions. The movement was soon politicized, and its focus shifted from mostly economic concerns to outright political demands, confronting the party-state (Temkina 1997: 23).

In 1990 there was a further organizational differentiation within the pro-democracy movement. Elections for soviets on the republican, *oblast*, city and district level in March 1990 stimulated popular mobilization and new political parties emerged (Fish 1995: 42–3). Democratic Russia was founded in October 1990 as an umbrella organization for the democratic movement, and local chapters quickly emerged (Fish 1995: 44–5). In early 1991, the killings in Vilnius – when Soviet troops seized the television centre – and the following crackdown on independent media marked the return to repression and the end of *glasnost*. An increased polarization between state and pro-democracy movement occurred, and strikes with political demands became increasingly common. Democratic Russia began to fragment in mid-1991 due to conflicts on strategies. Election campaigns – the referendum in March and the presidential election in June – still united the democratic forces (Fish 1995: 47–50).

The new groups and movements that emerged under *perestroika* and *glasnost* had a diverse character. Popular fronts in the capitals consisted mainly of left or democratic socialist intellectuals. In the provinces of Russia, popular fronts tended to be more populist, protesting against corruption, deprivation and pollution. In the Union Republics (especially in Estonia, Latvia and Lithuania) popular fronts were nationalist mass movements (Devlin 1995: 116–17). The core of the democratic movement in Russia was mainly concentrated in Moscow. It included the Social Democratic Party of Russia (SDPR), the Democratic Platform/Republican Party of Russia (RPR), the Democratic Party of Russia (DPR), the Russian Christian

Democratic Movement (RHhDD), Democratic Russia, and the Democratic Union (DU) (Fish 1995: 80). Popular mobilization was easier in large cities, but not primarily for reasons associated with modernization theory. People in large cities simply enjoyed greater anonymity. Furthermore they were less dependent on their workplace for consumer goods, and hence not so easily controlled by the party-state (Fish 1995: 166). Intellectuals were instrumental in the formation of the democratic movement. Political clubs were dominated by middle-aged male intellectuals (Devlin 1995: 79). In this way the 'democratic revolution' was superficial as it was a revolution from above. It was concentrated in the big cities. Country people, workers, women and the young were not much involved (Devlin 1995: 256–7).

However, far from all new groups and movements were concentrated in Moscow. Leningrad/St Petersburg and Sverdlovsk were two other centres for pro-democracy activism. In Leningrad, mobilization began in 1987 to protect the Hotel d'Angleterre. The protests were led by the ecological group *Spasenie* (Salvation) (Devlin 1995: 77). The Leningrad People's Front was a moderate democratic organization founded in June 1989 by part of the city's intelligentsia (Zdravomyslova 1996: 132). It effectively picked up problems, themes and symbols that resonated with the citizenry. Activists made references to Leningrad folk ideology and also used some Christian symbols (Zdravomyslova 1996: 134–5). Another important pro-democracy group was Memorial. Formed in 1988, it was one of the first independent organizations to be registered in St Petersburg (Interview HR4).[4]

Sverdlovsk, too, experienced an earlier and more extensive political mobilization than most other Russian cities. In November 1987 there were demonstrations in the city in support of Boris Yeltsin, who was born in this region (Fish 1995: 139–40). The Yeltsin issue stimulated mobilization, but focused on a single individual and drew attention from local issues (Fish 1995: 151). As in other Russian cities, there were two major currents within the new movements. First, political discussion clubs supporting *perestroika*. Second, more radical anti-regime groups including old dissidents (Fish 1995: 148). *Miting-87*, founded in January 1988, organized weekly meetings in the main square. The group split in the autumn of 1988. Most members founded a local chapter of the Democratic Union. Others founded the less confrontational but still radical club *Iskra* (Spark) (Fish 1995: 140). Voters' clubs were formed in early 1989. The umbrella organization Movement for Democratic Choice was set up in the summer of 1989, almost one year before Democratic Russia was founded on the national level (Fish 1995: 141). Most activity, however, was concentrated in the regional capital. The DPR claimed 150–200 members in the *oblast* in mid 1991, but other organizations had only tens of members and little or no presence outside the city (Fish 1995: 141).

In 1988–89 state authorities in Sverdlovsk sometimes used violent repression, especially against radical groups like the Democratic Union. Conservative officials controlled governments in Sverdlovsk *oblast* and city. The level of repression was significant but not extremely high (Fish 1995: 158–9). Many activists suffered sanctions at work, but official tolerance of private economic activity was greater in Sverdlovsk than in many other regions, and some new groups received donations from cooperatives. Collections taken at demonstrations were, however, the main source of funding for the democratic movement (Fish 1995: 181–2).

The issues taken up by the new social movements were the same as those addressed by dissidents since the 1960s. Helsinki human rights groups and individual dissidents like Andrei Sakharov, Vladimir Bukovsky and Roy Medvedev raised issues of human rights long before the liberalization introduced by Gorbachev. Nationalist movements have taken up many of the ideas expressed by Alexander Solzhenitsyn. Gender issues were raised in the 1970s by Tatiana Mamonova, among others (Butterfield and Sedaitis 1991: 2–3).

The first autonomous groups and movements in the mid-1980s focused on ecological issues, including Lake Baikal and a campaign against the diversion of Siberia's rivers. Such protests dated back to the 1960s, but they had been repressed. Environmental grievances and discontent were not new, but it was only under Gorbachev's reform policies that they could erupt into widespread social movement activity (Butterfield and Sedaitis 1991:3; cf. Ziegler 1991; Wolfson and Butenko 1992). The fire at the nuclear power plant in Chernobyl in April 1986 stimulated mobilization and strengthened the legitimacy of the movement. Unlike discussion clubs – which were initially confined mostly to the big cities – ecological groups emerged all over the country (Devlin 1995: 75). Greenpeace was founded as an officially endorsed organization in Moscow in 1987, but only a few independent groups associated themselves. In December 1988 the Social-Ecological Union (SEU) was founded as an umbrella organization, uniting 150 ecological groups from ninety cities (Devlin 1995: 78). There were both nationalist and democratic wings of the environmental movement. Nationalists were especially strong in the provinces (Devlin 1995: 76).

The nationalist movement *Pamyat* (Memory) organized the biggest unofficial demonstration in Moscow in May 1987 to protest a planned monument to the victory in the Second World War. Instead of being arrested, the organizers were invited to a meeting with the Party First Secretary for Moscow, Boris Yeltsin (Devlin 1995: 103).

The novelty of the independent groups led to the development of broad non-negotiable demands and difficulties in collective identity formation, which in turn made groups ineffective (Fish 1995: 96). A form of 'hyper democracy' was practised within the democratic groups because of a desire to depart from Soviet style and mistrust due to a fear of infiltration (Fish 1995: 117). This also made the pro-democracy groups ineffective. The Democratic Party of Russia and Democratic Russia were more successful in increasing membership as they focused exclusively on opposition to the regime, rejecting any appeals based on socio-economic, religious or other interests. Other groups focused on a particular social stratum and did not gain mass membership (Fish 1995: 112).

The democratic movement was influenced by anti-Stalinism and reform socialism rather than classical liberal theory. Its support was based on popular grievances with a corrupt and inefficient government rather than enthusiasm for liberal economic reforms and the break-up of the Soviet Union (Devlin 1995: 255). Nevertheless, there were not only 'new left' and social democratic but also liberal ideological tendencies within the movement (Devlin 1995: 80). Following the breakdown of the communist regime and the break-up of the Soviet Union, what used to be the democratic movement split into the traditional Russian categories of Westernizers (often more technocratic than democratic) and Slavophiles (nationalists who allied themselves with their neo-Stalinist enemies) (Devlin 1995: 256).

Unlike social movements in most other countries, those in Russia could not rely on support from already established independent organizations and they had great difficulties in securing material support (Fish 1995: 178). There were three sources of funds for groups on the local level (Fish 1995: 179): members' dues, which were very small and mostly voluntary; collections taken up at public meetings; and funds from non-state economic power, to the extent that it existed. Because of the extreme difficulties in mobilizing resources, solidarity rather than material incentives was behind people's decision to join the democratic movement (Fish 1995: 91). Despite mass participation in specific protest activities, the new groups typically failed to recruit a large number of members. The Democratic Party of Russia was less ineffective in gaining popular support than other groups. It had over thirty thousand members in mid-1991 (Fish 1995: 102).

Let us pay some more attention to the interaction between state institutions and the new independent groups and movements. The reforms initiated by Gorbachev were only a partial liberalization and authoritarian practices continued. Control and dependency in the workplace were particularly significant and did generally not decrease during the Gorbachev period. Enterprise managers used the power to dismiss or demote employees or to deny them access to goods in order to control their political behaviour. Often the threat of sanctions was enough to discourage oppositional activity (Fish 1995: 164). State institutions remained relatively closed and there were no opportunities for negotiations or pacts as in many other transitions (Fish 1995: 122). The more moderate 'popular fronts', however, were supported from above (Devlin 1995: 106). The state also established its own puppet organizations.

The decay of state institutions was an obstacle to the development of a strong and influential civil society. The state only possessed negative power. It was able to control, obstruct, harass and coerce, but could not take part in constructive negotiations with democratic societal forces (Fish 1995: 125). As there were no established channels for interest representation, the new groups had to concentrate on 'demonstration politics', i.e. mass public manifestations, independent publishing, etc. (Fish 1995: 128).

The establishment of new legislative institutions and partially free elections in 1989 presented pro-democracy activists with a difficult choice. Should they continue building a mass movement against the communist regime or should they focus on political representation within the reformed institutions instead of grassroots activism? Most activists chose to work within the reformed political society and managed to consolidate their position through the creation of electoral organizations. However, they were too weak to be able to negotiate a transfer of power with communist party reformers (Weigle 2000: 15). Despite their failure to play an active role in the last phase of the transition, new informal groups and social movements had an influence on both agenda-setting and policy-making. The democratic movement 'exposed the illegitimacy, brutality and ineffectiveness of the existing political system' (Fish 1995: 51). By 1990 the movements had taken the initiative away from Gorbachev and the reformist leadership that introduced *perestroika* and *glasnost*, and thus opened up the political opportunity structures (Butterfield and Sedaitis 1991: 1).

Transnational civil society actors played an important role in this process. Before the mid-1980s, Soviet dissidents used to have few transnational links, but support from the West was significant for some individuals. Exile to the West, however, weakened dissident groups. The peace movement and human rights groups got transnational links through the Helsinki monitoring process. After the Chernobyl disaster in 1986, ecological groups established transnational links too. Links with the opposition in Eastern Europe, however, remained weak (Sakwa 1998: 212).[5] It has been convincingly argued that transnational peace and human rights movements of the 1980s played an important role in the democratic revolutions of 1989 (Meyer and Marullo 1992; Chilton 1994; Evangelista 1999). The peace movement in the West put pressure on governments to constrain military build-up and allow a detente and thus provided opportunities for Soviet reform. Alternative ideas on international security, developed within the peace movement, influenced reform-oriented leaders in the Soviet Union. Western activists supported and cooperated with dissidents in the East (Meyer and Marullo 1992: 114).

It is now time for some theoretical reflections on the applicability of the concept of civil society. Did all the new groups and movements operate on a public arena that could be termed an emerging civil society? Fish (1995) answers in the negative. He lists a number of indicators of a *mature* civil society, including a capacity for aggregating, representing and articulating interests, access to and control of political arenas, and autonomy from the state (Fish 1995: 53–4). He concludes that independent organizations in Russia during the Gorbachev period did not score highly on any of these indicators. Hence, a *genuine* civil society had not developed (Fish 1995: 60). I agree that there was no *mature* or *genuine* civil society in the Soviet Union under Gorbachev, but was there no civil society at all? Hosking *et al.* (1992: ix), argue that the independent movements that emerged in the Soviet Union after 1986 'may not add up to a civil society' but they had a significant political impact.

Fish (1995: 61) uses the concept 'movement society' instead of civil society because societal initiatives in the Soviet Union were characterized by political campaigns rather than conventional interest associations and mass demonstrations instead of negotiations (Fish 1995: 62). This argument seems to be based on a too narrow understanding of civil society. What are political campaigns and mass demonstrations if not typical examples of civil society activities? Social movements are important civil society actors and it is hardly useful to separate a 'movement society' from civil society. I find it more useful to differentiate between different forms of civil societies – those dominated by social movements and those dominated by NGOs. Hence, I agree with Weigle (2000) that a 'nascent civil society' emerged in the mid-1980s when political opportunities were created through Gorbachev's reform policies. There was no rule of law protecting the autonomy of the emergent civil society. These early civil society activists faced opposition from hardliners and attempts at co-optation from 'softliners' within the ruling party-elite. Opportunities to establish a more mature civil society did not emerge until after the fall of the communist regime.

Independence movements in the Baltic republics

Unlike in Russia, there was a relatively strong civil society in the Baltic states in the interwar period. Under communist rule, civil society was crushed, but in the late 1980s and early 1990s many of the pre-war organizations reappeared when Gorbachev's policies of *perestroika* and *glasnost* provided political opportunities for independent organizing. Popular fronts for independence developed into mass movements. These movements were able to build on 'legal' national cultural traditions. Song festivals played an important role in the mobilization (Ruutsoo 2002: 397). Mass mobilization came earlier in Estonia and Latvia (where a more individualized civil culture had been inherited from the pre-communist period) than in Lithuania, but the independence movement in the latter country soon took the lead, helped by the more favourable ethnic composition (Ruutsoo 2002: 397).

The starting point in Estonia was February 1987 when an increase in phosphorite mining triggered protests. Students at the University of Tartu played an important role. Prominent members of the Estonian Communist Party, including Edgar Savisaar and Arnold Rüütel, joined the protests (Lagerspetz and Vogt 1998: 64). On 13 April 1988 *Eestimaa Rahvarinne*, the Popular Front, was established as an umbrella organization for various critical groups. Its ideological orientation was mainly moderate left and centre, and the front included prominent members of the Estonian Communist Party. It avoided dramatic confrontations with the Soviet Communist Party. The first goal of the popular front was democracy and more autonomy. It soon received a very large popular following (Lagerspetz and Vogt 1998: 64).

The re-emerging civil society in Estonia also included the Estonian National Heritage Society, founded in December 1987 with the aim of rewriting Estonia's history. A similar goal was the driving force behind the Estonian Group for Making Public the Molotov-Ribbentrop Pact, which went public in August 1987. Other new groups included the Estonian National Independence Party and Estonian Citizen's Committees (Lagerspetz and Vogt 1998: 65; cf. Hosking 1992).

The Latvian independence movement of 1987–92 has been rather well documented (e.g. Karklins 1994; Muiznieks 1995; Jubulis 2001; Pabriks and Purs 2002). The Latvian People's Front had about 110,000 members in October 1988 and 230,000 in spring 1989. More radical independence activists united in the National Independence Movement and the Congress Movement (Smith-Sivertsen 1998: 94).

As in Estonia, environmental concerns provided the impetus for the first independent protest activities in Lithuania. Moscow's plan to expand the chemicals industry was one factor behind the establishment of *Sajudis* in June 1988 (Lieven 1994: 220). *Sajudis* was initially a movement for *perestroika,* but it soon transformed into the main organization for independence (Zeruolis 1998: 122). Lithuania's path to independence was more dramatic, straightforward and militant than in Estonia and Latvia. The political identity of Lithuania was more consolidated, and hence popular mobilization had a more ideological and spiritual character (Ruutsoo 2002: 57). The Lithuanian declaration of independence in March 1990 was met by a military intervention in January 1991 (Lieven 1994: 250). Following the failed coup by hardliners within the Soviet Communist Party in August 1991, Latvia and Estonia also declared full independence, and the three Baltic states soon received international diplomatic recognition.

The independence process in the Baltic republics was very quick. It took less than two years from the first demand in April 1988 for an Estonian Popular Front to the Lithuanian declaration of independence in March 1990 (Lieven 1994: 219). The reason for this speed was primarily the mass character of the independence movements and the cumulative effects of protests, which undermined the will of the communist rulers. The most striking mass demonstration was the 'Baltic Way' of 23 August 1989, when two million Balts formed a human chain from Vilnius through Riga to Tallinn to demand independence (Lieven 1994: 219). Independent groups in the Baltic republics were also more successful in the elections than in other parts of the Soviet Union. Candidates supported by the popular fronts won overwhelming victories in Latvia and Lithuania in March 1989 (Butterfield and Sedaitis 1991: 5). However, politics suddenly lost its legitimacy in the Baltic republics after (or even before) the end of communist rule in August 1991 (Lagerspetz and Vogt 1998: 55) and a demobilization of civil society began when the independence movements had achieved their main goal.

The establishment of civil society groups in the USSR: further empirical indicators

An illustration of the development of a civil society in Russia and the Baltic states can be seen in Table 3.1. Of the civil society groups included in the study, only 2 per cent existed before the revolution in 1917. The organizations that have been able to survive the whole Soviet period include a few trade unions, women's groups and ethnic and nationalist organizations. Under communist rule before Gorbachev came to power there were almost no opportunities for the establishment of independent organizations. The organizations from this time (9 per cent of the sample) are mainly official trade unions and some environmental groups. Except for those organizations controlled by the party-state, there were some small dissident groups. When Gorbachev started his *perestroika* and *glasnost* policies, space opened up for independent groups and movements. This is reflected in the relatively large percentage of organizations in this sample that were established during the Gorbachev period – 31 per cent of all groups included in this study. There was a growth in the number of organizations in all sectors, but relatively few new women's groups. Eighty per cent of the women's groups in the sample were established after the breakdown of the communist regime and the disintegration of the Soviet Union. In total 57 per cent of the civil society groups in this study were established after 1991. This indicates that a majority of post-Soviet civil society groups are new. Only in the case of trade unions and labour organizations, and (with a small margin) environmental groups, do we find a majority of organizations established before the fall of the communist regime.

Table 3.1 Period of establishment by category of civil society group (%)

Category of civil society group	Pre-Soviet (–1917)	Soviet (1918–1984)*	Gorbachev (1985–1991)	Post-Communist 1992–
Human rights	0	4 (2)	30 (16)	66 (35)
Women	4 (2)	2 (1)	13 (6)	80 (36)
Labour	5 (3)	26 (17)	37 (24)	32 (21)
Environment	0	18 (7)	35 (14)	48 (19)
Ethnic/nationalist	4 (2)	0	46 (20)	50 (22)
Social welfare	0	5 (2)	29 (12)	67 (28)
Other	2 (1)	6 (3)	28 (15)	64 (34)
Total	**2 (8)**	**9 (32)**	**31 (107)**	**57 (195)**

Source: Democratization: Local and Transnational Perspectives Survey (DLTPS) 1999–2000.

Notes: The question was: 'When was the organization/group established (Month and year)?' Answers have been classified. N = 342. (Absolute numbers within brackets).

* The reasoning behind the time periods chosen should be obvious in the case of Russia. For the Baltic states another categorization, using the year of their annexation by the Soviet Union as a natural breaking point, would have been more logical. For the sake of simplicity and comparison, however, I use the same periodization for all respondents.

Table 3.2 Period of establishment of civil society groups by region (%)

Region	Pre-Soviet (–1917)	Soviet (1918–1984)	Gorbachev (1985–1991)	Post-Communist 1992–
Kaliningrad	0	0	10 (1)	90 (9)
Novgorod	0	5 (2)	16 (7)	79 (34)
Pskov	0	34 (12)	20 (7)	46 (16)
St Petersburg	6 (3)	8 (4)	36 (18)	50 (25)
Sverdlovsk	3 (1)	10 (4)	34 (13)	53 (20)
Harju	0	4 (1)	48 (11)	48 (11)
Ida-Viru	6 (1)	12 (2)	25 (4)	56 (9)
Pölva	0	15 (2)	15 (2)	69 (9)
Tartu	15 (3)	5 (1)	30 (6)	50 (10)
Riga	0	0	52 (13)	48 (12)
Valmiera	0	38 (3)	25 (3)	38 (3)
Kaunas	0	0	31 (9)	69 (20)
Vilnius	0	3 (1)	44 (14)	53 (17)
Total	**2 (8)**	**9 (32)**	**31 (107)**	**57 (195)**

Source: Democratization: Local and Transnational Perspectives Survey (DLTPS) 1999–2000.

Note: The question was: 'When was the organization/group established (Month and year)?' Answers have been classified. N = 342. (Absolute numbers within brackets).

Table 3.2 indicates that civil society first (re)emerged in the big cities in the Baltic republics (Riga, Harju and Vilnius have the highest percentage of civil society groups established between 1985 and 1991) and to a somewhat lesser extent in the Russian metropolitan areas of St Petersburg/Leningrad and Sverdlovsk. In more peripheral regions the development of new civil society groups came later, mainly after the break-up of the Soviet Union.

When examining the centre–periphery dimension for the different municipalities we get further indications that the growth of independent groups under *perestroika* and *glasnost* took place mainly in the centre. Thirty-five per cent of the groups in centre municipalities included in this study were established during this time. The same percentage for groups in peripheral municipalities is seventeen. Two-thirds of the groups in the peripheries were established after the fall of the communist regime.

Conclusion

Russia had no or little experience of civil society activities before the communists took power. By contrast, Estonia, Latvia and Lithuania had relatively strong and vivid civil societies in the inter-war period. All this was crushed under the totalitarian Soviet system. In the post-Stalin Soviet Union some dissidents existed, but they very tightly controlled and marginalized from the general public. Not until

Gorbachev initiated his reform policies in the mid-1980s did political opportunities for some independent organizing emerge. A large number of discussion groups were founded, mainly by the intelligentsia in the big cities. Ecological and nationalist concerns erupted into widespread protest activities. An independent labour movement organized political strikes. The most radical mass movements were found in the Baltic republics. The demand for independence received widespread popular support and the independence movements achieved their goals. The democratic movements in Russia were weaker than in the Baltic republics and the former client states, but they still had a considerable political impact. The independent movements took the initiative away from the communist reformers and opened up new political opportunities. Transnational civil society also had a significant influence on the reformist leadership and the whole transition process. However, the pro-democracy movement in Russia was not prepared to take power and after the break-up of the Soviet Union there was a dramatic decline in mobilization.

4 Actors and activities in post-Soviet civil society

This chapter provides an overview of major actors and activities in post-Soviet civil society. It starts with an analysis of the 'NGOization' of civil society after the breakdown of the communist regime. This section also summarizes previous research in this field. We then examine what is known about different civil society sectors. Drawing on survey data, post-Soviet civil society activists are presented and resource mobilization and other activities of civil society groups are analysed. Finally, case studies from three Russian regions complement the quantitative data.

The 'NGOization' of civil society in post-communist Russia and the Baltic states

Russian civil society actors played an important role in the collapse of the authoritarian regime, but politics soon turned into a struggle of a few persons around which political parties were founded (Patomäki and Pursiainen 1998: 20). Following the abortive putsch in August 1991, Yeltsin emerged with extraordinary legitimacy and power. The democratic movement in Russia, however, was unprepared for power. In the severe economic crisis, Yeltsin gave priority to economic transformation instead of political reform. His harsh policy towards the Communist Party as an organization was accompanied by accommodation towards *nomenklatura* officials (Fish 1995: 201). Hence, the political transformation in Russia was only partial, and the new political structures were not conducive to social movement activities.

The sudden collapse of the Soviet Union and the Communist Party power led to the break up of democratic coalitions, like Democratic Russia, and the creation of new parties with more conventional hierarchical leadership structures (Fish 1995: 210). The collapse of the Communist Party and the dissolution of the Soviet Union took away the 'enemy' of the democrats and their main source of unity. Economic and national issues replaced the political competition between 'Communists' and 'democrats' and the democratic forces had never been based on economic and national matters (Fish 1995: 214–15). Only one of the parties belonging to the democratic movement in the late Soviet period – the DPR – gained enough support to field a list of candidates in the December 1993 elections (Fish 1995: 232–3). This decrease in civil society mobilization was not unique to the Soviet Union. A similar tendency can be found in all transitions from communism (Smolar 2002: 52) and indeed in most other processes of democratization too.

There was not only a decline in movement activities, but also a process of regionalization. Local and regional chapters of democratic organizations became more autonomous from their mother organizations in Moscow and St Petersburg, and close cooperation of different groups on the local level became even more pronounced after the transition. This process was part of a general trend of regionalization and localization of power (Fish 1995: 211). Some local and regional workers' organizations also emerged after the coup attempt (Fish 1995: 216).

Weigle (2002) identifies four phases of civil society development in Russia: demobilization in the first years following the breakdown of communist rule, institutionalization of civil society (legally as well as mentally), development of civil society activism on local and regional levels, and the federalization of civil society with the Civic Forum in 2001. While the first three phases make sense when describing the development of post-Soviet civil society in Russia, the significance of Civic Forum is questionable. As will be argued in Chapter 5, this event is perhaps more accurately described as a (failed) attempt by the government to control and co-opt civil society groups. The demobilization of civil society is analysed in this section. The legal institutionalization will be discussed in Chapter 5. Analyses of civil society activism on local and regional levels are provided in both Chapters 4 and 5.

There is no lack of grievances that might stimulate civil society activity in post-Soviet Russia. Shocking (at least by Western standards) gender inequality (McIntosh Sundstrom 2002: 225), very bad conditions for workers (Crowley 2002), severe human rights problems (Weiler 2002), enormous environmental problems (Bridges and Bridges 1996), and a range of other severe social problems that are not adequately handled by the state would lead one to expect there to be a lot of civil society activism. Nevertheless, contemporary Russian civil society is typically described as 'weak, atomized, apolitical, and heavily dependent on Western assistance' (McFaul 2002: 109). This is not unique to Russia, but is rather a feature of post-communist civil society in general. Using data from the World Values Survey, Howard (2002) shows that membership in civil society groups is substantially lower in post-communist societies than in both older democracies and post-authoritarian countries. Russia and the Baltic states (together with Bulgaria and Ukraine) have the lowest percentage organizational membership of all countries included in the study (Howard 2002: 159). The pattern is the same for all kinds of organizations except for labour unions. Howard (2002) explains the lasting weakness of post-communist civil society with three factors: 1) A lack of trust in public organizations as a major legacy of the communist regime. 2) The persistence of friendship networks that developed under communist rule make people feel no need to take part in public social networks. 3) Disappointment with the performance of the post-communist regimes. Other, partly overlapping, reasons for the weakness of civil society in Russia include the Soviet legacy, the structure of the economy, institutional components of the state, policy decisions made by Yeltsin and Putin, and societal exhaustion (McFaul 2002: 111). Furthermore, civil society in Russia is weak because of the lack of strong federalism and an effective state, a developed middle class and a free enterprise system, and independent media (Weigle 2002: 126).

While all these obstacles to the development of a strong civil society in Russia are problematic from a democratic perspective, it should be noted that not only democratic civil society groups but also antidemocratic groups have problems mobilizing people because of the general distrust in public organizations (Howard 2002: 164). Distrust might, however, be too strong a word. Mishler and Rose (1997) argue that people in post-communist societies show scepticism rather than distrust towards civil society groups. Scepticism (or distrust) towards public organizations is closely related to what has been described as a relative lack of social capital. Marsh (2000a) has studied the regional variation of social capital in Russia. Inspired by Putnam, he uses the following indicators when measuring the level of 'civic community': voter turnout in elections to regional legislative assemblies (*sobranie*), referenda turnout in 1993 (concerning support for Yeltsin's reforms and the adoption of a new constitution), newspaper publishing and the number of 'clubs and cultural associations' (Marsh 2000a: 134–5). The result is somewhat counter-intuitive, with Pskov scoring the highest (5), Novgorod only 3 and St Petersburg a poor 2 on the 1–5 scale. The author, thus, draws the conclusion that several regions (including St Petersburg) 'seem to suffer from insufficient levels of civic community' and a lack of social capital (Marsh 2000a: 138).

Providing a more optimistic interpretation, Gibson (2001: 51) describes Russian society as 'characterized by broad, porous, and politically relevant interpersonal networks'. These networks might have been an alternative to more formal civil society organizations, but the existence of such interpersonal networks is also a good base for the development of more formal organizations. Marsh (2000b: 186) also argues that personal networks, *blat* – i.e. horizontal relationships based on reciprocity and implying a deep level of trust – are perhaps a Russian form of social capital.

Whether there is a specific form of Russian social capital or not, we can at least conclude that Russian civil society – at least in the form of a relatively large number of NGOs – does exist. Many foreign researchers have probably underestimated the size of civil society in contemporary Russia because they focus on NGOs with Western contacts, which are probably a small minority of Russian groups. By using Western liberal categories, one misses groups associated with the Soviet past. Furthermore, there has been a focus on the national level, to the neglect of local and regional civil society activity (McFaul 2002: 111).

The social movements of the late 1980s and early 1990s have been replaced by numerous small, but often professional NGOs. It should be stressed that there is hardly any group that could be described as a social movement organization in this study. Only NGOs and trade unions are represented. This is a reflection of the decline of social movements and the 'NGOization' of civil society in Russia and the Baltic states.

Estimates of the number of NGOs active in Russia range from 60,000 to 350,000 (McIntosh Sundstrom 2002: 207). The number has grown considerably during the last decade. According to one source there were 50,000 registered NGOs in 1993, nearly 66,000 in 1997, and in 2001 a prominent NGO activist claimed that there were 350,000 NGOs employing about one million people across Russia. However, it is estimated that only 70,000 of these NGOs are active (Weigle 2002: 123). Based on surveys, it has been estimated that only between 10 and 25 per cent of registered NGOs conduct regular activities (Patomäki and Pursiainen 1998: 35). But there are also many civil society groups that do not register as NGOs, and thus are not included in the statistics. Based on statistical evidence, internet discussion lists and their own empirical observations and interviews, Patomäki and Pursiainen (1998: 36) concluded 'there are plenty of civil society activities going on in Russia in the late 1990s'. But these activities are still limited to a relatively small minority of the population. This seems to be true also in the early twenty-first century. Given the small membership of most civil society groups (except for some trade unions etc., which tend to have very passive members) it is reasonable to speak about a civil society elite. This elite is composed of both old elites from the Soviet time and those who opposed the Soviet regime (cf. Dawn Hemment 2000: 259).

In the three Baltic states we find similar developments.[1] The process of demobilization or 'NGOization' is obvious. The density of civil society – measured as NGOs per million of population – seems to be higher in the Baltic states than in Russia. The number of NGOs in relation to the population seems to be particularly high in Estonia (while still lagging far behind the older democracies in Western Europe) (Gill 2002: 115). Ozolina (2003) also presents data confirming the more widespread participation in civil society groups in Estonia compared to Latvia and Lithuania. Data on membership in civil society organizations, however, is not entirely reliable in any of these countries.

The high expectations many people in Estonia had about material gains because of the transformation did not come true. On the contrary, prices went up very rapidly and there was a shortage of goods. The national unanimity of the struggle for democracy and independence was replaced by day-to-day political conflicts between former allies. Political scandals have further diminished people's belief in politics (Lagerspetz and Vogt 1998: 59). The major movements during the struggle for independence – *Rahvarinne* (the Popular Front) and the Citizens' Committees – moved from identity politics towards institutional politics (Lagerspetz and Vogt 1998: 60). There was a general demobilization of Estonian post-communist society, particularly among Russian speakers (Ruutsoo 2002: 352–61). A major study of civil society in Estonia characterizes post-communist civil society as generally weak when it comes to the articulation of common (as opposed to group-specific) interests and with very limited political influence. Most civil society groups are oriented towards recreational activities, health, self-improvement and cultural interests, but the poorest parts of the population are mostly excluded from participation in these associations (Ruutsoo 2002: 379–81).

After the successful struggle for independence in Latvia a common opinion was that there was no need for a new opposition in the form of civil society organizations (Ostrowska 1997: 89). Civil society activism naturally decreased, and civil society activities in post-communist Latvia are typically described as weak and mostly confined to small groups of intellectuals (Kaldor and Vejvoda 1997: 76) although there has been a slight increase in political participation through civil society initiatives since the late 1990s (Karklins and Zepa 2001).

Empirical data on the NGO sector in Latvia is available, especially through the Latvia Human Development Reports and some very useful publications by the Baltic Data House (e.g. Baltic Data House 1998a, b, c; Zepa 1999; see also Ostrowska 1997; Smith-Sivertsen 1998). Such studies indicate that there has been a marked decrease in civil society activity between 1991 and 1995. While the membership of NGOs drastically decreased, the number of NGOs increased. According to one source, there were 984 registered NGOs in 1995 and 1,849 in April 1997 (Ostrowska 1997: 90; cf. Karatnycky *et al*. 1997: 234). In January 1999 the number of registered NGOs had risen to 3,922 and individual membership also seemed to have increased slightly (Karklins and Zepa 2001: 337). In 1990 trade unions, sport associations, and cultural and artistic societies had most members in Latvia. In 1995 the membership in those organizations decreased 3–4 times, but they remained the organizations with the largest number of members (Ostrowska 1997: 90). NGOs representing 'post-modern' forms of interests – minority rights, green and feminist groups – typically have very few members, but they are the most active organizations due to international funding (Ostrowska 1997: 90). Most NGOs in Latvia are first and foremost service providers (Ostrowska 1997: 91). Organized labour is weak. There have been several unsuccessful strikes (Smith-Sivertsen 1998: 105). A recent NGO report based on survey interviews with representatives of a large number of Latvian NGOs describes the Latvian NGO sector as mainly consisting of newly established small organizations working on educational, social or youth issues (Centre for Non-Governmental Organizations 2002: 19).

Lithuania shares the same experience of demobilization and 'NGOization'. The level of participation in civil society groups seems to be lower in Lithuania compared to Latvia and Estonia (Ruutsoo 2002: 375), but there is very little research specifically on Lithuanian civil society.

The weakness of post-communist civil society in the Baltic states can be explained by the Soviet legacy, the hegemony of ultraliberal rhetoric (mainly in Estonia and

Latvia) which has further delegitimized collective civil initiatives, the individual-ization and social atomization associated with post-modern developments, elitist forms of governing and the political elite's lack of interest in political participation through civil society, and the exclusive citizenship policies in Estonia and Latvia (Ruutsoo 2002: 398).

Civil society sectors

Much previous research has focused on a specific sector of civil society. Some sectors – especially women's groups – have been thoroughly researched, whereas other sectors have been all but neglected by scholars. In this section I briefly review previous research on the different types of civil society groups included in the present study.

Human rights and democracy groups

There is plenty of research on the prominent role that human rights and democracy groups played during *glasnost* and *perestroika* (e.g. Sedaitis and Butterfield 1991; Hosking *et al.* 1992; Devlin 1995; Fish 1995). The situation for such groups in the post-Soviet context, especially under the contemporary Putin regime, is more underresearched. What we know is that during the 1990s human rights organi-zations emerged across the Russian Federation. Some have managed to generate significant publicity for their causes, and many NGOs have developed useful rela-tionships with local and federal authorities in order to solve human rights problems, notably in the prison system. Overall, however, these civil society groups are very weak compared to other social forces (Weiler 2002).

Women

Comparatively many foreign scholars have paid attention to women's organizations in Russia and much of this research consists of thorough empirical studies across many parts of the Russian Federation, so we know quite a lot about the development and problems of Russian women's groups. Dawn Hemment (2000: ch. 4) distin-guishes between three phases in the development of Russian women's organizations: a few dissidents in the 1970s and 1980s, the emergence of an independent women's movement in the early 1990s, and the development of 'third sector' women's NGOs in the mid- and late 1990s. In the late 1980s tiny feminist groups emerged in Moscow and St Petersburg. A new wave of women organizing as a response to the economic crisis came in the early 1990s (Sperling 1999: 18). Most women's groups at that time were set up as a form of protest against the dislocations of the market. In the 1990s there was a dramatic increase in the number of women NGOs. It is estimated that there were about 2,000 active women's NGOs in 1998. While a significant number of organizations, these groups only make up about 0.5 per cent of all NGOs in Russia (McIntosh Sundstrom 2002: 210). The new women's NGOs that are formed are mainly based on friendship and professional networks (Sperling 1999: 24). Most of these women's NGOs are not confrontational and they do not mobilize large numbers of women. There are also severe conflicts between different groups (Sperling 1999). The most pronounced ideological conflict is between, on the one hand, traditionalist organizations rooted in Soviet monopoly organizations and, on the other hand, new feminist NGOs (McIntosh Sundstrom 2002). In 1991 the Union of Russia's Women (URW) replaced the Soviet Women's Committee (SWC), which used to be the only recognized women's organization in the Soviet Union. Although no longer part of the party-state structure, independent women activists still consider the URW to be non-independent or at least too pragmatic (Sperling 1999: 21). These conflicts are real, but the distinction should not be overstressed. The Soviet Women's Committee actually acted as an incubator of new organizations independent from the state (Sperling 1999: 23). Despite the conflicts, McIntosh Sundstrom (2002: 211) argues that women's groups are more networked today than in the 1990s. It is fair to speak of a women's movement in contemporary Russia, she claims.

The contemporary Russian women's movement has been described as rigid, hierarchical, isolated from the people, professionalized, bureaucratic, Western oriented, and dependent on foreign funding (Dawn Hemment 2000: 253). Transnational links provide intellectual contacts, financial support and a degree of domestic legitimation, but such links are also problematic (Sperling 1999), something that will be discussed further in Chapter 6. Other problems for women's groups in Russia include a lack of economic infrastructure, a decline in social services that women relied on, institutional and psychological legacies of the Soviet regime and, not least, sexist attitudes towards women (Sperling 1999). McIntosh Sundstrom (2002) describes the weakness of the Russian women's movement as a lack of connections with ordinary citizens, negative public opinion, poor links between NGOs, and extreme political weaknesses. The public opinion problem is probably the most severe, and it is stressed by virtually all scholars writing about contemporary Russian women's groups. It is clear that there is a general aversion to women's organizations in Russia. The only exceptions are those groups that focus on domestic violence and sexual assaults, like crisis centres. A strong norm against violations of human physical dignity ensures public support for this kind of women's groups despite a general lack of support for feminism. Some women's business organizations have also been able to gain public respect (McIntosh Sundstrom 2002: 215). Russian women activists have severe problems in framing gender interests in a way that culturally resonates with the population. The concept of gender equality was appropriated by the communist regime and is still associated with women's double work, both within and outside the home. Feminism is a foreign concept that is hard to use in the sexist post-communist cultural environment, with traditional sex-role stereotypes being reinforced by the media (Sperling 1999: 95–7).

Berthusen Gottlick (1999) has interviewed leaders of women's organizations in St Petersburg. According to her, many women's groups are conservative and antifeminist. The driving force and motivation for organizing is the everyday pain caused by the transition to a market economy and the failure of the state to provide basic social welfare and protection (Berthusen Gottlick 1999: 242). She also concludes that there is a general acceptance of biologism among women activists. Although they generally seek to redistribute power and resources, most women activists deny that their work is political (Berthusen Gottlick 1999: 245–6).

These findings are confirmed by the present study. Among women activists interviewed, the word 'feminism' is usually avoided. 'Gender' seems to be a preferred and less threatening concept (Interview W3). The chairwoman of the Union of Women of Pskov, for instance, refers to her organization as a social – not a feminist – organization (Interview W2). It is worth noting that among the women's groups included in this study, 30 per cent (fourteen groups) claim not to work for women's rights.

Finally, we should note that women are active in most kinds of NGOs, not only women's groups. Forty-six per cent of the interviewed activists are women. Whereas political power (*vlast'*) is perceived as a masculine domain, women have found a niche in the non-governmental sphere (Dawn Hemment 2000: 21).

Labour

Research on Russian trade unions describes weak and accommodative collective actors, despite being the largest civil society groups when it comes to membership. The Federation of Independent Trade Unions of Russia (FNPR), the successor of the Soviet trade union, claimed 38 million members in the beginning of 2000 (Crowley 2002: 233). Although probably overstated, it makes the federation by far the biggest public organization in Russia. The FNPR inherited an enormous amount of property from the communist era. While giving it a substantial advantage compared to other unions (and civil society organizations in general) which do not have similar resources, it does make the FNPR politically weak, as the union avoids any confrontation with the government, fearing that its property may be privatized at any moment (Crowley 2002: 234). Unions during the communist period were essentially social welfare agencies closely related to the enterprise management. Traditional unions still have this function in contemporary Russia. Hence they can hardly be confrontational towards the management and typically try to prevent strikes (Crowley 2002: 239–40). It is a paradox that the FNPR is the largest social organization in Russia, and polls show that its main demands concerning wages and unemployment are very popular among the public, yet polls consistently show that the FNPR (and unions in general) are among the least respected public institutions in Russia (Crowley 2002: 230). The economic collapse has severely constrained the bargaining power of organized labour (Gill and Markwick 2000: 227). There have indeed been 'thousands of strikes involving millions of workers across a wide range of occupations', but they have been of limited duration and effect in a time of economic depression (Gill and Markwick 2000: 232). Furthermore, the majority of strikes have been by teachers. There have been very few industrial strikes (except for the mining sector) (Crowley 2002: 232). Most strikes have also been directed against the federal government or regional authorities, rather than enterprise managers. There has been a regionalization of industrial action. Workers, managers and local political leaders tend to cooperate against the central government (Gill and Markwick 2000: 230–1).

Trade unions are not only unsuccessful (or unwilling to take part) in industrial conflicts; they have little political influence too (cf. Crowley 2002: 234–5). In the early 1990s the FNPR was seen as part of the communist opposition, whereas independent unions, notably the Independent Miners' Union, were close allies of the Yeltsin government. Now the Putin government is hostile towards alternative unions, but has an increasingly warm relationship with the FNPR (Crowley 2002: 238–9). The FNPR has embraced market reform (Gill and Markwick 2000: 231). The trade unions' conciliatory policies towards the government and their failure to play a role in political society are obstacles to the development of a strong civil society (Gill and Markwick 2000: 236). In sum, traditional unions are not willing to fight for workers' interests, and alternative unions lack organization (Crowley 2002: 243). Alternative labour unions have little impact on the federal level, but some might be influential on specific enterprises (Crowley 2002: 232).

Environmental groups

Environmentalism (*ekologia*) has a broader meaning in Russian, including varieties of spirituality and daily life that are not associated with environmentalism in the West (Henry 2001: 19). Environmental issues played a key role in the early mobilization of independent groups under *glasnost* and *perestroika*. The party-state tended to tolerate environmental activism, as it was seen as less of a threat against the regime (Henry 2001: 12; Henry 2002: 185–6). Despite the general decline in movement activities, there are now environmental NGOs in all Russian regions. The problem is that they are often isolated from the public. It has been estimated that about 6 per cent of all NGOs in Russia are environmental groups (Henry 2002: 187). Henry (2002) distinguishes between two types of environmental groups in Russia: professional NGOs similar to Western advocacy groups on the one hand, and grassroots citizens' initiatives with a broader understanding of 'ecology' on the other hand. Grassroots groups typically have a more accommodating relationship with local government officials. They are often neglected by foreign donors (and scholars) because they are small and resource-poor, but they may prove to be more sustainable and make a more significant contribution to political participation than professional Western-funded NGOs, which tend to be elitist organizations isolated from the general public (Henry 2002). Grassroots groups 'recycle' Soviet-era administrative, cultural, or educational institutions. They have a strong focus on local problems. Few environmental NGOs are membership-based, and there is a lack of interest in reaching out to the public (Henry 2001: 18). During the 1990s the green movement in Russia became stronger and more professional. In the late 1980s and early 1990s they simply organized mass meetings against something. Now environmentalists take more concrete actions and work on more specific projects. While many NGOs have become more professional, most have little contact with or support from ordinary people. Public opinion in Russia is not much concerned with environmental problems (Interview E5).

Ethnic and nationalist groups

There is not much research on civil society groups based on ethnic or national identities. Neither organizations focusing on the culture and/or political and civil rights of ethnic minorities nor the more extreme nationalist and xenophobic organizations have received much scholarly attention. Umland (2002) has, however, analysed Russian political parties on the extreme right with a strong nationalist tendency.

Social welfare NGOs

While perhaps making up the largest section of post-Soviet civil society, organizations providing social services to various disadvantaged groups have not received much scholarly attention. An important exception, however, is White (1999) who provides a thorough examination of the emergence of charities and self-help groups in Russia under Gorbachev. In the post-Soviet context, many NGOs call themselves charity organizations because taxation is more favourable for such organizations according to the Russian law (Evgeniya Machonina, St Petersburg NGO Development Centre, seminar, 8 March 2001, Stockholm, Forum Syd). Many organizations in this category, like for instance societies for disabled people, are very similar to the old Soviet associations. They lack knowledge, language skills, etc. and have not been able to adapt to the new situation. Hence, they have not received much foreign funding (Interview S4).

Civil society activists

Before analysing the activities of different types of civil society groups, we should ask who the actual activists are. This section provides a brief description of some basic characteristics – sex, age, and level of education – of the respondents selected for this study.

Table 4.1 Percentage of women among respondents in different categories of civil society groups

Category of civil society group	Women
Women	100 (47)
Social welfare	57 (27)
Human rights	36 (20)
Ethnic/nationalist	36 (17)
Environment	36 (15)
Labour	35 (25)
Other	33 (19)
Total	**48 (170)**

Source: Democratization: Local and Transnational Perspectives Survey (DLTPS) 1999–2000.

Note: Absolute numbers within brackets.

There is a small overrepresentation of men, but the 48 per cent figure for women among the respondents indicates that many women hold prominent positions within the post-Soviet civil societies studied here. Two sectors have a female majority: women's organizations (of course) and social welfare groups. Within all other sectors about one third of respondents are women. This show that when women become active in civil society groups they often turn to what is traditionally considered women's areas.[2]

Generational differences might be of interest (see Table 4.2). Young people born after 1970 have no pre-*perestroika* experience as adults. Those in the 'young middle aged' category were born in the 1960s. They experienced their formative youth period during *perestroika* and had no permanent position in Soviet society before

Table 4.2 Age of respondents in different types of civil society groups (%)

Category of civil society group	−30 (young)	31–40 (young middle aged)	41–60 (older middle aged)	61– (older)
Human rights	13 (7)	16 (9)	47 (26)	24 (13)
Women	4 (2)	11 (5)	72 (34)	13 (6)
Labour	3 (2)	7 (5)	69 (50)	21 (15)
Environment	21 (9)	19 (8)	46 (20)	14 (6)
Ethnic/nationalist	6 (3)	15 (7)	57 (27)	21 (10)
Social welfare	11 (5)	28 (13)	48 (22)	13 (6)
Other	25 (14)	23 (13)	44 (25)	9 (5)
Total	**11 (42)**	**16 (60)**	**56 (204)**	**17 (61)**

Source: Democratization: Local and Transnational Perspectives Survey (DLTPS) 1999–2000.

Note: The question was: 'How old are you?' Answers have been classified. N = 367 (absolute numbers within brackets).

perestroika. The 'older middle aged' category includes those born in the 1940s and 1950s. They grew up under Soviet rule and are likely to have had a position within the Soviet system before *perestroika*. The older generation (born before 1940) has a long experience of the Soviet system.

A majority of respondents are between 41 and 60 years old, and only slightly more than one quarter are younger than 40. The relative lack of young people among the respondents may indicate a structural problem of post-Soviet civil society in that recruitment of new active members among the young generation seems to be limited. If this is indeed the case, the sustainability, renewal and vitality of many civil society groups might be threatened. We should, however, remember that respondents are selected among the leadership of the respective organizations and it may take some time for many younger activists to reach a leadership position within their organization. The average age of all civil society activists is most likely substantially less than for the civil society elite interviewed for this study. It should also be noted that the age profile differs considerably between different civil society sectors. Activists tend to be older in human rights and democracy-oriented groups (probably because of their historical roots in Soviet era dissident circles), and in trade unions (a category which also contain many old organizations). Women's groups and ethnic and nationalist organizations also seem to have fewer young representatives. The youngest activists are found within the category 'other' (which include some youth organizations), but also in environmental and social welfare organizations. This might indicate that it is easier for young people to rise to leadership positions within these kinds of organizations.[3]

The level of education among the interviewed civil society elites is impressively high (see Table 4.3). Eighty-one per cent claim to have completed higher education. This finding confirms statements in previous research about a highly educated post-Soviet civil society. Ethnic and nationalist as well as environmental activists seem to

Table 4.3 Respondents with higher education per category of civil society group (%)

Category of civil society group	Completed higher education
Ethnic/nationalist	89 (42)
Environment	88 (38)
Women	85 (40)
Human rights	80 (4)
Other	78 (45)
Labour	75 (51)
Social welfare	74 (35)
Total	**81 (295)**

Source: Democratization: Local and Transnational Perspectives Survey (DLTPS) 1999–2000.

Note: The question was: 'What is the highest level of education that you have received?' The answer 'Higher education' is shown. N = 365 (absolute numbers within brackets).

be particularly well educated. The level of education is somewhat lower among social welfare and trade union activists, but even within these categories three-quarters of respondents claim to have completed higher education.[4]

In sum, we can conclude that the post-Soviet civil society elite interviewed for this study is highly educated, largely middle aged, and includes almost as many women as men, although women tend to be concentrated in women's and social welfare NGOs and less well represented in other civil society sectors.

Resource mobilization

Post-Soviet civil society groups have severe problems in mobilizing both human and financial resources. Previous research has found that participation in civil society groups is limited to a tiny minority of the population (McFaul 2002: 115). Local surveys indicate that most Russians do not even know much about NGOs and do not see them as valuable (Patomäki and Pursiainen 1998: 36). There are relatively few volunteers within the Russian NGO sector. The hard socio-economic situation in the country forces people to seek a living by working for NGOs, especially if they are financed from abroad (Patomäki and Pursiainen 1998: 38).

While the post-Soviet society offers better opportunities for resource mobilization than during *glasnost* and *perestroika*, and many parties and organizations get financial support from private sponsors (Fish 1995: 234–5), most civil society groups find it very hard to get local funding. The history of state monopoly over the public sphere means that contemporary civil society groups have no tradition of public outreach and fundraising, nor any economic infrastructure for funding (Sperling 1999: 177). Individuals and businessmen who are willing to donate money to NGOs prefer charity organizations. Advocacy groups find it very difficult to get any form of local funding (McIntosh Sundstrom 2002: 222).

There is no reliable data on the funding of NGOs because many NGOs are unwilling to reveal their financial situation to researchers (cf. Ostrowska 1997: 91; Gorodetskaya 1998: 145). Asking about sources of funding rather than the exact amount, however, we can expect to get more accurate answers, although we cannot take them at face value. The same is true for questions about membership, which is probably overstated in some cases. However, having these reservations in mind, survey questions can cast some light on the problems of resource mobilization faced by post-Soviet civil society groups. Based on the result presented in Table 4.4, we can conclude that real mass organizations seem to be relatively uncommon in contemporary post-Soviet societies. Fifteen per cent of the respondents in this study claim to represent organizations with more than 1000 members on the local level. We should, however, not take these claims at face value. Respondents are likely to exaggerate the number of members, and lists of members may include many who have not actually paid their membership fees or registered as members. Not surprisingly, we find mass organizations mainly within the category of trade unions.

Table 4.4 Local membership in different types of civil society groups (% within each category)

Category of civil society group	Less than 20 (small)	21-100 (medium)	101-1000 (big)	More than 1000 (mass)
Human rights	32 (12)	35 (13)	16 (6)	16 (6)
Women	40 (14)	43 (15)	17 (6)	0
Labour	6 (3)	25 (12)	27 (13)	42 (20)
Environment	28 (9)	28 (9)	28 (9)	16 (5)
Ethnic/nationalist	14 (6)	28 (12)	49 (21)	9 (4)
Social welfare	33 (13)	20 (8)	28 (11)	18 (7)
Other	31 (13)	55 (23)	14 (6)	0
Total	**25 (70)**	**33 (92)**	**26 (72)**	**15 (42)**

Source: Democratization: Local and Transnational Perspectives Survey (DLTPS) 1999–2000.

Note: The question was: 'What is the approximate number of members of the organization/group on the local level (i.e. city, town or village)?' Answers have been classified. N = 276 (absolute numbers within brackets).

The large trade unions from the Soviet time have been able to keep many of their members, especially in Russia. The other extreme is women's groups. In this category we find no mass organizations, and 40 per cent of the women groups included in this study have fewer than twenty members. This finding supports previous research, which has stressed the special problems of gaining public support that women's groups face. Regional variation is not very big, but it should be noted that Estonia stands out as the country with most small civil society groups (42 per cent with fewer than twenty members). The same figure for all the other countries is 22 per cent.

Given the view in much previous research of post-Soviet civil society groups as largely uninterested in mobilizing new members (particularly when receiving foreign funding), the number of groups claiming to actively try to mobilize new members is surprisingly high. Eighty-seven per cent of respondents claim that mobilization of new members is one of their activities, and 48 per cent claim to do it often.[5]

Table 4.5 shows the number of employees that civil society groups claim to have. The relatively large number of employees is an indication of the professionalization of NGOs in the region. The numbers are, however, likely to be exaggerated. It is hard to believe that thirty-four organizations included in the study have more than fifty employees. This might be true for some of the large trade unions, but in other cases it might be a result of confusion between employees and members. Trade unions have most employees and women's groups least, following the same pattern as for number of members.

The relatively large number of salaried employees indicated by the survey is somewhat contradicted by qualitative interviews. For instance, a respondent in

Table 4.5 Number of employees of civil society groups (%)

Number of employees	
None	17 (56)
1–3	23 (76)
4–10	27 (89)
11–50	23 (75)
More than 50	10 (34)

Source: Democratization: Local and Transnational Perspectives Survey (DLTPS) 1999–2000.

Note: The question was: 'What is the number of employees of the organization/group?' The answers have been classified. N = 330 (absolute numbers within brackets).

Pskov claims that most NGO activists are volunteers, or at least have another income in addition to their work for the NGO (Interview S3). It is probably the case that there might be quite a few employees in an NGO, but they do not have full-time salaries. Many might indeed receive only symbolic payment, but they still count as employees.

When checking regional variation of number of employees, Estonia stands out as a country with comparatively small civil society groups on this indicator too. There is only one single organization in the Estonian regions that belong to the 'very big category' and 40 per cent have no employees at all. The percentage of groups with no employees in all the other regions (except Vilnius, which also has a large number of small NGOs) is well below 20.

In addition to members and employees, civil society groups try to mobilize financial resources for their activities. Fundraising is an important activity for most civil society groups. Eighty-nine per cent of the groups included in the study claim to do it, and 47 per cent claim to do it often, generating a relatively high level of 69 on the activity index from 0 to 100 (see Table 4.8). The lack of money is seen as the biggest problem for civil society groups, according to many respondents (e.g. Interview HR6).

Table 4.6 shows the main source of funding of different types of civil society groups. Contrary to what might be expected from previous research that has depicted post-Soviet civil society groups as weak on membership, poorly rooted in their local communities and heavily dependent on foreign funding, a large majority of respondents claim to have local sources like membership fees, private donations, and public subsidies as their main source of funding for their organizations. Fewer, but still a significant number, claim to rely mainly on foreign funding. While some respondents might have overstated the importance of membership fees and under-estimated reliance on foreign funding because they might perceive the former to be a more legitimate source of income, this result is a clear indication that many civil society groups have been able to find local resources for sustaining their activities.

Table 4.6 Main source of funding of different types of civil society groups (%)

Category of civil society group	Membership fees	Private donations	Public subsidies	Foreign donors	Own activities	Mother organization
Human rights	26 (14)	51 (27)	32 (17)	43 (23)	4 (2)	2 (1)
Women	46 (21)	22 (10)	17 (8)	33 (15)	11 (5)	2 (1)
Labour	87 (58)	12 (8)	15 (10)	3 (2)	6 (4)	0
Environment	29 (12)	32 (13)	32 (13)	37 (15)	10 (4)	5 (2)
Ethnic/nationalist	43 (20)	62 (29)	32 (15)	32 (15)	6 (3)	2 (1)
Social welfare	28 (13)	47 (22)	36 (17)	30 (14)	13 (6)	4 (2)
Other	41 (23)	43 (24)	38 (21)	21 (12)	9 (5)	2 (1)
Total	**45 (161)**	**37 (133)**	**28 (101)**	**27 (96)**	**8 (29)**	**2 (8)**

Source: Democratization: Local and Transnational Perspectives Survey (DLTPS) 1999–2000.

Note: The question was 'What is the main source of funding for the organization/group?' Some respondents selected more than one alternative so percentage of groups within each category adds up to more than 100. (Absolute numbers within brackets.)

As shown in Table 4.6, sources of funding vary considerably depending on civil society sector. Membership fees are important mainly for trade unions. Not so many human rights, environmental and social welfare groups rely on membership fees as their main source of funding. Private donations seem to be of most importance for ethnic and nationalist groups. Trade unions and women's groups seldom have private donations as their main source of funding. About one third of all organizations list public subsidies as a main source of funding, but considerably less within the categories of trade unions and women's groups. Foreign donors are important mainly for human rights and democracy groups, but also for environmental groups. For trade unions and labour organizations, foreign donors are not at all a significant source of funding. [6]

When examining the regional variation in funding (Table 4.7), we find that membership fees seem to be most important in Valmiera and least important in Novgorod. Private donations are common in Kaliningrad and Novgorod, but less important in most of Estonia (except Ida-Viru) and in Riga and Pskov. Public subsidies are the main source of funding for a majority of organizations in Ida-Viru and Pskov. Few organizations in Riga, Kaliningrad and St Petersburg seem to rely on public subsidies as their main source of income. Foreign funding is important in the metropolitan regions of St Petersburg and Vilnius (and also in Ida-Viru where the ethnic composition makes it likely that much of the foreign funding comes from Russia) but of very little significance in Pskov, Pölva and Kaliningrad.

Resource mobilization is most difficult for civil society groups in poor and peripheral local communities in Russia. As stated by one respondent, 'several thousand towns and villages in Russia do not even have electricity. There is simply no infrastructure for a civil society' (Interview HR6). Such economically depressed regions also tend to get very little foreign funding.

In sum, we can conclude that resource mobilization is a severe problem for much of post-Soviet civil society. Mobilization of new members is difficult, although more organizations than expected tend to give priority to this activity. With the exception of trade unions (which have been able to keep a substantial number of members, at least in Russia), the number of members as well as employees is relatively small for most civil society groups included in this study. Estonia in particular tends to have many small civil society groups. When it comes to mobilization of financial resources, this study points at a stronger reliance on local sources of funding than previous research has indicated. Membership fees, private donations and public subsidies are all claimed to be more common as the main source of funding than is foreign donors. Let us now examine how post-Soviet civil society groups use their (limited) human and financial resources for different activities.

Table 4.7 Main source of funding of civil society groups per region (%)

Region	Membership fees	Private donations	Public subsidies	Foreign donors	Own activities	Mother organization
Kaliningrad	46 (6)	77 (10)	8 (1)	8 (1)	0	0
Novgorod	36 (16)	56 (25)	24 (11)	36 (16)	7 (3)	0
Pskov	45 (17)	23 (9)	56 (22)	5 (2)	3 (1)	3 (1)
St Petersburg	40 (19)	48 (23)	15 (7)	46 (22)	6 (3)	6 (3)
Sverdlovsk	41 (16)	49 (19)	38 (15)	26 (10)	8 (3)	3 (1)
Harju	48 (11)	13 (3)	30 (7)	17 (4)	17 (4)	4 (1)
Ida-Viru	47 (8)	35 (6)	59 (10)	35 (6)	0	6 (1)
Põlva	62 (8)	8 (1)	38 (5)	8 (1)	38 (5)	0
Tartu	48 (11)	9 (2)	22 (5)	26 (6)	9 (2)	0
Riga	54 (14)	19 (5)	4 (1)	27 (7)	12 (3)	4 (1)
Valmiera	70 (7)	40 (4)	30 (3)	20 (2)	20 (2)	0
Kaunas	47 (14)	43 (13)	23 (7)	17 (5)	3 (1)	0
Vilnius	44 (14)	41 (13)	22 (7)	44 (14)	6 (2)	0
Total	45 (161)	37 (133)	28 (101)	27 (96)	8 (29)	2 (8)

Source: Democratization: Local and Transnational Perspectives Survey (DLTPS) 1999–2000.

Note: The question was 'What is the main source of funding for the organization/group?' Some respondents selected more than one alternative so percentage of groups within each region adds up to more than 100. (Absolute numbers within brackets.)

Civil society activities

Resource mobilization is necessary for civil society groups, but other activities should be central in order to achieve their goals. As stated above, previous research has tended to depict most civil society groups as accommodative towards political and economic elites. The time of mass mobilization for demonstrations and other public protest activities is over, and post-Soviet civil society is made up of NGOs, which (with few exceptions) do not engage in confrontational activities. For example, Sperling (1999: 6) has shown that demonstrations are rare among Russian women's groups. Seminars and conferences are the main means of organizing. Similar conclusions have been drawn about other civil society sectors. Another aspect of civil society activities that has been noted is the lack of networking among NGOs. Post-Soviet civil society is described as fragmented. Many NGOs work in isolation (Patomäki and Pursiainen 1998: 38). In this respect, there might be a difference between strong well-established and weaker NGOs. Old, established NGOs are typically ready to work together, whereas weaker NGOs are afraid of cooperation because they think they will lose resources, argues one prominent civil society activist in Russia (Interview HR6).

Results from the present survey support the view of a largely non-confrontational civil society, but networking with other NGOs in the country is a very common activity, casting some doubt on the argument about a fragmented civil society with isolated NGOs afraid of cooperation. The activity index in Table 4.8 shows that information gathering is the most common activity among the civil society groups included in this study. In fact, almost all organizations (98 per cent) have been involved in information gathering, resulting in a high 87 on the index from 0 to 100. Public education and networking with similar organizations within the country are other common activities. Fund seeking is also important although less so for trade unions (and ethnic and nationalist groups). With a substantial membership (and in some cases large properties inherited from the Soviet time) many trade unions do not have to apply for additional grants. Mobilization of new members reaches a surprisingly high 68 on the index. Given the low number of members of many NGOs one would have expected this to be an activity that more organizations did not care about. Mobilization of new members is most important for trade unions and labour organizations. Human rights and democracy groups are least interested in mobilizing new members, indicating that many groups in this category are small non-membership-based organizations relying on the work of a few committed activists. Lobbying political decision-makers is a less common activity, but a large majority (79 per cent of respondents) claim that their organization at least has done it, although seldom as a routine activity. Transnational networking is slightly less common than lobbying, but with considerable variation across civil society sectors. Social welfare organizations seldom take part in transnational networking (36 on the index) whereas environmental groups often are involved in such cross-border contacts (71 on the index). Writing petitions is not a particularly common

Table 4.8 Activities of civil society groups per category (index from 0 to 100)

Category of civil society group	Information gathering	National networking	Public education	Fund-seeking	Mobilization	Lobbying	Transnational networking	Writing petitions	Demonstrations	Boycotts or strikes
Human rights	90	79	82	81	54	59	54	46	24	12
Women	87	80	86	65	72	50	61	27	6	2
Labour	91	81	74	61	84	64	49	55	37	24
Environment	92	93	83	74	72	53	71	40	17	6
Ethnic/nationalist	81	87	77	62	62	55	57	32	14	2
Social welfare	79	79	72	70	69	63	36	35	10	2
Other	88	82	67	72	58	56	57	26	13	1
Total	**87**	**83**	**77**	**69**	**68**	**58**	**54**	**38**	**18**	**8**

Source: Democratization: Local and Transnational Perspectives Survey (DLTPS) 1999–2000.

Note: The question was: 'How often is the organization/group involved in the following activities?' The alternatives 'never', 'seldom', 'sometimes' and 'often' were given. The number of respondents selecting each alternative was multiplied by 0 for the first alternative, 33 for the second, 67 for the third and 100 for the last. The results were summed up and divided by the number of respondents. Thus we arrived at a measurement of frequency of different activities. 0 would mean never done by any of the groups. 100 would mean that all groups often are involved in this activity. N = 360–366 depending on activity.

activity, but trade unions and human rights groups in particular occasionally make use of this method. The more confrontational forms of activities – like organizing demonstrations, boycotts or strikes – are very unusual. Only trade unions and to some extent human rights and democracy groups appear to be somewhat confrontational in this respect. The overall picture, however, clearly confirms the non-confrontational character of post-Soviet civil society.

The regional variation in forms of activities is less pronounced, but there are some significant patterns. Writing petitions and the more confrontational activities of organizing demonstrations and strikes and boycotts are significantly less common in Estonia and the Russian region of Novgorod than in the other regions.[7]

When we look at the activities of individual activists, instead of organizations, the image of a largely non-confrontational post-Soviet civil society is confirmed (Table 4.9). Very few have been involved in the more confrontational activities like unofficial strikes and occupations of buildings, and a surprisingly large majority would never do these things. Post-Soviet civil society elites seem highly unwilling to act outside the present legal framework. Many are even unwilling to participate in common legal civil society activities like boycotts and lawful demonstrations, and 15 per cent would not even sign a petition. Less than half of the respondents have actually signed a petition.

Trade union and labour activists and human rights and democracy activists have most experience of, and are most willing to do, both the ordinary legal and more confrontational types of activities. Activists within women's groups, social welfare organizations and those belonging to the category 'other' show least activity in these respects. Civil society activists in Estonia are less active in general and particularly less willing to participate in more confrontational activities. Most active civil society activists (including confrontational activities) are found in St Petersburg, Kaliningrad and Riga. It is now time to focus more on regional differences, using qualitative data.

Table 4.9 Activities of respondents (%)

Activity	Have done	Might do	Would never do
Signing a petition	48 (174)	37 (137)	15 (55)
Joining in boycotts	14 (50)	41 (147)	46 (165)
Attending lawful demonstrations	39 (141)	40 (146)	21 (76)
Joining unofficial strikes	6 (20)	24 (86)	71 (256)
Occupying buildings or factories	2 (7)	9 (33)	89 (322)

Source: Democratization: Local and Transnational Perspectives Survey (DLTPS) 1999–2000.

Note: The question was: 'Here are some different forms of political action that people can take, and I'd like you to tell me, for each one, whether you have actually done any of these things, whether you might do it, or would never, under any circumstances, do it.' N = 362–366 depending on activity (absolute numbers within brackets).

Civil society in three Russian regions

In this section I provide a brief description of civil society in St Petersburg, Pskov and Novgorod and present some case studies of different NGOs in the respective regions. This analysis, mainly based on qualitative interviews, is intended to give more substance to the quantitative overview of resource mobilization and other activities of civil society groups given in the previous sections. It will also show the diversity of contemporary Russian civil society.

St Petersburg

It is hard to get any reliable information about the number of NGOs in St Petersburg. According to the city administration there are 8000 NGOs registered, but the estimation is that only about 1000 are active (Interview S4). Another representative of the city administration puts the figure of registered NGOs at more than 5000 (Interview S5). A leading figure within the St Petersburg NGO sector says that there were 3,800 NGOs in St Petersburg in 1994, but in 2001 the number had increased to about 11,000. She estimates that only about a quarter of these are really active (Interview HR6). Another prominent NGO figure claims that there were 16,000 registered NGOs in 2000, creating job opportunities for 10,000 people in St Petersburg (Evgeniya Machonina, St Petersburg NGO Development Centre, seminar, 8 March 2001, Stockholm, Forum Syd). NGOs in St Petersburg tend to be relatively independent compared to NGOs in small towns where they are typically controlled by the state (Interview HR6).

Olga Starovoitova: a key figure in St Petersburg's civil society

Olga Starovoitova (the sister of the famous politician Galina Starovoitova who was murdered in 1998) represents the St Petersburg branch of the International Charitable Foundation for Political and Legal Research, Interlegal. The organization aims at contributing to a better legal understanding through regular seminars and training programs for NGOs. It works in all six regions of North West Russia. Among other things, the organization has done work on the relationship between NGOs and the media (Interview HR6). Several activists are active in more than one organization, and Olga Starovoitova is a good example of this phenomenon. She is the leading figure in the St Petersburg Public Foundation for Galina Starovoitova. She is also active in Memorial, Civil Watch, Soldiers' Mothers, and the Neva NGO (one of the oldest NGOs in St Petersburg which educates social workers and NGO leaders) (Interview HR6). This personal overlapping across organizations indicates that the number of really active civil society activists might even be less than the number of NGOs.

Council of Veterans: the survival of a Soviet mass organization

The Council of Veterans of St Petersburg and Leningrad *Oblast* was founded in the 1950s. Its aim is to 'study and distribute knowledge about the heroical victory of the Soviet people during the war' (Interview O7). In the early 1990s the organization was restructured. Previously it included only war veterans, but now it also has police and labour veterans among its members. (This resembles the whole structure of the Ministry of Interior.) The organizational structure follows the administrative structure of the Russian Federation. The city organization in St Petersburg is divided into 20 district organizations, which in turn consists of municipal and basic groups. The Veteran organization claims to have 1,100,000 members in St Petersburg and 400,000 in Leningrad *Oblast*.[8] It claims to base its activities solely on voluntary work, having no salaried staff (Interview O7). The big office building in central St Petersburg is paid for by the city administration. In the 1990s when the organization had to pay itself it got financial support from individual deputies, industrial plants, banks and other 'rich organizations' (Interview O7). The main task of the organization is to provide social help for veterans. Other important activities are the publication of a newspaper and books on the experiences of war and labour veterans, and education of the younger generation. However, it seems difficult to get the younger generation interested, and the representative of the organization admits that membership is decreasing rapidly as old members die. 'Veterans are disappearing', as he puts it (Interview O7). War veterans from Afghanistan have their own organization, but they participate in the Council of Veterans too. Within Russia, the organization cooperates with groups with a similar orientation, e.g. the 'union of patriotic forces' and Cossack organizations (Interview O7). The First Deputy of the Head of Council is an old man wearing a large golden wristwatch with a portrait of Stalin. He served in the Soviet army for 40 years and used to be commander of the Soviet army in Poland (Interview O7).

Memorial: dissidents in defence of human rights

The All-Union Historical-Enlightenment Society, Memorial, was important in the formation of a civil society in Russia (Weigle 2000: 106–13). It started when a group of young liberal intellectuals in Moscow organized to promote the construction of a memorial complex to the victims of the Stalinist terror. Through publications, archival works and various forms of activism, the group tried to educate Soviet society about the communist repression. A founding conference was held in January 1989 and local branches were set up in many parts of the country. The party-state apparatus attacked the organization both through attempts to co-opt local organizations and through legal harassments related to registration and ability to mobilize resources.

The St Petersburg branch of Memorial, formed in 1988, was one of the first independent organizations to be registered in St Petersburg (Interview HR4). Its work is dedicated to victims of political oppression. The organization carries out historical research and runs a small museum documenting communist as well as Nazi atrocities and oppression. During *perestroika* there was a growing interest in history, but this vanished a few years after the breakdown of the Soviet Union. Memorial describes itself as a grassroots organization. It has three main orientations. First, as a social welfare organization it supports victims of political repression. This includes psychological and medical help too. Financial resources are very limited, but there are about 250 members who are involved in this work, and the organization claims to have an additional 2500 'veterans' who are not members but participate in some activities. The second orientation is a focus on human rights, including legal support to victims of human rights abuses, and political rehabilitation. In Moscow, this kind of human rights work is the main activity for Memorial. The St Petersburg branch of the organization does not have the same strong focus, but it does work on human rights problems, especially in relation to Chechnya. Another focus is support for imprisoned children and teenagers and the monitoring of their prison conditions. Memorial in St Petersburg also includes a small anti-fascist group. The third main orientation is research and information. Thirty-five people are involved in this work, and Memorial runs a museum and a library (Interview HR4).

It has been possible for the organization to receive grants for the human rights work, but more funds for the social work are needed. There is no support from the local government. Memorial has to rely on foreign grants and its own fundraising activities. Supported by the Berlin branch, the organization has organized a concert in order to get private donations. Some individuals and enterprises offer financial support. For research activities, Memorial has received grants from Russian scientific foundations. To a large extent, however, the organization relies on foreign funding (Interview HR4).

Today there is an association (described as a confederation by an activist) of different independent Memorial organizations (Interview HR4). There is a steering committee with representatives from different regions, which meets in Moscow every one or two months. The central office does not provide any funding for regional branches and gives only loose recommendations concerning activities. Nevertheless, the organization claims to have good cooperation with other regional Memorial organizations (Interview HR4). In St Petersburg, Memorial is close to the organization Civil Watch that was founded by members of Memorial and the Soldiers' Mothers of St Petersburg.

Soldiers' Mothers: broad public support for advocacy against physical abuse

Forced conscription to military service and systematic mistreatment of conscripts are widespread and severe problems in Russia. Organizations of Soldiers' Mothers, offering support for young men in the process of being conscripted and deserted soldiers, as well as their families, have thus met widespread support among large sections of the population – a situation that no other women's organizations could even dream of (cf. McIntosh Sundstrom 2001: 2). In the mid-1990s the Moscow-based Committee of Soldiers' Mothers had more than 300 local affiliates throughout Russia (Caiazza 2002: 124). The organization Soldiers' Mothers of St Petersburg is not one of those affiliated with the committee in Moscow, but it has nevertheless gained widespread support in the St Petersburg region. During the first decade of its existence, the organization estimates that about one hundred thousand people have asked for support (Interview HR5). In the mid-1990s the group of women in the Soldiers' Mothers of St Petersburg realized that they could not offer individual consultation for all the people who approached the organization. Instead they began with human rights meetings twice a week. Up to eighty people generally attend these meetings, which last about three hours. Using brainstorming techniques and role-play, the aim is to empower people and free them from fear. This human rights education is built upon a conscious individualistic approach. It takes as its starting point the universal declaration of human rights and chapter two of the Russian constitution, which deals with rights and liberties (Interview HR5).

Relations to the internationally praised Moscow Committee of Soldiers' Mothers are complicated. The two soldiers' mothers organizations in the two main cities of Russia seem to have different visions and personal disagreements. The Soldiers' Mothers of St Petersburg claim to have unique educational activities, and argue that they have a more philosophical approach than their sisters in Moscow. They accept only non-violent methods, and tend to disagree with their sister organization in Moscow concerning goals as well as tactics. The activists in St Petersburg, who have a strongly religious background, would like to see either a professional army or (ideally) a very different non-violent army to protect human rights (Interview HR5). This vision, however, was not elaborated.

The development of independent labour unions

The independent labour union, Council of Labour Unions – 'Unity' – emerged in 1988 as a union for cooperative entrepreneurs fighting for independence from the state. At that time there was no legal protection or social security for members of cooperatives. The traditional labour unions did not care about this new form of enterprise and the lack of a legal base benefited the authorities and was a disadvantage for the workers (Interview L2). This union now claims to organize 16,000 workers, or 25 per cent of the workforce in relevant small and medium-sized enterprises in St Petersburg and Leningrad *Oblast*. In order to recruit new members the union has created a social security NGO foundation providing support related to pensions and legal matters for members. It organizes both skilled and unskilled workers, and a representative of the union argues that in small and medium-sized enterprises there is no conflict of interest between different categories of workers.

There are fourteen persons employed by the union. The union claims to rely exclusively on membership fees and income from its own insurance business as well as earnings from property (Interview L2). Activists wanted to unite all labour unions in North West Russia and created an information centre for this purpose, but there was no real interest in other regions. There is already an umbrella organization based in Moscow uniting sixty-three labour unions in different regions all over Russia. This umbrella organization claims 1,700,000 members (Interview L2).

Free St Petersburg: failed mobilization

The Regional Political Party 'Free St Petersburg' was formed in 2000 by the same people who had been active in the 'Movement for the Autonomy of St Petersburg' for a few years. Far from being a political party with the objective of gaining votes in elections, it is a network of a few dozen intellectuals and activists concerned about the political situation in St Petersburg. The group emerged mainly as a reaction to the tendency to strengthen central power at the expense of the regions under Putins's rule. Registration of the party was delayed for more than a year because the party programme displeased the authorities (Interview O6). Before registering the party, they planned to join the Union of Right Forces, but this party only welcomed individual members. Attempts at uniting with other small parties failed because of the mutual fear of having the respective parties specific character extinguished. The party has not yet made any efforts to mobilize members. The movement that preceded the party made some efforts to mobilize people and increase its membership, but failed (Interview O6).

When the Movement for the Autonomy of St Petersburg ran a small election campaign for the city council in 1998 the cost was about $1500. They used their own money, but were also sponsored by a deputy of the city council (Interview O6). For general activities there is no funding. The group is trying to raise funds from private sources, but has not been successful (Interview O6).

Greenhipp: Green anarchists

The environmental group Greenhipp has never been registered as an organization. The anarchist attitudes of the most influential activist explain the lack of organizational structure. The self-proclaimed leader of the group estimates that there were about 300 members during 1988–90 (Interview E4). More than a decade later he claims to have almost ten people regularly working for the group and about fifty more who can be quickly mobilized for specific activities. But the time of mass mobilization has passed. During the 1990s there was very little interest in mass activities. People who become activists do it for personal emotional reasons rather than for achieving social and political results, he argues (Interview E4). The most important activity of Greenhipp is now to monitor nature protection areas, especially since Putin terminated the ministry of nature protection in 2000. In addition to the Nature Protection Society, Greenhipp also cooperates with some small environmental groups in St Petersburg. However, this seems to be of limited importance. The group claims to have better relations with Finnish environmental groups than with other local NGOs (Interview E4).

Shelter: caring for the homeless in St Petersburg

The organization 'Shelter' in St Petersburg supports homeless people. During the Soviet period, homelessness was connected to the prison economy as homeless people were imprisoned and used as forced labour. In December 1990 activists started to distribute food stamps for homeless people, and so 'Shelter' was founded (Interview SW1). The number of homeless people has not decreased since the fall of communist rule. Registration as a citizen is tied to a specific place of living. Most people 'sub-renting' a flat do not register, as the person really renting it wants to avoid the tax police. This is especially common among students who move to a big city. A representative of the organization Shelter estimates that 0.5 per cent of the population in St Petersburg is formally homeless, although many of them do in fact have somewhere to live. The organization tries to provide shelter for those who live on the street (more than 10,000 people in St Petersburg) and legal consultation for those who are not registered (more than 7,000 people) (Interview SW1). 'Shelter' tries to fund its own activities through publishing newspapers and books, and organizing concerts and other events. There is a partner organization in Odessa and another one is in the process of being established in Novosibirsk. Attempts to set up a similar organization in Nizhny Novgorod failed (Interview SW1).

Pskov

As in other Russian regions, there are no exact figures of the number of NGOs. According to NGO sources there are 1000–1200 registered NGOs in the Pskov region, but only about 300 exist other than on paper, and only 100–200 are really active. A large majority are based in the city of Pskov. There are fewer than ten active NGOs outside the city, according to one informant (Interview O4). According to the person responsible for NGO contacts within the Pskov city administration, there are 900 registered NGOs in the region, 500 of them in Pskov city. She estimates that only 300 NGOs exist in reality (Interview S3). There is less civil society activity in Pskov compared to Novgorod. Pskov's worse economic situation makes it hard to finance NGO activities, and most NGOs cannot pay any reasonable salaries to their staff. A respondent compares civil society in Pskov with a teenager, drawing a parallel to her own son who was born in 1985 when *perestroika* began (Interview S3).

Vozrozhdenie: an influential NGO centre

Founded in 1990, this organization has as its main goal to support other NGOs in the Pskov region. *Vozrozhdenie*, however, is also involved in psychological help for individuals and makes sociological studies on a commercial basis. The organization is very professional and has 15 salaried staff. Contacts with foreign funding agencies are very good (Interview O4).

Veche: a human rights and democracy group rooted in old dissident circles

The civil rights organization *Veche* in Pskov has its roots in the liberal dissident movement formed around Andrei Sacharov during *perestroika*. In Pskov the group organized demonstrations with up to 3000 people taking part. They protested against the economic blockade against Lithuania and supported the miners' strike in 1991. Since then, and more consistently since 1996, *Veche* has focused specifically on the protection of human rights. The organization has worked with specific events, for example the war in Chechnya (Interview HR2). Like many other human rights groups in Russia, *Veche* is not a membership-based organization. There are three people working full time for the organization and about ten more activists linked to the group. *Veche* works together with a number of other NGOs in the region, and in smaller towns outside the city of Pskov (Interview HR2).

Soldiers' Mothers of Pskov: a new regional organization of a successful movement

There are several different organizations of Soldiers' Mothers in Pskov. Some of them are closely linked to the local authorities and could hardly be seen as part of civil society. One of the more independent groups was established in 1998. The background was the personal experience of the founder. When her oldest son served in the army in 1994 he was sent to Chechnya. Through him she became aware of the bad conditions within the Russian military and she decided not to let her second son do his military service. She contacted the military and a Soldiers' Mothers Committee associated with the authorities, but she did not get any support. Her son had a physical dysfunction and according to the law he should not have to serve in the military, but it proved impossible to get hold of the right documents, and no doctors were willing to declare that he was not physically fit. In desperation she turned to a human rights organization in Moscow and the organization of Soldiers' Mothers in St Petersburg for help. She got some advice from them and also started to attend seminars organized by local human rights NGOs. Eventually her son was examined by a doctor in St Petersburg who verified that he suffered from a rather serious illness and was unfit to do his military service. After loads of bureaucratic paperwork the son was freed from the military.

The mother wanted to share her experience with others and wrote about it. In 1998 she registered the Pskov organization for Soldiers' Mothers. The NGO resource centre *Vozrozhdenie* assisted in the establishment of the organization and helped them with office space. The local authorities have refused to give the Soldiers' Mothers an office. The organization has only five members and financial resources are limited, although it has received some funding from the Open Society Foundation and EU TACIS programme (Interview HR3). The organization in Pskov is a member of a union of Russian Soldiers' Mothers committees. Relations to the Soldiers' Mothers in Moscow is good, but due to a conflict between Moscow and St Petersburg, the organization in Pskov has little contact with its sister organization in St Petersburg. Most support comes from other local NGOs, including *Veche* and *Vozrozhdenie* (Interview HR3).

Fragmented women's organizations

There are 5–6 active women's organizations in Pskov and some competition between them, although there is also some cooperation (Interview W3). The Union of Women of Russia is the continuation of the official Soviet women's organization. There are regional organizations all over Russia. Officially formed in 1990, the Union of Women of Pskov was the first women's organization in this region (Interview W2). The organization focuses on social and economic issues related to women. The Union of Women has no registered members, but the chairwoman in Pskov claims that there are active members in almost all municipalities in the region. Funding is a problem. There is little support from the central organization in Moscow.

The Union of Women's and Youth Initiatives claims to be the first post-Soviet women's organization in the Pskov region (Interview W3). The organization tries to influence local law-making related to women and youth. Other activities include educational and cultural programmes. The organization has also taken an active part in protests against the war in Chechnya and helped soldiers wounded in the war. The Union of Women's and Youth Initiatives claims to have about fifty-six members, but only five who work actively for the organization. They rely on private donations for specific activities and a small membership fee. Networking with some other NGOs in Pskov is intense.

Labour union in decline

The trade union for construction workers in Pskov was founded in the 1950s. Prior to that it was part of a broader union, including several different professions. Nowadays the union organizes not only workers but also engineers etc. employed within the construction industry. Membership of the union has dropped from about 20,000 in the 1980s to 2,100 in 2001. This is only 10 per cent of the total workforce within the declining construction industry in Pskov. The recruitment of new members is a big problem. The union attempts to provide legal assistance and inform workers about the union, but employers have a negative view of unions and try to stop their activities (Interview L1). The union deals with the same problems as other unions all over Russia, i.e. problems related to wages and working conditions. The union negotiates collective deals about minimum wages etc. Strikes are rare. During recent years there have been occasional cases of strikes lasting only an hour, often in solidarity with workers on strike in other parts of the country (Interview L1).

Novgorod

As in other regions, estimations of the number of NGOs vary considerably. In January 2001 there were 1395 NGOs, including political associations, in the Novgorod region, according to an NGO resource centre (Interview O1). Another NGO activist argues that there are only about 500 NGOs in the Novgorod region, most of them in the city of Novgorod. Most NGOs do only have a few members and many are not particularly active (Interview HR1). According to the vice-mayor, there are more than 600 NGOs in the region, including political and religious groups. 400–500 of them are active in the city of Novgorod (Interview S1). There seem to be relatively more charity organizations in Novgorod than in many other Russian regions.

The North-Western Community Development Centre: the spider in the NGO web

In 1998 the North-Western Community Development Centre emerged out of a charity organization called Health and Livelihood. The centre, with about ten staff, aims at supporting other NGOs in the Novgorod region with know-how, especially related to contacts with funding bodies and local authorities (Interview O1).

Environmental NGOs with little political influence

There are environmental NGOs in six out of Novgorod's twenty-one *rayons*. Most of these NGOs lack both personal and material resources. They have no paid staff and most of them do not have any office. Their legal knowledge is very limited and they have little or no influence on the local administration (Interview E1). The ecological club 'Ekologija' was established to develop a network of regional environmental NGOs. The organization has about twenty-five members, but only five or six are active (Interview E1).

Active environmentalism in a small town

There are about 140 NGOs (including political and religious groups) in Borovichy, a *rayon* with about 78,000 inhabitants. Most of these NGOs, however, are not very active (Interview E2). Borovichy's Ecology Club was founded in the late 1980s, but it did not register until 1995. A former engineer, now a teacher in geography and biology, leads the organization. It has 25 members. Half of them are active. The Ecology Club has been active on a wide range of environmental issues, including campaigns against a nuclear power plant and a polluting pig farm. A major activity is environmental education for young people. The group organizes excursions and seminars. About 200 children and youth attend this environmental school with three full-time and five part-time teachers employed. The school is funded by the local government, but it lacks technical equipment and money for excursions etc. The most pressing current problems that the organization works on include recycling of plastics (an industry making plastic bags from recycled plastics is under construction so this problem is in the process of being solved) and air pollution, especially from the bricks industry, a major industry located right in the centre of Borovichy (Interview E2). The Ecology club has close cooperation with other local and regional environmental groups. It gets most of its funding from a Moscow-based 'international fund for development', but only for specific projects. In addition to this it receives financial support from the local authorities for seminars and excursions. Membership fees and contributions from sponsors make up the rest of the budget, which amounted to about 3,000 USD in 2000. In 2001 it was far less because the specific projects had ended (Interview E2).

Closely related to the Ecology Club is *Nos 4*, an ecological organization founded in 1999. It focuses on education and organizing seminars. This small NGO has only 14 members. Its goal is to increase public awareness of the local environment. This includes not only ecological issues, but also the historical heritage at large. As in many other Russian environmental organizations, history and ecology are closely intertwined. The leader of the organization explains its philosophy as 'ecological sociology', which focuses on preserving cultural traditions and educating children. Traditional family and church values are important. One activity has been to persuade the military to leave a fourteenth-century monastery, which had been used by the military for decades. Members of the organization restored the monastery and schoolchildren helped clean up the surrounding area (Interview E3). The organization has monthly meetings with schoolteachers, informing them how education can be more ecological. Practical work includes the tidying of river beaches and tree plantation. The main problem for *Nos 4* is the lack of money. Members have written articles in the local newspaper in order to inform the public about the organization and its activities. The membership fee of 10 roubles a year is just symbolic. A local businessman sponsored the organization with 500 roubles so that it could register. Local authorities pay for excursions etc. and the organization has been given office space in the school. *Nos 4* has the same links to other ecological organizations regionally and in Moscow as the Ecology Club (Interview E3).

Staraya Russa: the recent development of civil society in the periphery

In Staraya Russa, a *rayon* with about 58,000 inhabitants in the Novgorod region, some NGOs have recently emerged. According to an NGO activist from St Petersburg who organized a seminar there in 1999, Staraya Russa had no experience of NGO activity at that time (Interview HR6). People active in NGOs there claim that there are about forty registered NGOs in the *rayon*, but of those only about a dozen are really functioning (Interview O3). The main problem for civil society groups is the almost complete lack of economic resources. Before 2000 there were few NGOs in the *rayon*, but since then some NGOs were set up with support from the NGO support centre in Novgorod. They also actively promoted the establishment of NGOs in small villages. Apart from areas dealt with by the old organizations – such as support for disabled, women and veterans – there are new organizations in the fields of children and youth, affiliated town contacts, animal protection, and refugees from Central Asia, as well as legal and ecological groups (Interview W1).

Some reasons behind the recent increase in civil society activity in Staraya Russa – apart from the obvious fact that economic resources were provided through the NGO support centre in Novgorod and foreign donors – include the inflow of well-educated and professional Russian refugees from former Soviet republics, the economic crisis which forced many people to try to find an income through work in NGOs, and an increased democratic awareness (Interview O2).

The NGO Resource Centre in Staraya Russa is part of the network of the North-Western Community Development Centre in Novgorod and claims to play a similar role as a resource centre for other NGOs but on a smaller scale (Interview O2). The group is also part of a wider network of NGO centres in several regions, including Moscow, St Petersburg, Novosibirsk, Krasnodar and Samara. The organization suffers from insufficient office space because the local administration is not willing to support it in any way (Interview O2).

Three NGOs dealing with consumer rights issues were set up in Staraya Russa. Altogether they have about forty members, but only a handful of them are active (Interview O3). The organization Consumer Rights conducts sociological studies and public opinion polls on consumer issues. Some of its work has been publicized in local papers, but local political leaders do not pay any attention to their activities. The department for consumer issues within the local administration, however, has secretly given the organization some support.

This section has given examples of the broad range of civil society activities that can be found in post-Soviet Russia and indicated some regional differences. Specific features of civil society in St Petersburg, Novgorod and Pskov are further analysed in Chapters 5 and 7.

Conclusion

Following the break-up of the Soviet Union, there was a clear pattern of 'NGO-ization' of civil society in Russia and the Baltic states. Broad popular movements were demobilized after having achieved their main goal. Several factors were important for the demobilization of civil society that occurred in Russia following the failed coup in August 1991 and the breakdown of the communist regime. First, the pro-democracy movement had achieved its only unifying goal – the demise of communist rule, and there was no basis to sustain mass collective action. Second, the impact of liberal economic reforms in the first year of the post-communist transition turned public opinion against liberalism – political as well as economic. Apathy and cynicism became widespread in the wake of socio-economic hardships experienced by most people while many within the old *nomenklatura* emerged as new capitalist elites. Furthermore, the lack of historical experiences of an institutionalized civil society and a public sphere protected and governed by the rule of law made the consolidation of a post-communist civil society very hard. Finally, it was natural for activists to take the step from civil society to political society and the state, the obvious arenas of power in the post-communist period.

Survey results indicate that contemporary post-Soviet civil society activists seem to be highly educated and largely middle aged. Within the sample for this study there are almost as many women as men on leading positions within civil society groups, although women tend to be concentrated in women's and social welfare NGOs and less well represented in other civil society sectors.

Previous research has depicted post-Soviet civil society groups as weak on membership, poorly rooted in their local communities and heavily dependent on foreign funding. The findings of this study do not fully support this view. Mass organizations are relatively uncommon. Women's organizations in particular tend to have few members, whereas trade unions typically are big. Small NGOs are especially common in Estonia. However, mobilization of new members is a common activity, according to most respondents. Furthermore, a large majority of respondents claim to have local sources like membership fees, private donations, and public subsidies as their main source of funding for their organizations. There seem to be at least limited opportunities for local resource mobilization in all regions, although the situation is worse in peripheral regions and municipalities than in metropolitan areas.

When it comes to other civil society activities, survey results demonstrate the largely non-confrontational character of post-Soviet civil society. A large majority of civil society groups included in this study concentrate on non-confrontational activities only. Information gathering, public education and networking are the most common activities. Demonstrations, boycotts and strikes are very uncommon, and most respondents say they would never join unofficial strikes or occupy buildings. Labour and human rights activists are somewhat more inclined to use confrontational methods than are other civil society groups. Confrontational activities seem to be especially uncommon in Estonia and the Russian region of Novgorod.

5   Civil society, the state, and other arenas

Conflict, cooperation, and unclear boundaries

The previous chapter showed that there is indeed a civil society in post-Soviet Russia and the Baltic states and that a lot of different NGO activities are going on in the region. Nevertheless, post-Soviet civil society is generally depicted as weak and the reasons for this are to be found in the relationships between civil society and the state as well as other social spheres, such as political and economic society. This chapter offers an analysis of these relationships based on the theoretical framework presented in Chapter 2 and empirical findings from the survey as well as qualitative research in three Russian regions. First, however, I summarize findings from previous research on state–civil society relations in Russia.

Civil society and the state in Russia

The relationship between state and civil society in Russia is complex and varies depending on the issue and the region. Civil society is not only 'against the state'. Nor is it located only within the state (Patomäki and Pursiainen 1998: 39). Overall, however, there has been a development from the 'against the state' pattern towards the 'within the state' pattern (Patomäki and Pursiainen 1998: 44). There is more cooperation between NGOs and state and municipal authorities, but also more efforts by state officials to use NGOs for their own ends. Relatively few civil society groups confront the state, and a large part of Russian civil society seems to be apolitical or even anti-political (Patomäki and Pursiainen 1998: 39–40).

Some characteristics of the Russian political system make the development of a strong, independent and influential civil society difficult. A presidential system with strong executive power, also on the regional and local levels, provides more limited opportunities for political influence by civil society groups than does a parliamentary system (McFaul 2002: 114). The rule of law and a functioning judicial system are other key facilitating factors for civil society, which have severe shortcomings in contemporary Russia. Furthermore, the Russian state is poor and ineffective, providing few incentives for civil society groups to interact with it (McFaul 2002: 114). The weakness of the Russian state in the 1990s led to a removal of political restrictions on civil society activities and the creation of an independent press, but it also meant that the state lacked the capability to carry out many state functions that were highly valued by many civil society groups. Hence, the strengthening of state power is not necessarily bad for Russian civil society (Squier 2002).

When analysing the relationship between state and civil society the legal framework is a natural point of departure. The laws regulating civil society in Russia include the constitution of the Russian Federation from December 1993, the Civil Code completed in December 1995, and three specific laws passed by the state *duma* and signed by President Yeltsin in 1995: the Law on Public Associations, the Law on Philanthropic Activities and Organizations, and the Law on Non-commercial Organizations (Weigle 2000: 359; McFaul 2002: 113). These laws have often proved discriminatory and obstructive to civil society activity, but they were nevertheless a big step forward, for the first time ever allowing Russian society to act legally independent from the state (McFaul 2002: 113). The problem is not so much the laws as such, but rather the fact that laws supporting civil society development are not always honoured by local and regional officials (Weigle 2002: 126). One legal problem that several NGO activists refer to is the regulation stating that 80 per cent of the income must be used for activities and not more than 20 per cent for paying staff, according to the law on non-commercial organizations (Elena Belokurova, personal communication, 22 October 2001). Labour organizations face the most severe legal restrictions. The 2001 Labour Code requires a union to organize at least 50 per cent of the workforce at a particular enterprise in order to be recognized as a legitimate representative of the workers. This effectively eliminates most independent labour unions that emerged after the fall of communism. Furthermore, it has become very difficult to organize legal strikes (Squier 2002: 175–6).[1]

All NGOs are supposed to be registered by the state. To officially register, NGOs must file an application with the local Department of Justice administration. This includes signatures of the members of its governing council, the statutes of the organization, excerpts from the minutes of its founding meeting, and information about the founders. There is a registration fee to be paid. Groups can be active without registering, but registration provides them with the official legal status that enables them to receive funding (Weigle 2000: 360). All NGOs were required to resubmit their registration by 30 June 1999. This provided state officials with an opportunity to get rid of critical organizations – particularly in the fields of human rights, labour and the environment (Squier 2002: 170–1). Many prominent organizations had their registration delayed or denied, but eventually the government adopted a less repressive approach to NGOs, and few NGOs now seem to have any problems registering (Squier 2002: 172).

Another form of state harassment against civil society groups is through the tax authorities. It is not uncommon for NGOs to be harassed by tax officials. This might be related both to the acceptance of foreign grants and the provision of services to

the public (Squier 2002: 173–4). Environmental groups considered to be oppositional, in particular, have been subjects of harassment from the tax police and the
Federal Security Service too. Several high-profile environmental activists have even
been charged with treason for activities related to environmental damage caused
by the military (Henry 2002: 199). State surveillance has increased again. Since
Putin came to power, telephones of many independent civil society groups are again
being tapped and monitoring of e-mail has become common (Fish 2002: 251). Only
NGOs considered to be politically against the government suffer these forms
of harassment. Less powerful or apolitical groups usually have no such problems
with the authorities. While lacking any significant elite allies, and hence having no
substantial political influence, women's NGOs have, for example, not suffered the
same form of harassment that many human rights and environmental NGOs have
been victims of. The reason is that most officials consider women's groups irrelevant
and weak (McIntosh Sundstrom 2002: 219).

While keeping a close eye on and harassing groups that are seen as politically threatening, the government also supports a cadre of loyal pseudo-NGOs or
GONGOs (Government-Organized Non-Governmental Organizations) that disrupt
the work of genuine civil society groups (Nikitin and Buchanan 2002: 160). One
example is the organization *Grazhdanskoe Obshchestvo* (Civil Society), which was
involved in the preparation of the Civic Forum. In 2000 the government formed
the *Zeleny Krest* (Green Cross) and KEDR (Constructive Ecological Movement of
Russia) in response to the call for a referendum on the importation of spent nuclear
fuel (Nikitin and Buchanan 2002: 149). The Kremlin-backed youth organization
Idushchie Vmeste (Walking Together) is, however, the most prominent example of a
GONGO (Squier 2002: 176).

'Walking Together' was founded after the presidential election in 2000 by
people working in Putin's election campaign. A representative of the organization
in St Petersburg admits that the primary goal was to support Putin (Interview
S6). The organization claims to be the first mass youth movement since the collapse
of the Soviet Union. There are branches in more than 30 regions, and in Moscow
alone the organization claims to be able to mobilize 10,000 people (Interview S6).
In St Petersburg there are only about 400 members, divided into local groups
with about 50 members each. The organization has campaigned for the new
labour code, which was opposed by the labour movement and widely seen as
extremely anti-labour. Despite the obvious close link to Putin and the Unity party,
'Walking Together' claims to be an NGO. A representative of the organization
points out that Unity has got its own youth organization, which is not related to
'Walking Together' (Interview S6). The council member interviewed was also head
of 'Young Salvors', a youth organization linked to the Ministry of Emergency.
He got to know Putin when working at the office of the Mayor in St Petersburg and
has also been a leader of the youth organization affiliated to 'Our Home Russia'
(Interview S6).

As indicated by the existence of GONGOs, the distinction between state and civil society is not so clear-cut. Civil society groups are hardly independent from state and economic interests. Many groups originated in the state or market sector and receive considerable funding from them (Weigle 2000: 356). NGO funds are sometimes used in other sectors and many NGO activists are state employees.

After 1993 the autonomy and self-organization of political and civil society has been institutionalized in constitutional law and legislative acts. The links between civil society, political society, and the state, however, are weak (Weigle 2000: 20). Many researchers of contemporary Russian civil society identify a lack of connection between civil society groups and state institutions as a major factor behind the weakness of civil society (McFaul 2002: 111). Civil society activists are aware of this problem, and since the mid-1990s many NGOs have given priority to developing contacts with local and regional governments (Weigle 2002: 128). Partnership between local governments and civil society groups is not uncommon (Weigle 2000: 371). 'Social-government' councils, bringing together civil society activists and local officials to address local problems have been established in many cities and towns throughout Russia (Weigle 2002: 128–9). However, there is not much evidence that such arrangements lead to any significant political influence for civil society groups. NGOs have occasionally been successful in influencing local or regional politics, but such sporadic victories seem to be dependent upon individual allies within the local or regional government (McIntosh Sundstrom 2002: 213).

When looking at post-Soviet Russian state policies on civil society, we can conclude that Yeltsin's government established the institutional foundations for a civil society, but it did not promote independent activities and did not recognize their potential (Weigle 2002: 132). Many civil society activists are even more sceptical towards the Putin government.[2] In spring 2001 Putin urged the presidential envoys in the seven new federal superdistricts to promote civil society activities. He also met with representatives of selected NGOs (Weigle 2002: 133). This led to a major event of state–civil society interaction – the Civic Forum, 21–22 November 2001. At this big conference Putin, cabinet members and government officials met with some 3,500 representatives of more than 300 NGOs (Nikitin and Buchanan 2002; Weigle 2002). First there were attempts to only invite moderate or non-political NGOs by the Kremlin, while ignoring (and thus marginalizing) oppositional human rights groups like Memorial and the Committee of Soldiers' Mothers. These attempts were rejected by civil society activists who established their own rules for participation in the Civic Forum. Some critical human rights organizations, however, still refused to have any contact with state officials (Weigle 2002: 133). The 'People's Assembly', an umbrella group of civil society organizations, rejected government attempts to have elections and appointments to representative organs at the Forum. In this way they hoped to avoid being co-opted by the state, while still engaging in a dialogue with state officials (Weigle 2002: 134). Local and regional civil society committees or conferences in sixty-one of the regions of the Russian Federation were involved in the preparations for the Forum (Nikitin and Buchanan 2002: 155; Weigle 2002: 134). According to one analyst, civil society groups in Russia showed their growing strength by rejecting Putin's attempts to determine the composition and orientation of the Civic Forum (Weigle 2002). The dialogue in itself, however, seemed to be disappointing, especially for more critical human rights activists. The Forum 'merely confirmed the depth of suspicion and frustration on both sides', according to one observer (Nikitin and Buchanan 2002: 159).

Many environmental activists also tend to be critical towards the Putin government. In May 2000, President Putin dissolved the State Committee on the Environment and the State Forestry Committee. Environmental NGOs criticized these committees for their failure to protect the environment in an adequate way, but they protested their dissolution, claiming that 'a flawed system of environmental protection was better than none at all' (Henry 2002: 200).

While NGOs in Russia generally have had very little political influence, there has been some impact on specific policy areas. Some human rights NGOs have, for example, had some positive impact on the prison system (Weiler 2002). A coalition of environmental groups managed to gather almost 2.5 million signatures on a petition demanding a referendum on the decision to import nuclear waste.[3] However, most of the limited political impact that civil society groups have had in post-Soviet Russia has been on local and regional levels. Following the breakdown of communist rule and the disintegration of the USSR, local government leaders in Russia tried to demobilize civil society activism in order to maintain political control. In Novosibirsk, for example, local administrations tried to make the NGO sector part of the local government apparatus (Weigle 2000: 362). The law is still typically perceived as a tool that local government leaders use to control the population rather than an instrument to protect citizen rights (Weigle 2000: 362). Nevertheless, most efforts by Russian NGOs to influence policies have been directed to the local level. Democratic elections have made local politicians more responsive to civil society groups (Weigle 2000: 362–3). It is easier for civil society activists to get access to officials in more peripheral regions and municipalities than on the federal level and in big cities, provided that the local and regional leaders are not outrightly hostile to independent NGOs (McIntosh Sundstrom 2002: 220–1). This is true not least in the environmental sector, because the Federal government is hostile towards many environmentalists. Hence, environmental NGOs see a greater likelihood of success when lobbying local and regional governments (Henry 2002: 195). In regions where environmentalists are not seen as oppositional to the political administration, some grassroots activists are even employed in the regional offices of the State Committee for Ecology (Henry 2002: 198).

Political opportunities and political influence

In this section I use survey data to cast some new light on the potential for political influence by civil society groups in post-Soviet Russia and the Baltic states. A first requisite for having any influence on state policies is to have contacts with state institutions. Table 5.1 provides an overview of the intensity of contacts between different sectors of civil society and state (and other civil society groups) on different levels. Hence, it gives a rough map of networks of civil society groups. The intensity of contacts with state and civil society groups on different levels show an expected pattern. Contacts are most intense on the local level and the intensity becomes less the further we move from the local level, with very low intensity on the international level. Furthermore, we can see that contacts with other civil society groups are somewhat more intense than contacts with government or state institutions on each level. When we examine different categories of civil society groups we observe that organizations within the category 'other' have most intense contacts on the local and especially the regional level. This is not surprising given the fact that several NGO resource centres are included in this category. Women's groups are least involved in local and regional networks, both with state and civil society actors. When reaching the national level and above, environmental groups have the most intense contacts – with the exception of international governmental organizations (read UN) with which human rights and democracy oriented groups have somewhat more contacts. Social welfare groups are most localized. The intensity of contacts is lowest for this category of civil society groups on the national level and beyond.

On average, there are contacts with local government and state institutions a few times a month. On the national level the intensity is only a few times a year, and on the regional level the intensity of contacts is somewhere in between. We may conclude that there are at least sufficient contacts with local (and to a lesser extent regional) authorities for civil society groups to have a potential to influence policies on these levels. However, we need to know more about the character of these contacts. Table 5.1 is constructed in order to provide a rough map of networks of civil society groups. Before continuing with a more elaborate analysis of state–civil society relations we should look at regional differences in the pattern of contacts.

Patterns of contacts differ significantly between regions (see Table 5.2). Not surprisingly, regions of the national capital have a higher degree of interaction with national state institutions as well as civil society groups on the national level. These regions are also those with most intense transnational contacts. Harju in Estonia stands out in this respect. Civil society groups in more peripheral regions (Pskov, Kaliningrad, Pölva) report most intense contacts on the local and regional level, but have very few transnational contacts. Some regions seem to have little contact with the national capital. This is especially true for Novgorod; a region where civil society groups report more intense contacts with foreign governmental and civil society organizations than with those based in Moscow. It is worth noting

Table 5.1 Civil society groups' contacts with state and civil society actors on different levels (average intensity on a scale from 0 to 100)

	Human rights	Women	Labour	Environment	Ethnic/ nationalist	Social welfare	Other	Total
Local government and state	45	33	44	42	37	47	55	44
Local civil society	48	45	44	52	48	55	47	48
Regional government and state	36	21	37	33	27	32	42	33
Regional civil society	46	23	32	31	28	41	46	36
National state	22	17	30	33	20	15	27	24
National civil society	29	23	27	36	27	18	31	27
European governmental	11	10	7	18	11	6	15	11
European civil society	18	17	12	26	10	11	19	16
International governmental	11	6	4	8	5	3	9	7
International civil society	17	12	10	22	8	5	12	12

Source: Democratization: Local and Transnational Perspectives Survey (DLTPS) 1999–2000.

Note: The question was: 'How often does the organization/group have contact with representatives of these organizations or institutions?' Organizations/institutions on different levels were listed as in the table. The alternatives given were 'Never/almost never', 'A few times a year', 'A few times a month', 'A few times a week', 'Almost every day'. The number of respondents selecting each alternative was multiplied by 0 for 'Never/almost never', 25 for 'A few times a year', 50 for 'A few times a month', 75 for 'A few times a week', and 100 for 'Almost every day'. The results were summed up and divided by the number of respondents (ranging from 312 to 351 for different questions and excluding Lithuania on the regional level). Thus we arrived at the measurement of average intensity of contacts shown in the table. 0 would mean never or almost never any contacts at all, whereas 100 would mean contacts almost every day for all respondents.

Table 5.2 Civil society groups' contacts with state and civil society actors on different levels per region (average intensity on a scale from 0 to 100)

	Kal.	No.	Ps.	St P.	Sv.	Ha.	I.-V.	Pö.	Ta.	Ri.	Va.	Kau.	Vi.	Total
Local government and state	44	46	57	37	54	43	41	50	39	38	40	39	35	44
Local civil society	58	55	53	56	51	39	44	54	54	38	44	38	36	48
Regional government and state	31	26	31	42	38	29	34	56	29	25	25	–	–	33
Regional civil society	45	38	28	47	42	19	31	58	36	25	25	–	–	36
National state	7	7	18	17	16	43	21	29	38	39	35	29	39	24
National civil society	20	11	20	29	24	32	23	44	34	35	15	32	40	27
European governmental	9	7	3	14	5	24	11	5	21	16	15	6	17	11
European civil society	16	11	3	24	11	20	5	10	32	26	12	11	24	16
International governmental	5	5	0	9	8	18	2	0	15	11	0	1	10	7
International civil society	15	11	1	17	14	22	2	4	20	21	10	8	16	12

Source: Democratization: Local and Transnational Perspectives Survey (DLTPS) 1999–2000.

Note: The question was: 'How often does the organization/group have contact with representatives of these organizations or institutions?' Organizations/institutions on different levels were listed as in the table. The alternatives given were 'Never/almost never', 'A few times a year', 'A few times a month', 'A few times a week', 'Almost every day'. The number of respondents selecting each alternative was multiplied by 0 for 'Never/almost never', 25 for 'A few times a year', 50 for 'A few times a month', 75 for 'A few times a week', and 100 for 'Almost every day'. The results were summed up and divided by the number of respondents (ranging from 312 to 351 for different questions and excluding Lithuania on the regional level). Thus we arrived at the measurement of average intensity of contacts shown in the table. 0 would mean never or almost never any contacts at all, whereas 100 would mean contacts almost every day for all respondents.

that only three groups in Novgorod account for almost all contacts with federal-level civil society organizations.

In order to understand if the relatively intense contacts with local government and state institutions – especially in peripheral regions – lead to any political influence for civil society groups, we need to analyse political opportunities and other aspects of political clout. The concept of political opportunities – as outlined in Chapter 2 – is a useful starting point for an analysis of state–civil society relations. We start with the conventional understanding of political opportunities as including three major aspects: openness of the government, the existence of elite allies, and the lack of harassment and repression.

Despite the more successful process of democratization in the Baltic states compared to Russia, political opportunities for civil society activities are not perceived as significantly better in Estonia, Latvia and Lithuania than in Russia. Instead the index of political opportunities shows a significant variation within countries, especially across Russian regions (see Table 5.3). Novgorod and Sverdlovsk are the regions with best political opportunities whereas Kaliningrad and St Petersburg have the worst political opportunities, as perceived by civil society activists. By contrast, perceptions of political opportunities are very homogenous across Estonia. All four Estonian regions score about the average on the index. As in Russia, there is a regional variation within Latvia and Lithuania too. There seem to be much better political opportunities in Valmiera than in Riga. Whereas political opportunities in Vilnius are average, they are much worse in Kaunas. Patterns are similar for all indicators, with some significant exceptions. Pölva would have reached an even higher level on the combined index if there had been more elite allies. Now the region scores very badly on this indicator. The opposite is true for Pskov. There seem to be quite a lot of elite allies, but the scores for openness and lack of harassment/repression are worse. Sverdlovsk scores very high on elite allies and openness, but a few civil society groups report systematic harassment and repression from local authorities.[4]

Differences between different categories of civil society groups are not as pronounced as between different regions (see Table 5.4). Unsurprisingly, political opportunities are best for politically less sensitive groups like social welfare NGOs and those in the category 'other', including NGO resource centres, youth organizations, etc. Activists working with human rights and democracy and ethnic and nationalist issues have fewer political opportunities. Ethnic and nationalist groups have significantly fewer elite allies than other civil society groups. Repression (like police actions and (threats of) violence) is uncommon. Most groups (five out of eight) that claim to have suffered repression are working in the field of human rights and democracy.

The analysis of perceptions of political opportunities, while very useful, is not sufficient. We should take the analysis a step further by asking about the actual personal overlapping between civil society and the local government. To

Table 5.3 Political opportunities for civil society groups in different regions (index from 0 to 100)

Region	Political opportunities (Total)	Openness of local government	Elite allies	Lack of harassment/ repression
Novgorod	77	80	56	94
Sverdlovsk	70	65	63	83
Valmiera	66	60	50	87
Pölva	63	59	35	95
Harju	61	48	48	88
Ida-Viru	61	48	47	87
Tartu	61	52	39	92
Vilnius	61	55	43	85
Pskov	60	48	52	81
Riga	54	43	35	83
Kaunas	52	45	43	67
St Petersburg	52	46	35	76
Kaliningrad	45	33	41	61
Mean	**61**	**54**	**46**	**83**

Source: Democratization: Local and Transnational Perspectives Survey (DLTPS) 1999–2000.

Note: The questions were: 'How do you perceive the local government?' Alternatives given: 'Open and transparent', 'Rather open', 'Rather closed', 'Very closed'. 'Does the organization/group have any allies (i.e. politicians who you feel are sympathetic to and supportive of your activities) within the local/regional government?' Alternatives given: 'Strong support from influential allies in local/regional government', Some sympathy from allies in local/regional government', No allies in local/regional government'. 'Has the organization/group suffered any harassment or repression initiated by local authorities during the last 2 years?' Alternatives given: 'No problem with local authorities', Occasional bureaucratic or legal problems (such as problems of registration, denial of permission for certain activities, etc.)', 'Systematic bureaucratic or legal harassment by local authorities', 'Repression including police actions or (threats of) violence against members of organization/group'.

For the first and third questions the number of respondents selecting each alternative was multiplied by 100 for the first alternative, 67 for the second, 33 for the third and 0 for the last. For the second question the number of respondents selecting each alternative was multiplied by 100, 50 and 0. The results were summed up and divided by the number of respondents (total 361, 360 and 359 respectively). Thus we arrived at a measurement of how civil society groups in different regions perceive openness, elite allies and harassment/repression.

Measurements of the three aspects of political opportunities are combined to produce an index of political opportunities (by adding the three indicators and dividing by three). 0 would mean a completely closed and highly repressive political system with no elite allies for civil society groups. 100 would mean a completely open and transparent political system with strong elite support for civil society groups and no harassment from local authorities.

what extent do members of civil society groups hold positions within the local government (or in political parties)? Table 5.5 indicates a rather strong connection between local governments and political parties on the one hand, and civil society groups on the other hand. Thirty-six per cent of all groups included in the study claim to have members within political parties and/or local government insti-

Table 5.4 Political opportunities for different kinds of civil society groups (index from 0 to 100)

Category of civil society group	Political opportunities (Total)	Openness of local government	Elite allies	Lack of harassment/ repression
Other	67	64	48	90
Social welfare	67	66	47	89
Women	64	53	46	93
Environment	60	53	47	79
Labour	60	49	51	81
Ethnic/nationalist	55	53	35	78
Human rights	54	44	47	71
Total	**61**	**54**	**46**	**83**

Source: Democratization: Local and Transnational Perspectives Survey (DLTPS) 1999–2000.

Note: The questions were: 'How do you perceive the local government?' Alternatives given: 'Open and transparent', 'Rather open', 'Rather closed', 'Very closed'. 'Does the organization/group have any allies (i.e. politicians who you feel are sympathetic to and supportive of your activities) within the local/regional government?' Alternatives given: 'Strong support from influential allies in local/regional government', Some sympathy from allies in local/regional government', No allies in local/regional government'. 'Has the organization/group suffered any harassment or repression initiated by local authorities during the last 2 years?' Alternatives given: 'No problem with local authorities', Occasional bureaucratic or legal problems (such as problems of registration, denial of permission for certain activities etc.)', 'Systematic bureaucratic or legal harassment by local authorities', 'Repression including police actions or (threats of) violence against members of organization/group'.

For the first and third questions the number of respondents selecting each alternative was multiplied by 100 for the first alternative, 67 for the second, 33 for the third and 0 for the last. For the second question the number of respondents selecting each alternative was multiplied by 100, 50 and 0. The results were summed up and divided by the number of respondents (total 361, 360 and 359 respectively). Thus we arrived at a measurement of how different categories of civil society groups perceive openness, elite allies and harassment/repression.

Measurements of the three aspects of political opportunities are combined to produce an index of political opportunities (by adding the three indicators and dividing by three). 0 would mean a completely closed and highly repressive political system with no elite allies for civil society groups. 100 would mean a completely open and transparent political system with strong elite support for civil society groups and no harassment from local authorities.

tutions. Surprisingly, women's groups are most closely linked to the formal political sphere. Environmental and ethnic and nationalist organizations have fewer members within parties and/or local governments.

Regional variations are more significant (Table 5.6.) Overlapping membership between civil society groups and political parties and/or local government institutions is very common in Estonia (especially in Pölva). It is also rather common in Lithuania, but less so in Latvia and significantly less common in several Russian regions. Only 11 per cent of the organizations in Novgorod have any members in political parties and/or local government institutions. This is due to the general lack of political parties in the Novgorod political system.

Table 5.5 Civil society groups with members holding positions in political parties and/or local government institutions (%)

Categories of civil society groups	Members holding positions in political parties and/or local government institutions
Women	47 (22)
Human rights	45 (24)
Other	41 (22)
Labour	38 (26)
Social welfare	28 (13)
Ethnic/nationalist	24 (11)
Environment	21 (9)
Total	**36 (127)**

Source: Democratization: Local and Transnational Perspectives Survey (DLTPS) 1999–2000.

Note: The question was: 'Do you or other members of the organization/group hold any position in political parties and/or local government institutions?' The answer 'Yes' is shown. (Absolute numbers within brackets.)

Table 5.6 Civil society groups with members holding positions in political parties and/or local government institutions per region (%)

Region	Members holding positions in political parties and/or local government institutions
Pölva	69 (9)
Tartu	52 (12)
Vilnius	49 (17)
Kaunas	47 (14)
Ida-Viru	44 (8)
Harju	42 (8)
Kaliningrad	42 (5)
Riga	42 (10)
Sverdlovsk	35 (14)
Valmiera	30 (3)
St Petersburg	29 (14)
Pskov	20 (8)
Novgorod	11 (5)
Total	**36 (127)**

Source: Democratization: Local and Transnational Perspectives Survey (DLTPS) 1999–2000.

Note: The question was: 'Do you or other members of the organization/group hold any position in political parties and/or local government institutions?' The answer 'Yes' is shown. (Absolute numbers within brackets.)

So far we can conclude that there are significant contacts between the state and civil society, especially on the local level. Political opportunities are perceived to be reasonably good in most regions and by most sectors of civil society. More severe forms of harassment and repression, at least, seem to be rare. There is also a surprisingly strong personal overlapping between civil society groups and local governments/political parties. All this indicates a potential for political influence by civil society groups, but we still do not have a clear picture.

Another indicator of political opportunities is the trust civil society actors have in state authorities. Table 5.7 shows significant differences across regions and the pattern is quite consistent. Civil society activists in Estonia have much more trust in all kinds of state institutions, and activists in Russia have much less trust. Activists in Latvia and Lithuania have a level of trust in state institutions lying in between Estonia and Russia. Trust in national state authorities is high in Estonia, with more than 70 per cent of respondents having some or a lot of trust (except for Ida-Viru with a slightly lower level, which is still significantly higher than in any region outside Estonia). Trust in federal authorities is low in the Russian regions and almost nonexistent in St Petersburg and Kaliningrad. Trust in regional authorities follows a similar pattern, with two interesting exceptions. First, civil society elites in Novgorod have much more trust in regional authorities than have civil society elites in other Russian regions. Second, there is surprisingly little trust in regional authorities in Valmiera. The specific case of Novgorod has already been discussed. The low level of trust in Valmiera is more difficult to explain.

The pattern of a lot of trust in Estonia and less trust in Russia is repeated for local authorities. Again we find more trust in local authorities in Novgorod than in the other Russian regions (but still less than in Estonia). Local authorities in Pskov and Sverdlovsk are also trusted by a majority of respondents, whereas trust in local authorities in Kaliningrad and St Petersburg is very low. Interestingly, civil society elites in Valmiera who had little trust in regional authorities have much more trust in local authorities.

Trust in courts is generally low in all countries except Estonia. Again, civil society elites in Kaliningrad and St Petersburg have least trust. A majority of respondents in Pskov have some trust in courts, placing the region above not only the other Russian regions but also Latvia and Lithuania. Civil society elites in Estonia (especially in the peripheral regions) find the police most trustworthy. Respondents in Russia have considerably less trust in the police – almost no trust at all in St Petersburg. There is a similar pattern – although with a higher level of trust – for the army. Especially in Lithuania there is more trust in the army than in other state institutions.

In sum, we can conclude that post-Soviet civil society elites in Russia, Latvia and Lithuania have relatively little trust in state institutions. More than 50 per cent of respondents (in many regions considerably more) have no or little trust in federal/ national authorities, regional authorities, courts and police. Only local authorities

Table 5.7 Civil society actors' trust in state authorities per region (% having some or a lot of trust)

Region	Federal/national authorities		Regional authorities		Local authorities		Courts		Police		Army	
Kaliningrad	8	(1)	15	(2)	8	(1)	15	(2)	23	(3)	46	(6)
Novgorod	15	(7)	53	(25)	61	(28)	33	(15)	27	(12)	53	(24)
Pskov	38	(15)	38	(14)	55	(22)	52	(21)	38	(15)	45	(18)
St Petersburg	2	(1)	15	(7)	17	(7)	22	(11)	10	(5)	37	(18)
Sverdlovsk	30	(12)	38	(15)	55	(22)	32	(13)	32	(13)	55	(22)
Harju	73	(16)	81	(17)	86	(19)	73	(16)	59	(13)	62	(13)
Ida-Viru	67	(12)	78	(14)	62	(10)	53	(9)	50	(9)	67	(12)
Põlva	77	(10)	85	(11)	77	(10)	75	(9)	69	(9)	83	(10)
Tartu	74	(17)	91	(21)	87	(20)	70	(16)	72	(16)	70	(16)
Riga	44	(11)	67	(16)	54	(14)	35	(9)	38	(10)	50	(12)
Valmiera	60	(6)	29	(2)	90	(9)	40	(4)	50	(5)	67	(6)
Kaunas	58	(18)	45	(14)	45	(14)	33	(10)	48	(15)	61	(19)
Vilnius	58	(21)	50	(18)	58	(21)	47	(17)	53	(19)	67	(24)
Mean	**40**	**(147)**	**49**	**(177)**	**55**	**(197)**	**42**	**(152)**	**39**	**(144)**	**55**	**(200)**

Source: Democratization: Local and Transnational Perspectives Survey (DLTPS) 1999–2000.

Note: The question was: 'How much trust do you have in the following institutions?' The answers 'Some trust' and 'A lot of trust' are combined and shown. N = 358–367 depending on institution (absolute numbers within brackets).

and the army enjoy somewhat higher levels of trust. The situation in Estonia is quite different. Here a large majority of interviewed civil society activists have some or a lot of trust in all state authorities. Trust is somewhat less common in Ida-Viru than in the other regions in Estonia. The results might be interpreted as a sign of better quality of state institutions in Estonia than in the other countries. The very low trust in all state institutions found among civil society elites in St Petersburg, for instance, may also be a reflection of a generally more sceptical and demanding civil society elite in this city. The trust that civil society elites have in state authorities does not automatically say anything about the quality of these authorities, but low trust never-theless indicates a problematic relationship between state and civil society.

When comparing different civil society sectors, the clearest pattern is that human rights and democracy groups have least trust in state institutions. Environmental groups are also more sceptical towards the state than other civil society groups. This is the expected pattern, as human rights and environmental groups are known to be more confrontational and critical towards the state. These kinds of groups have also suffered most from state harassment.

Do civil society elites seek support from the state despite the relatively low level of trust they have in these institutions? Table 5.8 shows the extent to which civil society actors seek support from state institutions compared to other public and private institutions. Forty-two per cent of respondents turn to local authorities and 36 per cent to higher-level state authorities when they need support. While not a majority, it is still a significant number of the interviewed civil society elites that find it worthwhile to ask for support from state institutions, especially compared to the very few respondents who turn to political or economic society. It should however be noted that most civil society elites seek support from other civil society groups.

In the regional comparison, civil society elites in Kaliningrad and Ida-Viru are most ready to seek support from the state whereas those in Riga and Kaunas seem to be much more sceptical about state support. It is also worth noting that civil society actors in Novgorod turn to local authorities to a much larger extent than average whereas they are not more willing than civil society elites in other regions to turn to higher level state authorities. Again the image of a close relationship between civil society and local authorities in Novgorod is confirmed.

Comparing different categories of civil society groups (Table 5.9), we find that ethnic and nationalist groups are generally most inclined to seek support from state authorities, especially on the local level. Interestingly, human rights and democracy groups have the highest percentage seeking support on the national level, but the lowest percentage on the local level. This might reflect a belief that human rights issues are mainly the responsibility of the national government. Environmental groups also turn more to national than local state authorities (a finding somewhat contradicting previous research on Russia), whereas all other civil society groups are more inclined to seek support from local authorities.

Table 5.8 Actors who civil society elites seek support from per region (%)

Region	National or regional authorities		Local authorities		National political parties		Local political parties		Local newspapers		Local business groups		Other civil society groups		The general public	
Kaliningrad	69	(9)	54	(7)	15	(2)	38	(5)	46	(6)	54	(7)	46	(6)	54	(7)
Novgorod	36	(17)	60	(28)	6	(3)	6	(3)	17	(8)	13	(6)	45	(21)	28	(13)
Pskov	30	(12)	42	(17)	2	(1)	12	(5)	25	(10)	12	(5)	65	(26)	28	(11)
St Petersburg	32	(16)	34	(17)	10	(5)	14	(7)	44	(22)	18	(9)	76	(38)	52	(26)
Sverdlovsk	50	(20)	45	(18)	15	(6)	10	(4)	32	(13)	8	(3)	70	(28)	45	(18)
Harju	32	(7)	46	(10)	23	(5)	18	(4)	18	(4)	0		54	(12)	46	(10)
Ida-Viru	50	(9)	61	(11)	33	(6)	17	(3)	33	(6)	17	(3)	61	(11)	28	(5)
Põlva	31	(4)	38	(5)	31	(4)	31	(4)	38	(5)	23	(3)	15	(2)	23	(3)
Tartu	39	(9)	48	(11)	13	(3)	9	(2)	35	(8)	26	(6)	56	(13)	44	(10)
Riga	27	(7)	15	(4)	12	(3)	8	(2)	38	(10)	12	(3)	65	(17)	38	(10)
Valmiera	40	(4)	50	(5)	10	(1)	20	(2)	30	(3)	20	(2)	50	(5)	30	(3)
Kaunas	29	(9)	26	(8)	13	(4)	6	(2)	39	(12)	13	(4)	52	(16)	36	(11)
Vilnius	31	(11)	43	(15)	34	(12)	31	(11)	34	(12)	6	(2)	54	(19)	37	(13)
Total	**36**	**(134)**	**42**	**(156)**	**15**	**(55)**	**15**	**(54)**	**32**	**(119)**	**14**	**(53)**	**58**	**(214)**	**38**	**(140)**

Source: Democratization: Local and Transnational Perspectives Survey (DLTPS) 1999–2000.

Note: The question was: 'When you as a leader are in a situation in which support from others is necessary, to whom do you usually turn?' More than one answer was accepted. The answer 'state, county or higher administrative officials' has been interpreted as 'national or regional authorities', 'city managers or top administrative officials at the local level' has been interpreted as 'local authorities', 'higher level party leaders' equals 'national political parties', the answers 'local party leaders', local elective officials' and ' special groups in local party organisation' have been combined as 'local political parties', 'local leaders of political movements', 'local civic, professional or reform groups concerned with local politics', 'local trade unions', 'local ethnic, religious or racial groups' and 'neighbourhood groups' have been combined as 'other civil society groups'. N = 368 (absolute numbers within brackets).

Table 5.9 Actors who different categories of civil society elites seek support from (%)

Category of civil society group	National or regional authorities	Local authorities	National political parties	Local political parties	Local newspapers	Local business groups	Other civil society groups	The general public
Human rights	40 (22)	29 (16)	22 (12)	24 (13)	34 (19)	14 (8)	60 (33)	44 (24)
Women	28 (13)	43 (20)	15 (7)	15 (7)	30 (14)	13 (6)	60 (28)	34 (16)
Labour	32 (23)	36 (26)	14 (10)	12 (9)	32 (23)	8 (6)	68 (49)	29 (21)
Environment	40 (17)	33 (14)	5 (2)	9 (4)	42 (18)	12 (5)	51 (22)	58 (25)
Ethnic/nationalist	39 (18)	63 (29)	24 (11)	15 (7)	37 (17)	15 (7)	63 (29)	35 (16)
Social welfare	36 (17)	51 (24)	4 (2)	8 (4)	23 (11)	13 (6)	51 (24)	34 (16)
Other	41 (24)	47 (27)	19 (11)	17 (10)	29 (17)	26 (15)	50 (29)	38 (22)
Total	**36 (134)**	**42 (156)**	**15 (55)**	**15 (54)**	**32 (119)**	**14 (53)**	**58 (214)**	**38 (140)**

Source: Democratization: Local and Transnational Perspectives Survey (DLTPS) 1999–2000.

Note: The question was: 'When you as a leader are in a situation in which support from others is necessary, to whom do you usually turn?' More than one answer was accepted. The answer 'state, county or higher administrative officials' has been interpreted as 'national or regional authorities', 'city managers or top administrative officials at the local level' has been interpreted as 'local authorities', 'higher level party leaders' equals 'national political parties', the answers 'local party leaders', local elective officials' and 'special groups in local party organisation' have been combined as 'local political parties', 'local leaders of political movements', 'local civic, professional or reform groups concerned with local politics', 'local trade unions', 'local ethnic, religious or racial groups' and neighbourhood groups' have been combined as 'other civil society groups'. N = 368 (absolute numbers within brackets).

When civil society elites seek support from political decision-makers in state institutions, how effective do they find these contacts? An indication of this is found in Table 5.10. The question concerns the effectiveness of personal contacts with decision-makers in general, but it is likely that respondents have their own personal experiences of such contacts with decision-makers within (mostly local) state institutions in mind when they answer. The average score of 77 on the index from 0 to 100 means that the average respondent considers personal contacts with decision-makers to be something in between somewhat and very effective. This is an indication that a majority of interviewed civil society elites think they have some political influence when contacting political decision-makers. The regional variation, however, is strong (except within Latvia which seems homogenous in this respect). Almost all respondents in Pölva find personal contacts with decision-makers very effective, and civil society elites in Kaunas also seem to have very positive experiences. By contrast, Ida-Viru scores 56 on the index, which is much lower than in any other region included in the study. In this region civil society

Table 5.10 Effectiveness of personal contacts with decision-makers according to civil society elites in different regions (index from 0 to 100)

Region	Effectiveness of personal contacts with decision-makers
Pölva	96
Kaunas	90
Harju	84
Novgorod	82
Riga	80
Valmiera	80
St Petersburg	78
Kaliningrad	73
Pskov	72
Tartu	72
Sverdlovsk	69
Vilnius	69
Ida-Viru	56
Total	**77**

Source: Democratization: Local and Transnational Perspectives Survey (DLTPS) 1999–2000.

Note: The question was: 'There are a number of ways in which people can influence decisions. We have listed some of them and would like to get your opinion on their effectiveness. Personal contact with decision-makers.' Alternatives given were: 'Not effective at all', 'Somewhat effective' and 'Very effective'. The number of respondents selecting each alternative was multiplied by 0 for the first alternative, 50 for the second, and 100 for the third. The results were summed up and divided by the number of respondents. Thus we arrived at an index of perceived effectiveness of personal contacts with decision-makers. 0 would mean that all respondents found personal contacts with decision-makers not effective at all. 100 would mean that all respondents found such contacts very effective. N = 366 (absolute numbers within brackets).

elites do not seem to find personal contacts with political decision-makers very effective.

Comparing different categories of civil society groups we find that less critical and confrontational groups in the categories of 'social welfare' and 'other' are most optimistic about the effectiveness of personal contacts with decision-makers whereas activists in human rights and democracy groups are less optimistic.

Another important aspect of political opportunities for civil society activities is the media situation. Civil society activists need media in order to reach out to the public. In regions where local and regional authorities control all or most media, opportunities for critical civil society activities are likely to be limited. Survey data give some insights into the relationship between post-Soviet civil society and media. Table 5.11 shows a relatively limited trust in media among post-Soviet civil society elites. The level of trust is similar for both regional and national TV and only slightly less for regional newspapers. Variations across regions are significant. A clear country pattern appears with all Estonian regions on top and all Russian regions at the bottom. The media situation, according to civil society elites, seems to be rather

Table 5.11 Civil society actors' trust in media per region (index from 0 to 100)

Region	Trust in media	Trust in regional newspapers	Trust in regional TV	Trust in national TV
Tartu	64	56	67	70
Harju	63	68	58	64
Pölva	62	59	62	64
Ida-Viru	58	52	60	63
Kaunas	56	56	53	59
Riga	56	58	58	53
Valmiera	54	53	57	53
Vilnius	50	40	54	56
Novgorod	37	38	40	32
Pskov	37	37	36	38
Sverdlovsk	34	31	38	33
St Petersburg	27	31	28	22
Kaliningrad	25	25	28	22
Mean	**43**	**39**	**45**	**45**

Source: Democratization: Local and Transnational Perspectives Survey (DLTPS) 1999–2000.

Note: The question was: 'How much trust do you have in the following institutions?' Alternatives given were: 'No trust at all', 'Little trust', 'Some trust' and 'A lot of trust'. The number of respondents selecting each alternative was multiplied by 0 for the first alternative, 33 for the second, 67 for the third and 100 for the last. The results were summed up and divided by the number of respondents. Thus we arrived at an index of trust in different media. 0 would mean no trust at all for all respondents. 100 would mean a lot of trust for all respondents. Measurements of trust in the three different forms of media were combined to produce an index of trust in media (by adding the three indicators and dividing by three). N = 338–365 depending on question (absolute numbers within brackets).

satisfactory in Estonia, slightly less so in Latvia and Lithuania, and much worse in Russia. Respondents in Kaliningrad and St Petersburg are particularly sceptical towards all forms of media.[5]

Returning to Table 5.8, we find that 32 per cent of the interviewed civil society elites would turn to local newspapers for support. This figure is much higher than similar figures for political and economic society, but somewhat lower than for state authorities. Given the very low level of trust in media among civil society elites in Kaliningrad and St Petersburg, it is surprising to see that civil society activists in these regions are most inclined to seek support from local newspapers. Activists in Novgorod, Pskov and Harju most seldom turn to local newspapers for support. Table 5.9 shows that environmental groups turn to local newspapers for support to a much larger extent than do other civil society groups. Social welfare groups are least inclined to seek support from local newspapers.

To what extent are civil society elites satisfied with their media contacts? Table 5.12 shows how effective respondents find the use of media. The average score is 72 on the index from 0 to 100, indicating a rather strong belief in the effectiveness

Table 5.12 Effectiveness of use of media according to civil society elites in different regions (index from 0 to 100)

Region	Effectiveness of use of media
Valmiera	90
Pölva	88
Kaliningrad	85
Harju	84
Tartu	80
Kaunas	79
Riga	75
Ida-Viru	72
Vilnius	72
Novgorod	68
Pskov	68
St Petersburg	64
Sverdlovsk	61
Total	**72**

Source: Democratization: Local and Transnational Perspectives Survey (DLTPS) 1999–2000.

Note: The question was: 'There are a number of ways in which people can influence decisions. We have listed some of them and would like to get your opinion on their effectiveness: Use of media.' Alternatives given were: 'Not effective at all', 'Somewhat effective' and 'Very effective'. The number of respondents selecting each alternative was multiplied by 0 for the first alternative, 50 for the second, and 100 for the third. The results were summed up and divided by the number of respondents. Thus we arrived at an index of perceived effectiveness of use of media. 0 would mean that all respondents found the use of media not effective at all. 100 would mean that all respondents found the use of media very effective. N = 366 (absolute numbers within brackets).

of the use of media among the interviewed post-Soviet civil society elites. Regional variations are, however, significant. With the (strange) exception of respondents in Kaliningrad, the Russian civil society elites seem to be less optimistic about the effectiveness of using media. Civil society elites in the more peripheral regions of Valmiera and Pölva, in Latvia and Estonia respectively, find the use of media most effective.[6]

Let us finally ask the respondents directly what they think about the general political influence of their organizations (Table 5.13). Representatives of civil society groups in general do not think that their organizations have got much 'clout'. Latvian respondents in particular are very pessimistic about their influence. The average score for civil society influence in general is a poor 38 on the index from 0 to 100. Only in the case of influence over other civil society groups does the score reach above 50, i.e. closer to 'some clout' than to 'little clout'. In general there is a perception of having somewhat more clout over local than regional authorities. For some regions the difference is significant (especially Valmiera, but also Harju, Vilnius, Tartu, Novgorod and Kaunas). Civil society activists think they have most influence on local authorities in Tartu, Pölva and Harju and least in Riga. Respondents say they have little influence over enterprises – be they state or private. Civil society influence on media seems to be very low in Ida-Viru and Novgorod and surprisingly high in Kaliningrad.[7]

It is interesting to compare this index of perceived influence of civil society groups with the index of political opportunities (Table 5.3). In Novgorod and Valmiera where political opportunities were considered to be among the best, civil society elites believe they have least influence. Even more strikingly, Kaliningrad came out on top of the influence index whereas it was at the absolute bottom in the political opportunities index. It is clear that good political opportunities do not automatically mean political influence for civil society groups. A shortcoming of the conventional understanding of political opportunities is that it does not incorporate any theoretical understanding of power and influence. The findings here indicate a need to reconsider the concept of political opportunities in order to pay more attention to aspects of power.

To sum up this section, we can conclude that there are relatively frequent contacts between post-Soviet civil society groups and state authorities, especially on the local level. A majority of interviewed civil society elites also seem to find such contacts effective. Political opportunities, conventionally measured as the degree of openness of the political system, the existence of elite allies and the lack of repression and harassment, are perceived as reasonably good in most regions and by most categories of civil society groups. Furthermore, there is a relatively strong personal over-lapping between civil society groups and local authorities and political parties. This indicates a fairly good potential for civil society groups to influence local politics. However, civil society elites in Russia, Latvia and Lithuania typically have low trust in state institutions. (Civil society elites in Estonia have considerably more trust in

Table 5.13 Influence of (and on) civil society groups per region (index from 0 to 100)

Region	Total civil society influence	Civil society influence on local authorities	Civil society influence on regional authorities	Civil society influence on other civil society organizations	Civil society influence on state enterprises	Civil society influence on private enterprises	Civil society influence on media	Local elites' influence on civil society
Kaliningrad	52	44	44	64	36	46	77	46
Põlva	47	52	51	58	31	36	54	56
Tartu	45	54	44	62	32	40	36	48
Vilnius	45	45	33	66	36	39	51	60
Harju	44	52	33	52	33	40	52	51
Sverdlovsk	41	44	41	55	31	34	42	46
Pskov	39	44	46	52	31	28	35	47
St Petersburg	37	41	43	59	25	17	39	46
Ida-Viru	33	42	42	50	17	22	23	31
Novgorod	33	40	31	45	27	28	29	43
Kaunas	32	37	28	42	26	23	34	58
Riga	30	24	24	44	31	23	37	47
Valmiera	26	43	23	30	26	30	33	30
Total	**38**	**42**	**37**	**53**	**29**	**30**	**40**	**48**

Source: Democratization: Local and Transnational Perspectives Survey (DLTPS) 1999–2000.

Note: The question was: 'How do you assess the clout of the organization that you represent with respect to the following institutions? Local authorities, Regional authorities, Civil society organizations/groups, State and/or collective enterprises and/or companies, Private enterprises and/or companies, Newspapers, radio, TV.' Alternatives given: 'A lot', 'Some', 'Little', 'None at all'. The number of respondents selecting each alternative was multiplied by 100 for 'A lot', 67 for 'Some', 33 for 'Little' and 0 for 'None at all'. The results were summed up and divided by the number of respondents (total 351–363 depending on question). Thus we arrived at a measurement of how civil society groups in different regions perceive their own influence over other institutions. 100 would mean a lot of clout/influence and 0 none at all. Measurements of the different aspects of influence of civil society groups are combined to produce an index of civil society influence (by adding the six indicators and dividing by six). A similar index of other local elites' perceived influence over civil society is provided as a reference point. (N = 1052).

the state.) Despite the low trust, many civil society activists (more than 40 per cent of the respondents) are willing to turn to local authorities for support. Another aspect of political opportunities is the media situation, and in this respect Russian civil society activists face severe problems. Trust in all kind of media is very low in Russia. The situation in the Baltic states is quite different. Civil society elites in Estonia, Latvia and (to a lesser extent) Lithuania have a largely positive view of the media. Post-Soviet civil society elites generally asses their own political clout as fairly limited. Taken together, all indicators point at political opportunities for civil society in Estonia being better, and civil society elites there also think they have somewhat more political influence. Pölva, in particular, scores very high on most indicators, perhaps reflecting the benefits of a relatively small community where many people know each other personally. Regional variation is most pronounced within Russia. Novgorod stands out as a region with comparatively good political opportunities for civil society on most indicators, but civil society elites there do not think they have much influence anyway. Political opportunities in Kaliningrad, and especially in St Petersburg, seem to be bad by virtually all indicators. Let us focus more on regional differences, using qualitative data.

State–civil society relations in three Russian regions

The analysis above – as well as previous research – has indicated that there are significant regional variations in conditions for civil society groups in Russia. Here we will look more closely into this issue through a comparison between our three Russian regions: St Petersburg, Pskov and Novgorod. This analysis is based mainly on qualitative data derived from interviews with representatives of civil society groups and local/regional authorities.

St Petersburg

The political system in St Petersburg is described as 'closed' by many activists. There is no real openness, claims a leading activist (Interview HR6). However, there are conflicts on the elite level, which some civil society groups might be able to take advantage of. There is a conflict between the governor and the city *duma*. The structure of the city *duma* is quite fluent. *Yabloko* is the only fixed faction (Elena Belokurova, personal communication, 25 April 2001). The governor and regional government are described as having no ideology at all (Interview O6). Neither Yakovlev nor any other governor has opposed Putin's reforms. Nevertheless, there is a sharp conflict between the governor and representatives of the federal government. This split on the elite level creates some opportunities for civil society activists. Political elites need support and new ideas and are thus open to civil society groups, when they think that it will strengthen their own position vis-à-vis their elite opponents. Since the representatives of the President emerged as a second centre of power, conditions for civil society in St Petersburg have actually improved. The elite division might not be seen by the general public, but it is important for civil society activists and the media, according to one activist (Interview O6).

There are several people who work with aspects of civil society relations within the St Petersburg city administration, mainly within the department of mass media and public relations (Interview S4; Interview S5). The city has very limited funding for NGOs. Since 2001, however, NGOs can get financial support through individual deputies instead of the department working with NGO relations. The city administration also organizes competitions in which NGOs compete for funding (Interview S5).

In interviews with representatives of the city administration it became very clear that authorities favour social welfare NGOs, which are seen as providing important services for citizens, especially for disabled and disadvantaged children. Environmental NGOs are seen as more confrontational and problematic (Interview S4; Interview S5). Furthermore, NGOs concerned with 'anti-bureaucratic structures' are singled out as problematic. They are said to constantly criticize the city administration, not in a constructive but in a scandalizing way (Interview S5). The respondent refused to give any concrete examples of such NGOs.

In addition to funding some NGOs, which are seen as useful, the city administration tries to engage with civil society groups in several ways. The city administration and NGOs organized joint meetings in preparation for Putin's 'Civic Forum' in 2001 (Interview S4). The concept of 'social partnership', implying cooperation between the local government, enterprises and NGOs, is stressed by the city administration (Interview S4). Many NGOs have adopted this discourse, but ecological, human rights and the more radical women's groups remain critical (Elena Belokurova, personal communication, 22 October 2001). In a similar way, the representative of the President created a 'public council', but no NGOs wanted to be involved (Interview HR6).

In 1997 the city administration decided to stop allowing NGOs to rent office space at highly subsidized rates. Since the beginning of the 1990s NGOs had paid only a small portion of the market value.[8] A coalition of NGOs formed to protest the decision. Representatives of more than 400 NGOs met and signed a petition to the governor. They got support from some deputies. This initiative was successful and led to a continuation of the favourable renting conditions for NGOs (Interview HR6). However, some NGOs, which the authorities dislike, are refused office space. In the mid-1990s, in particular, many groups lost their offices. There was also police harassment against oppositional civil society groups, for example organizations funded by foreign religious funds, ultra-nationalist organizations and NGOs protecting homeless children. Environmental and human rights NGOs do not need an office or tend to have their own property so they are less dependent on the authorities (Elena Belokurova, personal communication, 22 October 2001).

As in other Russian regions, the media situation is not particularly supportive of independent and critical civil society activities. The authorities control all newspapers in St Petersburg except one. The only independent paper, *Dela*, appears only twice a week. It is distributed freely, but only read by a small circle of politically aware oppositional activists. Several of its journalists are associated with the 'Movement for the Autonomy of St Petersburg' (Elena Belokurova, personal communication, 23 October 2001). Compared to the media situation in the city of Sosnovy Bor, however, St Petersburg's media appear as relatively open to civil society agendas. The environmental organization Green World, based in this small nuclear city on the Baltic Sea coast, gives press conferences in St Petersburg in an effort to reach out to the public, and activists are mostly satisfied with the St Petersburg media. The organization has a list of media persons to contact on the regional level. The local newspaper in Sosnovy Bor is not independent and Green World cannot get anything published there (Interview E5).

In order to get a deeper understanding of state–civil society relations in St Petersburg, we will now look into the experiences of some specific NGOs.

The environmental group Greenhipp in St Petersburg has an interesting history. It has its origin in the famous café Saigon at Nevsky Prospekt where hippies, anarchists, punks and other dissidents gathered in the late 1980s. When people from the youth section of the old Soviet nature-protection society joined, a focus on environmental issues developed. A small group of young people started to undertake direct action. For example, they blocked a road into a nature-protection area where illegal *dachas* were being built for the regional elite (Interview E4). Some local officials within the otherwise conservative nature-protection society provided the radical 'hippies' with an official organizational umbrella, which gave them some protection in relation to the authorities. They also trained them in writing petitions and other typical NGO activities. Nevertheless, illegal demonstrations and direct actions dominated, and people were often arrested. At café Saigon people were arrested every Tuesday. The rest of the week they were OK, if they did not take part in demonstrations (Interview E4).

In the last years of the Soviet Union, radical environmentalists were heavily repressed. In December 1990, the leader of a group of environmentalists trying to protect the Tungilman river was hanged in prison. According to the police she committed suicide, but her fellow activists are sure that she was killed by the police (Interview E4). The Greenhipp leader also tells about activists being beaten, kidnapped and even killed when they disclosed corruption related to false forest maps.

Greenhipp has few contacts with local government, but there has been some support for nature protection from a few regional parliamentarians belonging to the Communist party. The group has not been able to raise any local funds. Police harassment was widespread in the 1980s and early 1990s, but since then activists have not had more problems with the police than have ordinary citizens (Interview E4).

Asked about Memorial's relationship to the state, a human rights activist answered that there is no relationship at all, but at least at the moment they do not arrest us (Interview HR4). However, a few deputies in the city council and the state *duma* do support Memorial. Like many members of the organization, they are former political prisoners. Under *perestroika*, Memorial managed to get one of its members elected to the state *duma*, but since then there has been no effort to influence formal politics. Based on his own experiences, a veteran activist of Memorial argued that it was worse to be in the state *duma* than to be in prison. 'In prison you could have good people around you, but not in the *duma*.' (Interview HR4). This tendency to strongly reject inclusion into the state or formal political sphere is mostly found among human rights activists, especially in St Petersburg.

The Council of Veterans, being an organization closely associated with the previous regime, has different but also similar experiences of the state compared to the (former) dissidents in Memorial. The Council of Veterans got financial support from the governor Yakovlev after the election in 2000 (Interview O7), probably as compensation for electoral support. The organization does not have to pay anything for its large building. There is also support from the governor of Leningrad *Oblast* and the committees of social security within both city and *oblast* administrations also support the organization (Interview O7). While relatively successful in getting financial support, the Veterans have been less successful in influencing politics. The organization tries to influence individual deputies, but there are no important political power-holders who are really supportive of ideas put forward by the Veterans. This is especially true for the federal level. The main channel of influence is the so-called 'consulting council of veteran issues', which is headed by the governor. They meet about four times a year (Interview O7).

An independent labour union activist in St Petersburg says that neither the city nor the federal government perceive unions as good partners. There is no interest in labour issues at any level of political power (Interview L2). Nevertheless he hopes to be able to achieve goals through negotiations – strikes are not useful. There has been some limited success in influencing policies. A new law on 'social partnership' in the city has led to an agreement between enterprises, labour unions and the authorities on how to bring new law proposals on labour issues to the city *duma*. Labour activism has moved on from confrontation to negotiation. During the transition, the legal base of labour unions has been changing all the time and this has contributed to a decrease in membership (Interview L2).

The organization Soldiers' Mothers of St Petersburg did not receive any funding for the first four years. Initially the activists were given office space in a NGO building. The Christian Democratic Party provided an office, but due to disagreements on tactics the Soldiers' Mothers had to move. This time the Republican Party offered an office. When the Soldiers' Mothers of St Petersburg received funding from the Soros Foundation they could rent an office of their own. When interviewed in 2001, the co-chairwoman said that the contract for the organization's office would expire the following year and they were afraid that the local administration would not renew it (Interview HR5).

The state strategy of confronting independent NGOs by creating quasi–NGOs is common within the field covered by organizations of Soldiers' Mothers. Many Soldiers' Mothers committees around Russia have been set up by the military and are not independent organizations. Whereas the Soldiers' Mothers of St Petersburg is an independent organization highly critical of the military, the Committee of Soldiers' Mothers support the state and military by encouraging faithful service in the army (Berthusen Gottlick 1999: 247). Naturally, the Soldiers' Mothers of St Petersburg does not have any contact with such quasi-NGOs (Interview HR5). In St Petersburg the organization claims to have good cooperation with a group of young officers who worked for military reform and the protection of human rights within the armed forces (Interview HR5).

The experiences of different NGOs outlined above gives a picture of a range of problems in state–civil society relations, ranging from a lack of state support for NGO activities to systematic harassments of NGOs perceived to be oppositional. If the political climate in the city of St Petersburg is not supportive of independent civil society activity, it is at least not particularly hostile either. The situation is much worse in the nearby small city of Sosnovy Bor on the Baltic Sea coast. There, the environmental organization Green World has a mission to change the mentality of people living in the Baltic Sea region of Russia concerning environmental problems (Interview E5). The organization claims to have more than twenty active members and an additional sixty in the associated organization 'Children of the Baltics'. Green World combines human rights and environmental approaches in its struggle against the nuclear power plant in Sosnovy Bor. Activists have tried to influence local authorities to adopt a local Agenda 21, and arranged seminars on the dangers of nuclear power. This is a very sensitive issue in the small city dominated by the military and the nuclear power plant (Interview E5).

Despite very difficult conditions, Green World has been at least partly successful in some of its activities. In 1996, the organization learnt about a leakage in the power plant and informed the authorities about it. There was no adequate reaction, so activists published information about the incident in both Russian and English. When the problem became public the local authorities were forced to deal with it. The man who told Green World about the leakage, however, lost his job at the power plant (Interview E5). Another successful campaign was carried out by Green World in cooperation with environmentalists from St Petersburg when a small lake with a lot of bird life was threatened by drainage due to the construction of a channel. The construction, which involved military interests, did not follow the legal procedures. The environmental activists managed to stop the construction work and took responsibility themselves for repairing the damage that had already been caused (Interview E5).

There have also been severe setbacks for the organization. One activist lost his job because of his work for Green World. The organization has been stopped from organizing public meetings. Activists complain about a general apathy among citizens (Interview E5). There is substantial harassment from the state apparatus. Police and tax inspectors have searched the Green World office several times. The regional Department of Justice and the Federal Prosecutor have started investigations into the foreign funding of the organization. Green World has even been accused of supporting Chechen 'terrorists'. Generally there is a lot of psychological pressure on NGOs in Russia, and Soviet practices have not disappeared, claims a representative of the organization (Interview E5). The level of pressure on an organization, however, depends on its activities. Anti-nuclear power campaigns involve considerable political risk. It is particularly difficult to work with environmental issues in the city of Sosnovy Bor. Because of the concentration of nuclear power plants and secret military-related enterprises, the city is still almost a closed zone. Foreigners need a special permit to visit Sosnovy Bor. For media contacts, activists have to go to St Petersburg. Most contact with the outside world is through e-mail. The status as a closed city has created a special mentality among citizens and authorities alike (Interview E5). Nevertheless, Green World claims to have secret support from some mid-level officials in the city administration. They have supplied information related to the investigation of the nuclear power plant. The power plant interests control the city council in Sosnovy Bor so no positive response is to be expected there. Neither does the organization receive any support from the regional *duma*. A deputy in the state *duma* working with human rights issues, however, has shown some interest in the activities of Green World. On the local and regional level no political party is seriously concerned with environmental problems. Since 2001 all local politicians have joined Unity (Interview E5).

Green World is the only environmental NGO in Sosnovy Bor. (In fact there does not seem to be any other politically active NGO at all – only some charity organizations.) However, the nuclear enterprise has set up its own 'NGO' in order to counter criticism from Green World. This 'false NGO', which includes some academics, has published memorandums on 'sustainable development' and 'Agenda 21' in favour of nuclear power. It uses the same methods as real NGOs. Whereas Green World has created a 'coalition for a clean Baltic', the 'NGO' set up by the power plant has announced a 'coalition for a nuclear Baltic'. Green World has decided it is more effective to concentrate on its own campaigns instead of battling with the 'false NGO'. Instead of depicting itself as against nuclear power, Green World emphasizes that it is in favour of renewable energy (Interview E5).

Pskov

According to a centrally placed NGO figure in Pskov, before 2000 local and regional authorities tended to ignore civil society groups. Local authorities were slightly better to deal with than regional authorities. Relations between state authorities and civil society groups appear to have changed in 2000 when the regional leaders realized that NGOs could be used in the interest of political power. NGO resources were mobilized and utilized during the election campaign. Now there is an interdependent relationship between regional authorities and some NGOs. NGOs have, for example, organized seminars with authorities, teaching officials how to apply for funding from TACIS. Lawyers active in NGOs have contributed to the crafting of new laws (Interview O4).

The leader of the NGO centre *Vozrozhdenie*, Shlosbek, is also chairman of *Yabloko* in Pskov and an influential person within both political and civil society (Interview HR3). He has been chairman of the city's 'NGO committee' since 1997 (Interview S3). Shlosbek was closely allied to the former mayor, Prokofiev, who lost the election in March 2000. The new mayor does not support Shlosbek and his NGO centre, but there is more support for other NGOs now (Elena Belokurova, personal communication, 25 April 2001). An official within the city administration working with NGO relations also claims that the election of a new mayor led to changes within the city administration and a stronger focus on NGOs (Interview S3). The local government is described as open, but unreliable in the sense that promises are not kept (Interview W3).

Most civil society groups in Pskov feel obliged to register with the department of law. Without a formal registration, the group cannot open a bank account and it is impossible to get funding. Only groups that are closely linked to and supported by the authorities – like some Soldiers' Mothers groups – can afford not to register (Interview HR2). The cost for registering is only a symbolic half rouble, but if the organization has any commercial activity it costs 1000 roubles to register. About 60 per cent of the NGOs do have some kind of commercial activities, according to the authorities. This may be as little as taking a fee for participation in workshops organized by the organization (Interview S3). NGOs have to submit their statutes when they register. They are not allowed to do anything that is not explicitly stated there. Hence, most NGOs have very extensive statutes (Interview S3).

Since 2000, the city administration has one person whose only task is to work on NGO relations. Every three months she has to report to the department of justice which NGOs in the city are active. The city administration had a budget of 200,000 roubles for funding NGOs in 2000 (Interview S3). There were two major projects. First, the creation of a 'coordinating council' with 19 NGOs to 'discuss NGO ideas'. Second, the establishment of a fund with contributions both from the city administration and local enterprises from which NGOs could apply for funding (Interview S3). The city administration thinks that it is better for NGOs to have local funding instead of relying on international funding agencies, but because of the poor economic situation in Pskov there has not yet been a decision to make this project permanent (Interview S3). A committee of representatives of the city administration, NGOs and local businesses decides which NGO projects shall get funding. The main criterion is that the project should be relevant to the city (Interview S3).

From the perspective of state authorities, many NGOs lack competence and need guidance (Interview S3). The state tries to gain control over civil society. There are systematic efforts at coopting NGOs. Local NGOs are dependent upon local authorities and/or local businessmen. This is a tendency found all over Russia, but it is especially obvious in smaller cities like Pskov (Interview O4). Although there does not seem to be any systematic repression of civil society groups in Pskov, more outspoken dissidents have suffered various forms of harassment. The two leading activists in the human rights group *Veche* both lost their jobs in 1992 due to their political work in the organization. They have been unemployed since then (Interview HR2). This used to be an efficient way to silence dissidents under the communist regime, and the practice to some extent seems to have survived in the post-communist context. The *Veche* activists also tell about a former head of the local radio station who was sacked for political reasons and accused of having tax debts. After two years of court proceedings he was freed, but during that time he had no opportunity to criticize the authorities. He now works for Radio Free Europe (Interview HR2).

From the perspective of the authorities, there are not many oppositional NGOs in Pskov. The only exceptions are some aggressive NGOs that are set up in connection with election campaigns. Other NGOs are not in conflict with the city administration (Interview S3). Civil society activists, however, argue that conditions for civil society in Pskov are more difficult than in many other parts of Russia because of the strong military influence in the region, its history as a very patriotic region, the relative low level of education and the bad economic situation (Interview HR3). Furthermore, the media situation in Pskov is not at all open and democratic. Civil society groups find it almost impossible to get publicity on the issues they work with. It is not uncommon for NGOs to have to pay newspapers in order to get an article published (Interview HR3). The reason for this might be related to corruption in general rather than any politically motivated censorship, but often payment is not enough, as newspapers are controlled by the authorities and reluctant to publish anything critical of the political power. *Pravda Pskov* is controlled by the governor and serves as his mouthpiece. The local authorities own the other local newspaper, *Pskov News* (Owens 2002: 108). Some NGOs, like the human rights group *Veche*, try to publish their own paper, but due to financial problems this is very irregular and of very limited distribution (Interview HR2). However, according to a representative of the city administration, there are now 'NGO pages' in the local newspaper (Interview S3).

Despite difficult conditions for critical civil society groups, several NGOs report successful cooperation with local or regional authorities. The human rights group *Veche*, for example, has a positive experience of cooperation with local authorities in a specific project. In an effort to democratize the judicial system in Pskov, *Veche* initiated a project to computerize the court. Initially the court refused to cooperate, but when the regional law department realized that they would be provided with free computers – funded by the Eurasia Foundation – the project could start, although one of the judges refused to take part. The creation of a database created more order and also made the court more open, as it was possible to get access to documents in the database. *Veche* had earlier paid attention to a case of a man being taken into custody for three months without anyone taking responsibility. This could not happen with the new reformed and computerized court, claims the project leaders (Interview HR2).

The Union of Women has an agreement with the social committee within the local government in Pskov, which pays for an office and journeys related to conference participation etc. According to its chairwoman, the amount is so small that it does not create a situation of dependency limiting the autonomy of the organization. The organization has never been denied funding it has asked for from the local authorities. 'We do not ask something that is not reasonable', says the chairwoman (Interview W2).

An example of the blurring of the distinction between the state and civil society is the organization 'Regional Centre for People's Creativity', which is presented as an NGO, but in reality is a part of the regional authorities, funded through the regional department of culture. It supports 'Houses of Culture' throughout the region (Interview O5). There are almost 500 'Houses of Culture' or 'Clubs' in the region, 460 of them in small towns and villages. Each 'Club' only has between one and ten members, but in the whole region there are about 1200 people employed. The cultural clubs are funded by the municipalities. During the 1990s the number of clubs decreased because of financial problems, but now the situation is stable. The clubs arrange festivals (like 'Stars of the Countryside') and give scholarships to talented children. They are also involved in educational activities related to the cultural sphere. They study local popular culture, including songs, dances, and ways of living. Such cultural clubs are a heritage from the Soviet Union. They used to be an integrated part of the party-state. Since the late 1980s they have tended to focus on folkloristic culture instead of ideological propaganda (Interview O5). The 'cultural houses' have been described as very democratic public spaces, open to everyone and available all over Russia, where children are educated and people can discuss, learn and practise different cultural expressions (Interview O5). In the 1990s, local people united and demanded that the politicians should open 'cultural houses' that had been closed due to financial problems. Culture has traditionally been the responsibility of state authorities and there are not many conventional NGOs that cooperate with the 'cultural houses' (Interview O5).

The Pskov Centre for People's Creativity has 40 people employed. Its budget is about one million roubles per year. To complement this the Centre applies for scholarships from the Ministry of Culture (Interview O5). The regional and local funding for culture should, according to the law, be 6 per cent of the region's and municipality's budget, but in practice it is far less. Furthermore, a large part of the budget for culture is used to restore monuments, pay salaries and rent office facilities (Interview O5).

Novgorod

The political situation in Novgorod is typically described as stable. There are no strong political parties in Novgorod. None of the deputies in the local or regional *duma* sit on party mandates (although some are members of political parties) (Interview S1). Another peculiarity of Novgorod city is that the chairman and vice-chairman of the city *duma* are also mayor and vice-mayor. There is not a similar mixture of law-making and executive functions on the regional level (Interview S1).

The local and regional governments in Novgorod have been described as 'fairly welcoming to NGOs' (McIntosh Sundstrom 2002: 215). The local media regularly contains letters to the administration and answers from the responsible politician or bureaucrat. Political decision-makers are accessible by telephone. There is a community council with the governor, and every third month there is a 'city gathering' when the mayor and his assistants meet the general public and inform them about their work. Representatives of NGOs are also invited to these meetings (Interview S2). NGOs can turn to local authorities or individual *duma* deputies with their suggestions and demands. Members of the local and regional parliaments meet their electorate several times a month. All assembly meetings are open to the public (cf. Petro 2002: 34–44).[9] Nevertheless, there is widespread political passivity. Only a tiny minority of citizens bother to try to influence politics. The leader (in this case Governor Prusak) is very influential because the general public is politically passive (Interview HR1). The fact that the regional and local administration is open, and that decision-makers are accessible to the general public, does not mean that they really pay attention to popular demands. One civil society activist describes the community council as a 'decorative agency'. It is only useful for getting information. We have no real influence. There is never any concrete action as a result of our demands and discussions, she argues (Interview E1).

Unlike in Pskov and St Petersburg, there does not seem to be any conflict between regional and local authorities that civil society groups might take advantage of. According to a representative of the local government, NGOs cannot play out the city against the region (Interview S2).

According to the vice-mayor of Novgorod city, there is a good relationship between the local authorities and NGOs. There are common projects, mainly related to social welfare, and the local authorities provide direct support to NGOs, including financial assistance, tax redemption, office facilities, etc. Furthermore, the local authorities create a political framework for NGO activities and give moral support (Interview S1). There is a law on 'social tasks' which sets aside funding for NGOs in the city of Novgorod. The budget is less than 1 per cent of the total municipal budget. NGOs apply for funding, and the city *duma* decides about overall priorities. Sixty per cent should be funded by the organization, but in practice some activities are funded almost completely by the local authorities (Interview S1).

According to the vice-mayor of Novgorod city, NGOs help politicians see issues from another perspective, they bring foreign funding to Novgorod and they perform functions that the municipality could not afford. However, he also thinks that many NGOs cause problems for the authorities because they demand too much. There have also been some problems with specific NGOs, e.g. the houseowners' organization, which tries to stop new construction in the city. Sectarian religious organizations also create problems. There has been a group of Satanists who have destroyed graveyards (Interview S1).

On the regional level, there is a department for media and NGO relations. There are two officials within the city administration who are responsible for issues related to NGOs, but they have a wider mandate, also working on media and public relations in general (Interview S2). An official within the city administration makes a distinction between three kinds of civil society groups. First, there are political organizations. They ask for permission to arrange public meetings, campaigns, etc., but otherwise they have little contact with local authorities. Second, there are labour unions and employers' associations. They are involved in negotiations with local and regional authorities, and there is a committee with representatives from the three spheres. Interest organizations representing labour and employers also participate in the work of municipal committees, for instance concerning housing and social issues. Third, there are voluntary organizations (including women, youth and other interest groups, sports clubs, etc.) Most NGOs register in order to obtain a legal status and get financial support. The administration cooperates with about fifty NGOs, but the official responsible for NGO contacts claims to know all 500 NGOs in the city (Interview S2). Local authorities support and cooperate with those NGOs that solve concrete tasks for the benefit of the citizens. These include mainly social welfare organizations, not least those focusing on children and disabled. Ecological NGOs are more demanding and more difficult to deal with. Nevertheless, the official responsible for NGO issues claims that the authorities do not treat NGOs differently because of their orientation (Interview S2).

Members of 'establishment-oriented NGOs' typically describe relations between authorities and civil society groups as good. There are plans to let NGOs take over some tasks of the local government. The Red Cross, for instance, handles some social services for pensioners, within a project funded by the local government (Interview O1). A leading NGO figure admitted that there were practical legal problems, but he could not see any problems of principle with this kind of privatization of social services (Interview O1).

Concerning the political influence of civil society groups, a representative of an NGO resource centre makes a distinction between, on the one hand 'professional organizations' – like his own – which have good contacts on all levels of power and succeed in influencing policy, and, on the other hand 'populist organizations' which are involved in permanent protests, but do not achieve anything (Interview O1). Hence, well-connected NGOs claim to have political influence. Another example is the 'Women's Parliament', which managed, after long hard work, to get a plan for promoting women's entrepreneurship into the regional Social Chamber's recommendations for economic policies, and eventually had it accepted by the regional government (McIntosh Sundstrom 2002: 212).

The quality of the regional media in Novgorod is not perceived as high. There is almost no criticism of the administration, but this is not due to censorship or political pressure but a lack of responsibility and competence among journalists, according to a prominent civil society actor (Interview HR1). Journalists are still influenced by the Soviet tradition of only writing about how 'good' everything is. The governor and the mayor have even criticized journalists for being too uncritical (Interview HR1). There is one newspaper owned by the regional administration, one owned by the local administration in Novgorod and one privately owned. According to one civil society activist, the newspapers controlled by the authorities are similar to those existing under communist rule. They do not publish anything related to civil society issues. Relationship to the privately owned newspaper is better. It may occasionally publish material from NGOs (Interview E1). Regional radio and television tend to be perceived as somewhat more open and democratic than newspapers. Several NGOs claim to have good relationships with journalists in these media (Interview E1).

The political climate in the city of Novgorod, thus, seems to be rather open for general NGO activities that are not perceived as threatening by the authorities, whereas more oppositional groups have experienced more problems. Let us now examine the situation in two peripheral municipalities in the Novgorod region.

Borovichy is a small town with about 59,000 inhabitants located in the north-eastern part of Novgorod *oblast.* Borovichy's Ecology Club was founded in the late 1980s as a reaction to a concrete case of environmental damage on the local level – pollution from a pig farm. Like several other new environmental groups, it had its origin in the Soviet Nature Protection Society. The group managed to gather 11,000 people in a protest movement, petitioning the authorities to close down the farm. The local authorities initially refused to listen to the protests, but the massive protests forced the local government to take a more compromising attitude. Representatives of the ecological club were invited to participate in seminars. There was still little support from local politicians, but the protest movement had contacts in Moscow and in the affiliated town of Binghampton in the United States. Eventually the pressure on the local government grew so strong that the pig farm was closed down (Interview E2).

In the 1990s the ecological club has been campaigning against a nuclear power plant in the neighbouring Tver region. A river flowing through Borovichy was allegedly polluted by the power plant. The group took the initiative to an inter-regional meeting and sent a delegation to the power plant. It became obvious that radioactivity was too high, and the authorities had to inform the public. The power plant is still operating, but now there are regular inspections and the public is informed if radioactivity is dangerously high (Interview E2). The organization has tried to stop the construction of new reactors at the site, but in vain. The construction of new nuclear power plants rests on federal decisions and a small local environmental group has no power to stop it (Interview E2). Another big campaign in the 1990s has been on air pollution from the big brick industry in Borovichy. Two-thirds of the municipal budget comes from the now privatized brick industry so the leadership of the enterprise is very influential (Interview E2).

There is not much support for environmental groups among the local political leadership in Borovichy. It is possible to meet political leaders and discuss environmental issues, but mostly they ignore the concerns of the environmentalists. The ecological club focuses on local issues and has not tried to influence the regional *duma* or the governor (Interview E2). The ecological NGO *Nos 4* in Borovichy claims to have support from the vice-mayor and the youth department within the local government. Support comes in the form of payment for journeys, excursions, etc. and printing of publications (Interview E3).

Environmental organizations in Borovichy report difficulties in reaching out to the public through the media. The local authorities control the only local newspaper. Prior to 1996 there happened to be an editor sympathetic to the environmental movement so it was rather easy to get critical articles published, but when he was replaced by a relative of the mayor, critical articles tended to be censored. Regional television has an even more negative attitude towards environmental groups, according to this activist (Interview E2).

Another small town in the Novgorod region is Staraya Russa with a population of about 40,000. People active in NGOs in Staraya Russa argue that they have no relationship with the local administration. 'They [the local administration] do not disturb us, but neither do they help us. They simply do not see us.' (Interview W1) Only in connection with elections do NGOs get some attention from local politicians. NGOs have run their own candidates in elections, but not yet succeeded in winning any seat in the local *duma* (Interview O2). Nevertheless, it seems to be possible for NGO people to contact the mayor directly and they may also attend *duma* meetings (Interview O2).

This section has analysed state–civil society relations in St Petersburg, Pskov and Novgorod and given examples of different types of state–civil society interaction, ranging from cooperation to co-optation and confrontation. A concluding comparative analysis of civil society in these three regions is offered in Chapter 7. We will now examine the more general pattern of relationships between civil society on the one hand and political and economic society on the other hand in the post-Soviet context.

Civil society and political society

There has been a general trend of civil society actors taking the step into political society in the post-Soviet context. This trend was already evident before the transition in the Soviet Union, and culminated in the elections of 1993 and 1995 when a very large number of civil society organisations, many of which were very small, tried to organize themselves as political parties and get their own parliamentary representation (Kisovskaya 1998: 154). Furthermore, key figures in civil society have become political leaders. For example, the environmental movement in Russia has produced several prominent political leaders, including Boris Nemtsov of the Union of Right Forces (Henry 2001: 20) and Alexei Yablokov – the former adviser to Yeltsin and Minister for the Environment (Sakwa 2002: 326). Russian civil society groups are also said to be active in local politics, writing agendas for political parties and providing expert advice in different fields. According to a central NGO figure in St Petersburg, all political parties have some civil society connections, but *Yabloko* is the party with most extensive civil society links (Jevgenija Machonina, St Petersburg NGO Development Centre, seminar 8 March 2001, Stockholm, Forum Syd).

However, political parties in post-Soviet Russia are fundamentally distrusted by the public (White 2000: 270) and many Russian civil society groups do not find it useful to interact with political parties. Political parties tend to be for the sake of elections only. Generally, they have no institutionalized structures and few if any grassroots connections (Patomäki and Pursiainen 1998: 35). There is also a tendency to compete with civil society groups through the creation of quasi-NGOs. The Unity Party has created its own 'NGOs', including pioneer organizations like *Komsomol* etc. This is seen as a serious problem by civil society activists (Interview HR6).

We have some survey data that can help us get an overview of relationships between civil and political society in the post-Soviet context. First we can see how much trust civil society elites have in political parties (Table 5.14). It is clear that there is a general lack of trust. On average only 19 per cent of the interviewed civil society elites have some trust in political parties. In Latvia and the Russian regions there is very little trust. Civil society elites in Lithuania and Estonia have considerably more trust in political parties, but in no region are there more than 50 per cent having some or a lot of trust.[10] When interpreting these results, we should remember that the character of political parties differs significantly between regions. From a democratic perspective, low trust in democratic political parties is problematic, but low trust in parties with a more dubious democratic character like the Liberal Democratic Party and the Communist Party of Russia (which play an important role in Pskov) must be interpreted as positive for democracy.

Returning to Table 5.8, we find another indication of the lack of confidence in political parties. Only 15 per cent of respondents say they turn to political parties

Table 5.14 Civil society actors' trust in political parties per region (% having some or a lot of trust)

Region	Trust in political parties
Vilnius	47 (17)
Tartu	44 (10)
Pölva	42 (5)
Kaunas	37 (11)
Harju	30 (6)
Ida-Viru	22 (4)
Pskov	20 (8)
Sverdlovsk	8 (3)
St Petersburg	6 (3)
Riga	4 (1)
Novgorod	2 (1)
Kaliningrad	0
Valmiera	0
Mean	**19 (69)**

Source: Democratization: Local and Transnational Perspectives Survey (DLTPS) 1999–2000.

Note: The question was: 'How much trust do you have in political parties?' The answers 'Some trust' and 'A lot of trust' are combined and shown. N = 363.

(on either the national or local level) for support. Vilnius and Pölva – two of the regions with most trust in political parties – also have most civil society groups seeking support from political society. Table 5.9 shows that environmental and social welfare organizations are least likely to turn to political parties for support. Human rights and democracy groups are somewhat more inclined to seek support within political society.

Despite the general distrust in political parties, one out of five respondents is a member of a political party. Within the category 'other', one out of four respondents belongs to a political party. Among representatives of social welfare organizations less than one out of ten has party membership. Regional variation is significant in this respect. Almost half of the (very few) respondents in Kaliningrad claim to be party members, whereas only 6 per cent of those in Novgorod say they have any party membership. This emphasizes the very weak position of political parties in Novgorod.

McFaul (2002: 115) argues that Russian NGOs have tended to avoid the electoral process altogether. Many respondents interviewed for this study, however, claim that their organizations have been active in election campaigns. In St Petersburg, NGOs that aim to influence politics try to get good relations with *duma* deputies. There is some support from members of *Yabloko*, but political parties mostly only show an interest in NGOs during election campaigns. State officials try to mobilize NGOs for their own purposes (Interview HR6). Each member of the St Petersburg city *duma* can spend a small part of the city budget on projects of their own choice in their respective districts. This system, which has been in place since the mid-1990s, creates incentives for NGOs to seek financial support from individual parliamentarians. The practice has been widely criticized, as it may lead to corruption (Elena Belokurova, personal communication, 23 October 2001).

The independent labour union Council of Labour Unions 'Unity' in St Petersburg got support from new parliamentarians on both regional and federal level when it was established in the late 1980s. Today there is no political party that really cares about labour issues. Many parties have a 'mask of social democracy', but not in their practical policies, argues a labour activist (Interview L2). No national union in Russia has allied itself with the communists (Gill and Markwick 2000: 235), but some labour unions in Pskov get support from local branches of the Communist Party and the Agrarian Party and to some extent also from *Yabloko*. On the federal level there is no party that supports labour unions, but there is a pro-labour *duma* group with representatives from different parties. The construction workers union in Pskov does not support any particular party in elections, but many unions are actively involved in the campaign for individual candidates (Interview L1).

Not only labour unions, but also other NGOs have a close relationship to political parties and typically take an active part in election campaigns. There is, however, a feeling among many civil society activists of being exploited by the politicians. 'NGOs are flowers to put on your jacket during elections. Then they are thrown away', says a Russian women activist (Interview W2). A women's NGO in Pskov has some cooperation with the youth organization of the Unity Party. The chairwoman actively supported the Union of Right Forces in the elections, but the organization claim to have good relations with all parties, except for the communists and nationalists (Interview W3). Another women's organization – the Union of Women in Pskov – has a different ideological profile and hence partly different political allies. On specific issues – e.g. a campaign against contract employment – the Union of Women in Pskov finds allies within the Communist Party, but there has also been support from Unity (Interview W2). It is interesting to note that both the new anti-communist women's NGO and the old women's organization with roots in the Soviet system claim to have good relations with Unity. The reason may be that the party has no clear ideology and is perceived as an instrument of power, making it a useful and influential ally.

Unlike in St Petersburg and Pskov, political parties in Novgorod are so weak that they do not make any useful allies for civil society groups. In Novgorod ideological differences between parties fade away when discussing concrete issues on the regional level. Not even the communists are against the governor or the mayor (Interview HR1). On specific issues there has been some opposition from the Communist Party and traditional labour unions (Interview HR1). In the regional parliament there are no party representatives at all. It consists of mayors from the different municipalities and managers of enterprises. They are all dependent on the governor and thus there is no critical opposition at all (Interview E1; Interview O1).

It has been argued that the Communist Party can be seen as a 'civil society substitute' in many parts of Russia, especially in the so-called Red Belt (Kurilla 2002). In many small cities of these mostly agrarian regions in southern Russia there is virtually no conventional civil society organization. Nevertheless there are many groups working on local problems and trying to defend public interests against state authorities. Those institutions are not considered as part of civil society as they exist within the Communist Party, but they do in fact function as civil society groups. This situation can be found in many other post-communist contexts too. Smolar (2002: 59) even writes about a 'new socialist civil society', arguing that 'real social-ism' lives on in the institutions of civil society. This tendency is not strong in the regions included in this study, because of the relative weakness of the Communist Party in these regions (with the exception of Pskov, where several civil society groups claim to have good relations to the Communist Party). Unlike in the Red Belt, the regions of this study, including Pskov, have many new civil society groups, which have not emerged out of Soviet organizations related to the Communist Party. Nevertheless, several Soviet organizations have survived, and form part of civil society in these regions.

In sum, there seems to be a fundamental lack of trust in political parties among post-Soviet civil society elites. In Latvia and the Russian regions there is almost no trust at all in political parties. Despite the widespread distrust in political parties, one out of five civil society respondents is a party member. In Novgorod, where political parties are extremely weak or even non-existent, only 6 per cent of the interviewed civil society elites claim to be members of a political party. Despite a deep mutual scepticism between actors in civil and political society, there seem to be considerable interaction, at least during election campaigns. However, the general weakness of both political and civil society is problematic for the devel-opment of democracy.

Civil society and economic society

Russian civil society activists tend to see the realm of civil society as distinct from, although related to, the economy (Weigle 2000). In practice, the distinction between civil and economic society tends to be blurred in the activities of many NGOs. Civil society groups seek funding from enterprises in order to sustain their activities. Several NGOs have their own economic activities in order to earn money. Civil society activism has also become a source of income for individual activists. Regional differences are, however, significant.

Civil society elites' trust in private companies is generally much higher than their trust in political parties (see Table 5.15). Nevertheless, a majority of respondents have little or no trust in private companies. Private companies seem to be most

Table 5.15 Civil society actors' trust in private companies per region (% having some or
a lot of trust)

Region	Trust in private companies	
Tartu	83	(19)
Harju	70	(14)
Pölva	67	(8)
Kaunas	61	(17)
Vilnius	56	(20)
Riga	48	(12)
Novgorod	44	(19)
Ida-Viru	41	(7)
Pskov	26	(10)
Sverdlovsk	21	(8)
Valmiera	20	(2)
St Petersburg	20	(9)
Kaliningrad	17	(2)
Mean	**42 (147)**	

Source: Democratization: Local and Transnational Perspectives Survey (DLTPS) 1999–2000.

Note: The question was: 'How much trust do you have in the following institutions?' The answers
'Some trust' and 'A lot of trust' are combined and shown. N = 349.

popular among civil society elites in Estonia (except for Ida-Viru). A majority of
respondents in Lithuania also have a favourable opinion of private companies. There
is less trust in Latvia (especially in Valmiera) and least trust among civil society elites
in Russia (except for Novgorod where market reforms seems to have been more
successful than in many other Russian regions).[11]

Returning to Table 5.9, we find that only 14 per cent of respondents turn to local
business groups for support, indicating a low confidence in economic society among
civil society activists. Twenty-six per cent of the representatives of organizations
belonging to the category 'other' turn to local business groups for support whereas
only 8 per cent of the interviewed trade union and labour activists do the same.

The relatively high level of trust in private companies (compared to other Russian
regions) found among civil society elites in Novgorod is a reflection of the general
economic development in that region. The investment climate in Novgorod is
favourable and the region attracts a large amount of foreign investment. This,
according to an NGO representative, is also supportive for civil society (Interview
O1). It should, however, be noted that this positive effect on civil society can be
seen mainly in the city of Novgorod. Civil society groups in peripheral municipalities find it very difficult to get funding from enterprises. The only NGO in
Staraya Russa that has been successful in local fundraising is a group supporting
disabled children (Interview O2). Even in the city of Novgorod, funding from local
enterprises is generally not an option for environmental and human rights NGOs.

Occasionally the environmental group *Ekologiya* used to receive some limited funding from local enterprises, but for several years this has not been an option. Private enterprises have no interest in supporting environmental NGOs (Interview E1). When sponsoring civil society groups, local businessmen tend to choose apolitical charity organizations.

In contrast to Novgorod, Pskov has few socially responsible local entrepreneurs who sponsor NGOs (Interview O4). For human rights groups critical of the regional and local authorities it is impossible to get any funding. Local businessmen are dependent on good relations with the political power-holders and are afraid of being associated with regime critics. Besides that, they do not care about human rights anyway (Interview HR2). Nevertheless, the human rights group *Veche* tries to work together with some entrepreneurs in a project aiming at providing legal support for small-scale enterprises (Interview HR2).

In Pskov there are several NGOs with local businessmen as members. These organizations work with the development of entrepreneurship and there is also a trade union for small and medium enterprises. The person responsible for NGO relations within the city administration views the involvement of businessmen in civil society groups as very positive. They care about the city and they can increase funding for NGOs (Interview S3). The city administration wants to unite civil society and economic society. Local businessmen have, for instance, assisted in the administration of humanitarian aid received through local NGOs. There are plans for a meeting to discuss the cooperation between the political power, NGOs and local businessmen (Interview S3).

Such cooperation between the state, civil society and economic society is common in contemporary Russia, although many civil society activists are afraid of co-optation. Tripartite councils are especially common in the labour sector. A form of 'social partnership' involving labour unions, employers and state authorities is being implemented. It is modelled roughly on the West European corporatist system, but with a much weaker position for labour (Crowley 2002: 236; Kubicek 2002). Labour unions are naturally the part of civil society that has most inter-action with economic society and this interaction is often conflictual. At the turn of the century a new wave of privatization – now of smaller enterprises – led to more industrial conflicts. Smaller enterprises were not of any great interest in the first wave of privatization and workers usually kept their shares, but now new businessmen have begun to buy shares and take over small enterprises. This has caused conflict between the new owners on the one hand and workers and old owners/heads on the other hand. There have been many media reports of such conflicts, including blockades of enterprises. The new owners typically call in the police. They have the law behind them and usually win (Elena Belokurova, personal communication, 22 October 2001).

The distinction between civil society and economic society is being blurred when NGOs take on commercial activities. Such activities are important for the ability of organizations to sustain themselves (Berthusen Gottlick 1999: 246; Evans Jr. 2002: 329). It is, for example, not uncommon that NGOs in Latvia are used as a basis for business activities (cf. Ostrowska 1997: 91). *Vozrozhdenie*, (recreation) in Pskov is a support centre for other NGOs in the region, but it is also a commercial institute working on sociological and political analyses. This enables the organization to have fifteen salaried staff (Interview O4). In a similar way the NGO resource centre in Novgorod runs a parallel consulting agency working with management and organizational development on a professional and commercial basis (Interview O1). The commercial and non-commercial activities, however, have to be kept separate, as Russian taxation law does not permit NGOs to have an income.

Another economic aspect of civil society activism is that it is income generating for professional NGO activists. With increasing foreign funding, NGOs have become an important source of income for many people. Women, in particular, tend to find work for a living within the NGO sector (Elena Zdravomyslova and Anna Temkina, personal communication, 5 October 1999). Asked why he, having degrees in both engineering and management, still chose to work within an NGO instead of a private company, one respondent answered that he earned more in the NGO than he would have done in most private companies (Interview O1). This indicates that the reason for being active in NGOs might sometimes be more related to material self-interest than a sense of solidarity and political conviction. Work for an NGO may give the individual not only economic benefits but also power and prestige, enhancing the social position of the NGO activist (Zaleski 2001).

In sum, the boundaries between civil and economic society often tend to be blurred in the post-Soviet context. Several NGOs have their own profit-making activities and civil society activism has become a source of income for many individual activists. Civil society groups seek funding from local enterprises, and state authorities promote 'partnership' between civil and economic society. Post-Soviet civil society elites have more trust in private enterprises than in political parties, but they still seem to be rather sceptical, especially in Russia and Latvia.

Conclusion

This chapter has analysed the relationship between civil society and other social spheres. The state provides the legal framework for civil society and applies various strategies of control, co-optation or (more seldom) repression. The concept of political opportunities was applied in order to examine how the formal political system conditions civil society activities. We found that political opportunities, conventionally measured as the degree of openness of the political system, the existence of elite allies and the lack of repression and harassment, are perceived as reasonably good in most regions and by most categories of civil society groups. Going beyond the conventional understanding of political opportunities, however, we found that civil society elites in Russia, Latvia and Lithuania have low trust in state institutions. The media situation in the Russian regions covered by this study does not seem to be supportive of civil society activities. Local and regional – not to mention national – media are controlled by powerful political and economic interests. Activists in all sectors of civil society find it hard to put their issues on the public agenda through the media. According to the survey findings, trust in all kinds of media is very low in Russia. The situation in the Baltic states seems to be quite different. Civil society elites in Estonia, Latvia and (to a lesser extent) Lithuania have a largely positive view of the media. Despite perceiving political opportunities to be reasonably good, post-Soviet civil society elites, as observed in this study, generally think they have little political influence.

State–civil society relations generally seem to be best in Estonia and most problematic in some of the Russian regions (especially Kaliningrad and St Petersburg). Novgorod (and to a lesser extent Sverdlovsk) stands out as regions with comparatively good political opportunities for civil society on most indicators. This is true for apolitical or uncontroversial civil society activities, but there is no indication that critical oppositional civil society groups should have any better political opportunities in Novgorod than in other Russian regions.

This study points to the problematic relationships between political and civil society in the post-Soviet context. There is a deep-rooted mutual scepticism between actors in civil and political society. Civil society interaction with political parties seems to mainly take the form of support in election campaigns. The general weakness of both political and civil society is problematic for the development of democracy.

Furthermore, this study indicates that boundaries between civil and economic society often tend to be blurred in the post-Soviet context. Civil society activism has become a source of income for many individual activists and several NGOs have their own profit-making activities. Some civil society groups are dependent on funding from local enterprises and state authorities often promote 'partnership' between civil and economic society.

The reliance on government, corporate or foreign funding and the lack of a self-sustaining economic base reduces the autonomy of civil society groups (Weigle 2000: 368). Only a few of the NGOs included in this sample found it important to guard their independence and stress their autonomy in relation to both state and economic forces. The environmental groups *Ekologija* in Novgorod and Green World in Sosnovy Bor and the human rights organization Memorial in St Petersburg are examples of civil society groups that have clear borders with the state and market sectors and reject inclusion. In most cases civil society tends to be mixed with political society (in the form of political parties) and economic society (in the form of private companies) as well as state authorities. Inclusion in the state in the Russian regions often takes the form of participation in various institutions for 'social partnership', an arrangement that more confrontational civil society activists describe as efforts by the state to co-opt civil society groups.

Unclear boundaries between the different social spheres tend to be more common in small cities and towns than in metropolitan areas because of the relatively small number of people involved in different public activities in small cities. For example, cooperation between actors within the state, political, civil and economic society is easier in Pskov because most people know each other (Interview S3).

6 The transnationalization of local civil society

Whereas Russian social scientists have paid relatively much attention to problems of civil society and social movements, there does not seem to be any research at all on the transnational dimension of this field (Belokurova 1999).[1] Several foreign scholars, however, have stressed the transnational linkages of Russian civil society groups, especially the dependency on foreign funding. Patomäki and Pursiainen (1998) argue that Russian civil society is also a transnational phenomenon, including global concerns (e.g. peace and ecology) and implying the spread of ideas across state borders, systematic education of civil society activists, and financial support. Whereas many Russian NGOs are eager to strengthen transnational ties and receive foreign funding, parts of Russian civil society (especially communist and nationalist forces) are critical towards transnational financial and ideological linkages (Patomäki and Pursiainen 1998: 48). This chapter aims at providing new data and a fresh analysis of the transnational dimensions of local civil society developments in post-Soviet Russia and the Baltic states. We will first examine the problem of transnational funding and then look into other forms of transnational networking.

Transnational funding

Several studies have stressed the importance of foreign funding for civil society groups in Russia. A representative of the St Petersburg city administration even claims that without foreign funding it would have been impossible to speak about a Russian civil society (Interview S4). This might be an overstatement, but there is no doubt that significant sections of contemporary Russian civil society would not exist without support from abroad.

Foreign funding of emerging civil society groups in the Soviet Union started in the 1980s. During the Gorbachev period new NGOs sometimes received donations from abroad. Contributions went to organizations in Moscow and there was rarely any substantial trickle down to groups in the provinces. Activists decided that resources were most effectively used by the headquarters in the capital. Local organizations mostly had to rely on their own resources, which also had the positive effect of making them more independent (Fish 1995: 179).

Sources of foreign funding to Russian NGOs include USAID, Soros's Open Society Institute, the Eurasia Foundation, the National Endowment for Democracy, the Ford Foundation, the McArthur Foundation, the Mott Foundation, and the European Union TACIS program (Weigle 2000: 353). 'Free' trade unions were set up with substantial support from the US government through the AFL-CIO (Gill and Markwick 2000: 230). More than 13,500 NGO activists have participated in the USAID-sponsored training program (Henry 2001: 5). Russian women's groups are heavily dependent upon foreign funding (Sperling 1999: ch. 7; Henderson 2000). More than 70 per cent of environmental groups included in a broad study on environmental organizations in Russia had received foreign aid (Henry 2002: 187).

What have been the effects of more than a decade of substantial foreign aid to post-Soviet civil society groups? There has undoubtedly been a growth in the number of civil society groups because of foreign funding (Weigle 2000: 352–3). This, however, does not automatically mean that civil society has become stronger. New NGOs have been created in order to increase possibilities to get foreign funding, as funding agencies tend not to fund the same organization repeatedly (McIntosh Sundstrom 2002: 211). In a study of environmental groups in Russia, Henry (2001) concludes that foreign funding has secured the survival and internal development of NGOs, but these organizations have hardly been able to achieve substantive goals or contribute to increased political participation. Similarly, Henderson (2003) found that Russian women's groups that relied on foreign funding were professional, but lacked a grassroots constituency. The same situation can probably be found within other civil society sectors too.

The main effect of foreign funding has been the transformation of a 'societal movement' to NGOs. The formalization and professionalization of civil society activities leading to the 'NGOization' of civil society discussed in Chapter 4 is a trend driven by foreign funding (cf. Richter 2002). Dawn Hemment (2000: 5) argues that civil society aid draws NGOs into service provision, but my own findings indicate that most foreign funding goes to advocacy groups rather than charity organizations. Nevertheless, the tendency is clear that civil society activists who began as an opposition to the state and political elite have been forced into a close relationship with local state officials (Dawn Hemment 2000: 5). The 'third sector', which has been installed by Western design, according to Dawn Hemment (2000: 252), is a constrained space. It emphasizes notions of charity and voluntarism but demands professionalism. It claims to represent the local and grassroots but is mainly elitist. It introduces a market logic to non-governmental activity when NGOs compete for scarce resources. Nevertheless, it would be wrong to see Russian activists as passive victims of Western attempts to design a 'third sector' in Russia. Many activists have managed to use resources selectively and make use of an independent space at the margins (Dawn Hemment 2000: 257).

Other problems related to foreign funding include suspicions that foreign funding is an attempt to undermine Russia's sovereignty, conflicts between NGOs due to competition for scarce resources, and the tendency that transnational funding further strengthens large NGOs and ignores small indigenous groups (cf. Weigle 2002: 125). Environmental groups, in particular, have been depicted by state authorities as a front for foreign interests furthering non-Russian goals (Henry 2001). Foreign funding of Russian women's NGOs has provided necessary resources, but it has also had negative consequences. Foreign funding agencies have given priority to Western-style feminist groups over more traditional social welfare groups, which are more connected to the Russian society. Thus, a civil society elite has been created (Henderson 2000: 66). Competition for foreign funding limits cooperation between women's groups in Moscow. There is less fragmentation in the provinces where foreign funds are less available (Sperling 1999: 258). Similarly, Ferree and Risman (2001) argue that foreign funding helped build local organizations and strengthen regional and national networking, but it also caused a fragmentation within the women's movement and fostered competition and jealousy. It also encouraged bureaucratization.

The results of the survey and qualitative interviews for the present study show that foreign funding is indeed important for parts of post-Soviet civil society, although perhaps not as significant as indicated by previous studies. While a prominent civil society figure in Russia claims that about two-thirds of the funding for NGOs in Russia comes from foreign funding agencies (Interview HR6) only slightly more than one quarter of the organizations included in the survey declare that their main source of funding is foreign donors. This indicates that while probably being the single most important source of funding for civil society activities in general (at least in terms of the amount of money), there are plenty of civil society groups that rely more on other sources. As Table 6.1 shows, there are large differences between different types of civil society groups in this respect. Human

Table 6.1 Foreign donors as the main source of funding for different categories of civil society groups (%)

Category of civil society group	Foreign donors as the main source of funding
Human rights	43 (23)
Environment	37 (15)
Women	33 (15)
Ethnic/nationalist	32 (15)
Social welfare	30 (14)
Other	21 (12)
Labour	3 (2)
Total	**27 (96)**

Source: Democratization: Local and Transnational Perspectives Survey (DLTPS) 1999–2000.

Note: The question was: 'What is the main source of funding for the organization/group?' The answer 'foreign donors' is shown. N = 358 (absolute numbers within brackets).

rights and democracy oriented NGOs are most dependent on foreign donors. Forty-three per cent of groups within this sector have foreign funding as their main source of funding. Many environmental organizations (37 per cent) also rely on foreign donors as their main source of funding. Trade unions and labour organizations stand out as the only category of civil society groups which do not have any significant foreign funding. Regime-critical NGOs in politically sensitive fields – like human rights and environmental issues – rely almost exclusively on foreign funding. They are not able (or willing) to seek support from either state or private sources within the country. NGOs in politically non-sensitive fields – e.g. charity organizations and some women's organizations – also get a large share of the available foreign funds, but they also tend to be able to find local funding in the form of private donations, sponsorship by local enterprises or support from local authorities.

Differences between the four countries are very small when it comes to reliance on foreign funding, but there is some significant regional variation. Forty-six per cent of the groups in St Petersburg and 44 per cent in Vilnius state that their main source of funding is foreign donors. Novgorod and Ida-Viru also show a significant share of groups mainly dependent on foreign funding (approximately 35 per cent each). On the contrary the regions of Kaliningrad, Pskov and Pölva have almost no organizations claiming to rely mainly on foreign funding. This is partly a centre–periphery pattern. Thirty per cent of organizations in centre municipalities have foreign funding as their main income whereas the same percentage for organizations in peripheral communities is 18 per cent.

What difference does foreign funding make? Do civil society groups that rely on foreign donors as their main source of funding have different activities compared to other civil society organizations? Table 6.2 shows that civil society groups with foreign donors as their main source of funding are much more engaged in trans-national networking, fund seeking and public education than are other civil society groups. The first two activities are obviously part of applying for foreign funding and thus the difference between the categories is not at all surprising. The frequent involvement in public education by groups with foreign donors as their main source of funding can be explained by the priority foreign funding agencies give to this activity. In this respect foreign funding seems to increase civil society groups' outreach to the general public. When it comes to actively involving more people in civil society activities, however, foreign funding seems more problematic. Membership mobilization is significantly less common among civil society groups with foreign donors as their main source of funding. This result gives support to the argument that foreign funding takes away incentives for civil society groups to reach out to the general public and mobilize people in the local community. Activities aimed at influencing political decision-makers – including lobbying, writing petitions, organizing demonstrations, boycotts or strikes – are less common among civil society groups with foreign donors as their main source of funding. Differences

Table 6.2 Activities of civil society groups with and without foreign donors as their main source of funding (% often involved in activity)

	Foreign donors as main source of funding	Foreign donors not main source of funding	Difference
Information gathering	77 (72)	74 (190)	3
Public education	76 (73)	48 (124)	28
National networking	74 (71)	68 (176)	6
Fund-seeking	67 (64)	41 (106)	26
Transnational networking	55 (53)	27 (68)	28
Mobilization	39 (37)	52 (133)	−13
Lobbying	30 (28)	36 (93)	−6
Writing petitions	14 (13)	18 (46)	−4
Demonstrations	4 (4)	6 (17)	−2
Boycotts or strikes	1 (1)	2 (4)	−1

Source: Democratization: Local and Transnational Perspectives Survey (DLTPS) 1999–2000.

Note: The question was: 'How often is the organization/group involved in the following activities?' For each activity respondents were asked to select one of the alternatives 'Never', 'Seldom', 'Sometimes' or 'Often'. The answer 'Often' is shown. N = 350–356 depending on activity (absolute numbers within brackets).

are small, but the pattern is consistent.[2] Foreign funding does not seem to increase politicization of civil society. Post-Soviet civil society groups in general, and those having foreign donors as their main source of funding in particular, are overwhelmingly engaged in less straightforwardly political activities such as information gathering, public education, networking and fund-seeking.

One might ask what is cause and effect here. Does foreign funding make civil society groups less inclined to influence politics and less radical and confrontational? Or do foreign funding agencies give priority to those groups that are already less politically active and confrontational? Both interpretations might be plausible, but given the fact that more radical human rights, environmental and feminist organizations are the main beneficiaries of foreign funding it is less likely that the tendency found is a result of foreign funding agencies' selection of moderate NGOs. It is more likely that foreign funding has a depoliticizing effect on the activities of civil society groups. NGOs receiving foreign funding have to give priority to fund-seeking and transnational networking as well as public education, which is the priority of most donors. Hence, there is simply less time (and less need) to mobilize new members, lobby politicians and engage in more confrontational activities.

The qualitative interviews confirm many human rights and environmental NGOs almost complete dependence upon foreign funding. In addition to human rights, environmental and some women's NGOs, NGO resource centres are significant beneficiaries of civil society aid from abroad. The centre for support to NGOs in Pskov, *Vozrozhdenie*, has extensive (about 90 per cent of its budget) funding from a range of foreign funding agencies, including TACIS, Eurasia, NED, Soros's Foundations, Sida and the Friedrich Nauman Stiftung. According to one of its leading members, you are almost guaranteed funding if you know how to apply and have simple, easily understood ideas about a local problem. But most NGOs do not have this competence and many turn to *Vozrozhdenie* for assistance. Fund-seeking is a permanent aspect of the organization's activities and it takes up a considerable part of its time (Interview O4). Similarly, the North-Western Community Development Centre, a resource centre for NGOs in the Novgorod region with about ten staff, is mostly funded by Western funds. (In 2001 USAID was the major donor and before that it was TACIS). As a professional organization the centre has the capacity to write applications in a way appreciated by foreign donors. Its general director claims that all except one proposal have received funding. The centre aims at increasing local funding and recently it has become easier to receive financial resources from local companies (Interview O1).

There have been some positive effects of foreign civil society aid from the perspective of state authorities as well. A representative of the St Petersburg city administration admits that foreign funding of NGOs has solved some significant problems in the city. As an example she mentions a TACIS-funded NGO project on drug abuse. The city administration has also been active in this field and cooperation has been good. Another positive example is an NGO working for parents with disabled children, also funded by TACIS (Interview S4).

A representative of St Petersburg city administration points out that European and US funding agencies have been working separately with NGOs and the state. She thinks this is understandable because there were simply no clear state structures in the early 1990s, but the negative consequence has been that a lot of funding has been given to NGOs that were created just to receive foreign aid. She argues that the European Union has been more successful than other foreign funders because it worked with good NGOs from the beginning. Ideally, the city administration should offer foreign funding agencies advice on which NGOs are suitable to fund. Mostly funding agencies have approached NGOs directly, but recently some have asked the city administration for advice (Interview S4). A priority would then be old social welfare organizations providing services for disabled people and other disadvantaged groups in society. Since 1999 such organizations are included in the 'social program' of the city administration and they are given support in order to increase their ability to receive foreign funding (Interview S4). According to a representative of St Petersburg city administration, the roles of the city administration in relation to NGOs seeking foreign funding are to provide contacts and provide further funding after the project has ended for those NGOs that have proved themselves competent (Interview S4).

Generally, the impact of foreign funding tends to be mixed. An obvious problem, pointed out by many civil society activists, is that funding depends on the priorities of funding agencies, not the local people or civil society activists. The

Ford Foundation, for example, has a reputation for giving priority to feminists (Interview HR6). A recent trend among funding agencies is to give priority to provincial NGOs rather than those active in the big cities. The Centre for Support for Women Entrepreneurs – 'Happiness' – in the small municipality Staraya Russa in the Novgorod region, for instance, was set up in 1998 with money from USAID and IREX (Interview W1). This trend, while benefiting NGOs in peripheral regions, has caused problems for many NGOs in the big cities (Interview HR6).

From the perspective of civil society activists, the main problem with foreign funding is that it can be used only for specific projects during a limited period. Activities have to be short-term and issue-specific. Funding agencies often require that the project should continue after the actual funding, but without money it is impossible (Interview HR2). That makes the long-term development and even survival of the organization highly uncertain. If the funding agencies do not like a certain type of activity their funding will cease (Interview O4). This is a problem stressed by most informants. The effect is that long-term activities as well as routine costs for office equipment etc. are hard to finance (Interview E5). Nevertheless, a survey of Russian women's groups showed that 69 per cent had used foreign grants for office equipment and 44 per cent had used it for paying salaries (Henderson 2000: 71).

Having examined the mixed blessings of foreign funding of NGOs, we now turn to other forms of transnational civil society networking.

Transnational networking

While important, funding is far from the only aspect of transnational interaction of civil society groups. There is some extensive networking between civil societies in different countries, ranging from the exchange of information to the coordination of political campaigns. Transnational networking may include both relatively formalized and sustained networks between well-established organizations and more occasional forms of interaction between civil society groups. The Baltic Sea region, including North Western Russia and the Baltic states, also has its share of transnational civil society networks. Karlsson (2002) identified twenty-one 'regional INGOs and transnational networks' in the Baltic Sea region, (excluding both subregional INGOs and INGOs with participation beyond the Baltic Sea region).

Ecological concerns are probably the most transnationalized civil society sector. Most local and regional ecological organizations in Russia have become branches of Western and international organizations. They tend to be based in Moscow and St Petersburg rather than in the places of the worst ecological disasters (Belokurova 1999). The Russian women's movement has wide international contacts too (Temkina 1997: 27; Sperling 1999: ch. 7).

Supporting the trend of increased transnational civil society networking is the development and spread of electronic communication. However, it is still a very small minority of the population that has regular access to e-mail. A document on the Baltic Sea Information Society Project[3] estimated that only about 2 per cent of the population in St Petersburg used the internet in 1999. There were 300,000 computers, although many of them were old. Five per cent of the households had PCs at home. The availability of electronic communication is without doubt much more limited in more peripheral regions of Russia. Hence the lack of access to the internet is an obstacle to more widespread transnational civil society networking.

Nevertheless, there are many transnational links and they do have significant impact on local civil society groups in Russia and the Baltic states. We should, however, not see this as only a foreign influence on post-Soviet civil society groups. Transnational networking is not a unidirectional process. Ferree and Risman (2001), studying a set of seminars for Russian women's activists organized by US women's organizations, argue that ideas and resources flowed both ways and that there were reciprocal benefits.

We should also have in mind that transnational networking might have different effects upon different kinds of organizations. For example, transnational support for Russian women's and soldiers' rights organizations has been equally strong, but the effect has differed significantly. Soldiers' rights organizations have been strengthened through transnational links whereas such links have tended to increase the isolation of Russian women's organizations from the general public. The reason is that domestic norms and transnational principles converge in the case of soldiers' rights NGOs' advocacy against physical abuse, whereas Western feminism is perceived as conflicting with Russian values (McIntosh Sundstrom 2001).

With the exception of women's NGOs, our knowledge of the extent, form and effects of transnational networking of post-Soviet civil society groups is still limited. There is need for more data on this issue. Fortunately, our survey, as well as qualitative interviews, can provide some new insights in this respect. First, we can note that there is reason to use the popular concept of a 'global civil society' with some caution. Only nine of the civil society groups included in the study claim to be part of an organization with global membership. Transnational links of the large majority of civil society groups are more geographically limited. There is also a substantial part of post-Soviet civil society that does not have any transnational links at all. In the index of civil society activities in Table 4.8 transnational networking reaches 54 on the scale from 0 to 100. This means on average somewhat closer to 'sometimes' than 'seldom' transnational networking. Variations between different groups are, however, profound. Twenty-six per cent of the civil society respondents claim that their organizations are never involved in networking with similar organizations in other countries. One third of the organizations are, according to the respondents, often involved in transnational networking. Supporting previous research findings, environmental groups stand out as most active in transnational networking (reaching 71 on the index in Table 4.8). Social welfare organizations seem to be least transnationalized (36 on the index). The combined indicator for women's groups is misleading, as 46 per cent of respondents in this category claim that their organization is often involved in transnational networking (the highest percentage for any category of civil society groups), but there is also a substantial number of women's groups who never network transnationally (26 per cent). We have to distinguish between the transnationalized feminist organizations and the localized traditional women groups.

Table 6.3 shows no fundamental differences between countries when it comes to transnational networking of civil society groups. Variations within countries, however, are significant. The main metropolitan regions are the most transnationalized whereas more peripheral regions have significantly fewer transnational links. Harju is the most transnationalized region, followed by Riga, St Petersburg, Kaliningrad and Vilnius. The only peripheral region coming close to the level of transnational networking of the metropolitan areas is Tartu in Estonia. With its big university and strong tradition of student activism, the relatively high level of transnational networking in this region is not that surprising. All the other (more peripheral) regions have substantially less transnational contact. Civil society groups in Novgorod seem to be much less transnationalized than average, but we should remember the

Table 6.3 Transnational networking of civil society groups per region (index from 0 to 100)

Region	Transnational networking
Harju	83
Riga	77
St Petersburg	75
Kaliningrad	74
Vilnius	73
Tartu	68
Valmiera	53
Pölva	43
Sverdlovsk	43
Kaunas	41
Pskov	32
Ida-Viru	30
Novgorod	30
Total	**54**

Source: Democratization: Local and Transnational Perspectives Survey (DLTPS) 1999–2000.

Note: The question was: 'How often is the organization/group involved in networking with similar organizations/groups in other countries?' The alternatives 'never', 'seldom', 'sometimes' and 'often' were given. The number of respondents selecting each alternative was multiplied by 0 for the first alternative, 33 for the second, 67 for the third and 100 for the last. The results were summed up and divided by the number of respondents. Thus we arrived at a measurement of frequency of transnational networking. 0 would mean never done by any of the groups. 100 would mean that all groups are often involved in transnational networking. N = 362.

relatively large number of social welfare groups in peripheral municipalities included in the Novgorod sample. The centre–periphery dimension is obvious concerning transnational networking. Forty-two per cent of organizations based in what is classified as central municipalities say they are often involved in transnational networking, whereas only 5 per cent of organizations in peripheral municipalities make the same claim.

When more specific questions about how often the groups have transnational contacts are asked it becomes evident that such contacts are seldom of any intense or regular character. Only 4 per cent of the respondents claim to have transnational contacts more than a few times a month. Among women's groups, trade unions and labour groups and ethnic and nationalists groups not a single respondent say that they have transnational contacts more than a few times a week. Again, environmental organizations stand out as those with most frequent transnational contacts. The regional variation is significant. No single respondent in Pskov, Ida-Viru and Valmiera says that they have transnational civil society contacts more often than a few times a year.

Where are the foreign civil society groups that Russian and Baltic organizations network with based? Seventy-nine respondents claim to have contact with civil society organizations in former Soviet republics. One hundred and thirty respondents state that they have contact with European-based organizations, and 106 say they have contact with global organizations.[4] While most transnational civil society networking seems to be of an East–West nature, this indicates that a substantial share of transnational contacts of post-Soviet civil society groups is with organizations in other parts of the former Soviet Union. Geographic and cultural proximity is important, not least for culturally oriented groups. Naturally, most interest in Russian culture is found in countries with a large Russian-speaking population like Belarus and Latvia. There is also a cultural exchange between Pskov and neighbouring municipalities in Estonia. Relations to Estonia used to be problematic in the 1990s, but they have improved (Interview O5). There may also be political reasons for transnational networking within the borders of the former Soviet Union. The chairwoman of the Union of Women of Russia in Pskov emphasizes the close relations with women's organizations in Belarus. There is a geographical and cultural proximity to Belarus, she argues. But she also states that 'Belarus has managed to keep something that Russia lost with *perestroika*. Russia has a lot to learn from Belarus.' (Interview W2).

Affiliated city cooperation is an important base for transnational civil society cooperation. Civil society groups in Novgorod have intense contacts with the city of Örebro in Sweden. There have been almost fifty joint seminars in Novgorod and Sweden (Interview HR1). Pskov has similar contacts with Norrtälje in Sweden. The Pskov Regional Centre for People's Creativity, a coordinating body for 'cultural houses', also claims some other transnational contacts through affiliated city cooperation (Interview O5).

Table 6.4 Means of communication for transnational civil society contacts

Means of communication for transnational civil society contacts	Absolute number of respondents
Personal meetings	102
Surface mail	100
E-mail/internet	88
Telephone	77
Fax	73

Source: Democratization: Local and Transnational Perspectives Survey (DLTPS) 1999–2000.

Note: The question was 'Approximately how often and in what way does the organization/group have contact with representatives of these organizations or institutions?' Respondents were asked to select as many as appropriate of the following alternatives: 'Personal meetings', 'Surface mail', 'Telephone', 'Fax', and 'E-mail/internet'. Answers for 'European civil society organizations' and 'International civil society organizations' are combined.

Through what means of communication do civil society activists interact transnationally? The number of respondents claiming to have transnational contacts through personal meetings, surface mail, telephone, fax and e-mail respectively are shown in Table 6.4. It is worth noting that personal meetings (presumably during international conferences and foreign visits) are the most common form of transnational interaction. Surface mail is still more common than e-mail, but e-mail is used by more organizations than those who rely on telephone or fax. The findings indicate that we should not overstate the significance of electronic communication for transnational networking of civil society groups.

The forms of communication for transnational civil society contacts also show some variation depending on category of civil society group and region. Only slightly more than one-quarter of the women's groups list personal meeting as a form of transnational interactions as compared to 62 per cent for all civil society groups. Only about one-third of ethnic and nationalist groups and trade unions and labour organizations with transnational contacts use e-mail whereas three-quarters of the environmental groups do. The use of e-mail is, not surprisingly, more common in the large cities than in the peripheral regions.

All NGOs included in the qualitative sample had some transnational contacts – even those selected because the survey showed a lack of such contacts – indicating a very recent transnationalization in the period between the survey interviews in 1999/2000 and the qualitative interviews in April/October 2001. The Soldiers' Mothers in Pskov, for example, did not have any transnational relations, because they did not have the communication resources necessary for transnational contacts. In April 2001, however, the organization was connected to the internet (Interview HR3). Most of the organizations included in the sample for qualitative interviews to some extent relied on (or had relied on) foreign funding. Almost all were involved, at least in occasional exchange of information, with sister organizations abroad. Transnational cooperation in specific projects was common, but sustained cooperation not limited to a specific project was rare.

Information exchange seems to be the most common form of transnational civil society contacts. Even groups with very limited transnational links tend to share some information with similar organizations abroad, at least occasionally. For instance, the Regional Political Party 'Free St Petersburg', which has only sporadic transnational contacts, claims to be involved in some information exchange with political party representatives in Finland and Germany (Interview O6). New labour unions claim to have learnt a lot from older unions in Western Europe through such transnational exchange of information. The independent labour union 'Unity' in St Petersburg, as part of a federation of labour unions in the region, has contacts with labour unions in Italy, Denmark and Sweden. Transnational contacts have mainly taken the form of exchange of information. There have been study trips to Denmark and England in which heads of enterprises participated too. Russian labour activists view these foreign contacts as positive. Foreign unions are older and there is much to learn from their experiences, not least when it comes to the recruitment of new members (Interview L2). For other groups the exchange of information is not enough, but more substantial transnational cooperation is difficult to achieve, even for rather big organizations with substantial foreign funding. *Vozrozhdenie* in Pskov, for instance, has extensive transnational contacts, but its representative still finds them insufficient. Transnational contacts take the form of information exchange only. Real partnership and cooperation would be useful, but this has not been achieved on the transnational level. Most cooperation occurs with similar organizations in other Russian cities, he argues (Interview O4).

The internet is important for the transnational exchange of information, but large sections of post-Soviet civil society lack computers. Most NGOs in Pskov do not have their own computer with access to the internet, but they can use the facilities of *Vozrozhdenie* or another NGO centre. Many also use the public internet offices available (Interview S3). The human rights group *Veche* in Pskov has contacts with organizations in the USA, Sweden, Poland and Belarus, but there does not seem to be any form of more sustained cooperation. The activists describe the transnational links of the organization as 'many name cards, a few visits, but nothing more' (Interview HR2). However, they feel a strong need for better transnational contacts. In April 2001 *Veche* had started to create a website in order to reach out with its information. This is a way to overcome the language and information problem that has been an impediment to more developed transnational cooperation (Interview HR2). Some of the larger NGOs in St Petersburg have very professional websites (e.g. Memorial – http://www.memo.ru/eng/index.htm).

International conferences are important arenas for transnational networking. The 1995 UN women's conference in Beijing was important for many Russian women's organizations. It gave inspiration and also showed how international conventions could be used for local civil society advocacy (Interview W2). Several transnational civil society networks also organize their own conferences. The organization 'Shelter' in St Petersburg, for instance, is part of a transnational network of organizations publishing papers by homeless people. The strongest transnational ties are to Scotland. This relationship dates back to the first conference of 'street papers' in London in 1995. Since then there have been conferences every year. In 1998 the annual conference was held in St Petersburg. A feeling of transnational solidarity is the most important outcome of these conferences (Interview SW1).

Education abroad is another form of transnational networking. Many post-Soviet civil society activists have been trained through programs in the US or Western Europe. The Union of Women's and Youth Initiatives in Pskov has no foreign funding, but its chairwoman has participated in a leadership programme in the US, sponsored by the Open Society Foundation. (Interview W3). In Novgorod there is an association for people who have participated in American NGO programs. In 2001 it was claimed that this association had 350 members (Interview O2).

Cooperation in specific projects is not uncommon because much transnational funding is devoted to such purposes. Most foreign-funded NGOs have these experiences. Even old organizations without any foreign funding may be involved in transnational cooperation for specific projects. The Council of Veterans has an international department headed by a former vice-minister of foreign affairs. The organization has contacts with veteran organizations in England, Germany and former Soviet Republics. There is an exchange between veterans who participated in the same war. They have a common interest in the protection of war cemeteries. There has been a big project in cooperation with Germany. Approximately 25,000 German soldiers are buried outside St Petersburg. For Russian veterans it is easier to work together with Germans than other nationalities that fought for Hitler. The Germans were perhaps forced to fight for the Nazis, whereas other nationalities chose to do so, argues a representative of the Russian veterans (Interview O7).

Membership in a more formal transnational network leads to more regular transnational interaction, not limited to a specific project during a rather short time. The ecological club *Ekologiya* in Novgorod is a member of the International Social Ecological Union, a network of more than 200 organizations in Russia and the former Soviet Union, but also including NGOs from the USA and some European states. The union has organized seminars in different Russian cities (Interview E1). *Ekologiya* also has some less permanent transnational contacts. The organization is, for instance, involved in a Russian–Dutch project (Interview E1). Centrally placed organizations in the regional capital tend to provide transnational links for smaller groups in the regional periphery. Borovichy's Ecological Club has most of its transnational contacts through a regional ecological organization based in the city of Novgorod. These contacts include an East European nature-protection project led by a Dutch NGO and transnational funding which the club won in competition with other groups in the region (Interview E2). An environmental youth organization in the town of Borovichy in Novgorod region sent three representatives to Örebro in Sweden where they participated in environmental research in Lake Hjälmaren (Interview E2). Similarly, the ecological NGO 'Nos 4', also in Borovichy in Novgorod region, has contacts with an organization in the United States which adheres to an ideology of 'ecological sociology' and works with orphans and single parents. The contact was established through an NGO resource centre in Novgorod (Interview E3). The pattern is clear. For civil society groups in the periphery, membership in transnational networks tends to go through bigger organizations in the regional capital.

Sustained transnational cooperation – beyond the routine exchange of information and occasional cooperation in a specific project – is rare, especially outside the big cities. In St Petersburg, however, we find some high profile civil society groups with substantial activities on the transnational level. The Soldiers' Mothers of St Petersburg cooperates both with religious groups in other European countries (like the Pax Christi International based in Belgium) and with transnational human rights organizations like Amnesty International. In Finland, local Amnesty groups have arranged a speaking tour for deserters from the army. The group has written reports to UN commissions and the Council of Europe about the torture of conscripts in Russia (e.g. Soldiers' Mothers of St Petersburg 1999). Together with the League of Women Voters the organization has protested against the war in Chechnya. Foreign volunteers who speak Russian work for the organization. There are also close links to Poland (Interview HR5). The Russian human rights organization Memorial is also involved in sustained forms of transnational cooperation. The organization has a branch in Berlin. It started as a society of support for the St Petersburg Memorial. The Russian and German organizations have cooperated on an exhibition about the KGB prison in Potsdam. Memorial has also cooperated on specific projects with the Polish organization *Charta*. Relations with German groups are best, partly because of the shared understanding of what it means to live under a totalitarian regime, argues a representative of the organization (Interview HR4).

More radical environmental groups in Russia tend to have close links to transnational environmental networks. Green World in Sosnovy Bor is linked to Children of the Baltics (consisting of teachers and youths in the Baltic Sea region), Coalition Clean Baltic (a coalition of twenty-six NGOs), and the Social and Ecological Union (Interview E5). In 1999, Green World organized a bicycle trip from Sosnovy Bor to Helsinki, where activists took part in an environmental movement conference. On the way they organized meetings with local NGOs, media and authorities. In 2000 they made a similar trip to Tallinn (Interview E5). Green World is one of rather few post-Soviet civil society groups that systematically try to take advantage of transnational opportunities, probably because of the extreme lack of local political opportunities for civil society activism in the almost closed city of Sosnovy Bor. Its campaigns typically follow the same pattern. When becoming aware of an environmental problem the organization urges the local authorities to take action. When there is no reaction, the group tries to reach out to the public, both locally and abroad. Through publications, in English as well as in Russian, information is spread. Environmental activists in other countries are informed, and they urge their governments to put pressure on the authorities in Sosnovy Bor (Interview E5).

By now it should be clear that post-Soviet civil society groups are involved in quite extensive transnational networking, although it is seldom intense or sustained. How important is this transnational networking for local activists? Only 12 per cent of respondents in the survey saw transnational contacts as completely unimportant, indicating that most of those groups who did not have any regular transnational contacts would like to establish such foreign links. Supporting the findings from the survey, all respondents to the qualitative interviews have a positive view of transnational cooperation. The importance of the exchange of information and experiences is typically stressed. In some cases civil society groups have been successful in reaching their goals thanks to transnational cooperation. One example of successful transnational civil society activism is the case of the threat of environmental damage related to a planned motorboat rally on a lake in the Novgorod region. The lake is protected as a nature reserve, but the regional government chose to allow the rally anyway. Local environmental NGOs protested, but seemingly in vain. One week prior to the rally the NGO *Ekologiya*, through an e-mail message, turned to transnational civil society groups for support. Using the list of addresses of NGOs provided by the Social Ecological Union, *Ekologiya* managed to reach out to civil society groups on a global scale. The regional administration received a large number of faxes and e-mails demanding that the rally be cancelled in order to preserve the sensitive environment in the lake area. The power-holders yielded to this transnational pressure, and the rally was moved to another area. Inspired by this positive experience *Ekologiya* established its own website and tried to expand its transnational contacts (Interview E1).

Another example of successful transnational civil society interaction is also taken from the environmental field. Contacts with the affiliated town Binghampton in the United States seem to have been instrumental for an environmental protest movement in the small town of Borovichy in Novgorod region in the late 1980s. People from Binghampton visited Borovichy, and a representative of the Ecological Club was part of the Russian delegation to Binghampton. There was support from the US in the protest against a polluting pig farm and the exchange of experiences (including an exchange of letters after the visits) helped the development of the Ecological Club in Borovichy (Interview E2).

Views about transnational civil society contacts, while basically positive, are typically mixed among post-Soviet civil society activists. Prominent St Petersburg activist Olga Starovoitova (Interview HR6) expresses a common view when she argues that pragmatically, the main advantage of international contacts is funding. However, it also has a positive effect in establishing common values. Discussing the main advantages of transnational cooperation, an environmental activist (Interview E5) nicely sums up what many other respondents have also argued. The main advantages are:

1   The moral and psychological support it gives. (It is especially valuable for someone who lives in a closed city to feel that he or she is a member of a wider, open world.)
2   The opportunity to gain more leverage on local authorities through the organization of transnational campaigns.
3   Access to funding. (It is not possible to find financial support for radical environmental activities within Russia.)

Finally, we should examine possible differences in activities between groups having many transnational links and other groups. Comparing the two extremes – groups which often are involved in transnational networking and groups which never network transnationally – we find that the former category of civil society groups are more active in all respects except lobbying (see Table 6.5). Groups with a lot of transnational networking are also very much involved in networking on the national level. These transnationalized civil society groups are also much more engaged in fund-seeking, public education and information gathering than are groups that never do any transnational networking. There are no significant differences between the two categories concerning more openly political activities, such as mobilization,

Table 6.5 Activities of civil society groups, which often or never are involved in transnational networking (%)

Activities (done often)	Groups often involved in transnational networking	Groups never involved in transnational networking	Difference
National networking	92 (111)	36 (35)	56
Information gathering	85 (101)	63 (59)	22
Public education	74 (89)	43 (40)	31
Fund-seeking	62 (75)	30 (29)	32
Mobilization	50 (60)	45 (42)	5
Lobbying	32 (39)	36 (34)	–4
Writing petitions	18 (21)	14 (13)	4
Demonstrations	8 (10)	6 (6)	2
Boycotts or strikes	2 (2)	1 (1)	1

Source: Democratization: Local and Transnational Perspectives Survey (DLTPS) 1999–2000.

Note: The question was: 'How often is the organization/group involved in the following activities?' For each activity respondents were asked to select one of the alternatives 'Never', 'Seldom', 'Sometimes' or 'Often'. The answer 'Often' is shown. N = 355–361 depending on activity (absolute numbers within brackets).

lobbying, writing petitions, organizing demonstrations and boycotts or strikes. Transnational networking generally seems to be related to increased activity, but only less political and confrontational types of activity. Comparing Table 6.5 and Table 6.2, it is interesting to note that unlike groups with foreign donors as their main source of funding, groups which are often involved in transnational networking are not less active in mobilization of new members. This is an indication that it is not transnational contacts per se, but the dependence on foreign funding that makes civil society groups neglect the mobilization of new members locally.

Conclusion

Writing about foreign aid to Russian women's NGOs, (Henderson 2000: 78) concludes that '[a]n international civil society is developing, not in conjunction with, but perhaps at the expense of domestic civic development'. The results presented here give some support for this view, but the argument has to be modified. The 'NGOization' of civil society is indeed partly driven by foreign funding, but the importance of foreign funding for post-Soviet civil society should not be overstated. A substantial share of civil society groups included in this study claims to have been able to mobilize local resources. By contrast, some human rights, environmental and feminist groups are highly dependent upon foreign funding. What they have in common is a more critical attitude towards local and national power centres, which makes it impossible for them to receive local funding. In this respect, on the one hand, international donors have helped sustain critical civil society activities that would otherwise not have survived. On the other hand, survey data show that membership mobilization is significantly less common among civil society groups with foreign donors as their main source of funding. Activities aiming at influencing political decision-makers are also less common among mainly foreign-funded civil society groups. Hence, we can conclude that foreign funding tends to strengthen civil society groups that have comparatively little public support and relatively limited political influence. Furthermore, foreign funding risks increasing resource inequality within civil society as funds mainly reach professional NGOs in metropolitan areas, whereas small civil society groups in the periphery are neglected (although several funding agencies recently have given priority to NGOs outside the major cities).

Other forms of transnational networking do not seem to have a similar negative impact on membership mobilization. On the contrary, those organizations that are most transnationalized tend to be more active in almost all respects. Comparing civil society sectors, environmental groups have most transnational networking. Many local environmental organizations are in fact part of a transnational environmental activist network. Transnational civil society links are common in the metropolitan regions, but relatively rare in more peripheral regions, not to mention peripheral municipalities. Another finding is that the importance of the internet and e-mail for transnational networking should not be overstated. More respondents mention personal meetings and surface mail as important means of communication for transnational civil society contacts. Information exchange is the most common type of transnational civil society interaction. Participation in international conferences, education abroad and cooperation in specific projects are other types of transnational civil society interaction, experienced by several respondents. Several civil society groups are members of formal transnational networks, but more sustained transnational cooperation is relatively rare.

7 Civil society and democratization

A multilevel analysis

This concluding chapter puts together the findings from previous chapters and analyses the relationship between civil society and democratization in post-Soviet Russia and the Baltic states in line with the analytical framework outlined in Chapter 2. The first section provides a summarizing overview of the development of post-Soviet civil society. We then examine some qualitative and quantitative indicators of democracy. This leads to a multilevel analysis of civil society and democratization, which finally results in a presentation of three models of post-Soviet civil society and democracy, and some more general conclusions.

The development of post-Soviet civil society

The movement society of the turbulent years of *perestroika* and *glasnost* was replaced by an 'NGO-society' after the breakdown of the communist regime and the break-up of the Soviet Union. Processes of demobilization and institutionalization are typical following regime transitions. The conditions that make civil society successful in the opposition to an authoritarian regime are very different from the conditions that make the consolidation of civil society in a liberal democracy possible (cf. Weigle 2000: 30). Hence, the 'NGOization' of post-Soviet civil society is not a unique or unexpected development, but it is still not un-problematic for the process of democratization, as it tends to be associated with a decline in popular political participation.

Nevertheless, there are plenty of civil society activities going on in contemporary Russia, Estonia, Latvia and Lithuania, and the number of NGOs has increased dramatically during the last decade. However, post-Soviet civil society is generally described as weak and the findings of this study support this view, although with some qualifications. Relatively few people are engaged in civil society activities and most civil society groups have failed to mobilize members. Nevertheless, membership mobilization is a prioritized activity for many groups included in this study and trade unions in particular still have a large membership. Resource mobilization is problematic and many NGOs are completely dependent on foreign funding. However, a large majority of groups included in this study claims to have local sources as their main source of funding. Foreign funding is vital mainly for small – but important – sectors of civil society, including critical human rights, environmental and feminist groups. With the exception of a few groups in the above-mentioned categories, post-Soviet civil society is largely non-confrontational. Information gathering, public education and networking are the most common activities.

The development of civil society seems to be more problematic in Russia than in the Baltic states. While a legal framework for civil society has been established in post-Soviet Russia, there are many obstacles to the consolidation of civil society, including resistance from public officials, a political culture of apathy and distrust, and a legal system oriented towards protecting those in power rather than making them accountable to an organized public (Weigle 2000: 338).

The emergence of civil society groups can be explained by the existence of political opportunities. *Perestroika*, as analysed in Chapter 3, provided the general political opportunity for all kinds of civil society activities. More specific political opportunities, discussed in previous chapters, include protection and advice from old Soviet organizations (e.g. the Union of Women of Pskov, Greenhipp) and foreign funding (e.g. consumer and women's NGOs in Staraya Russa). Personal experiences of problems are also an important factor explaining the emergence of some civil society groups. In this case Soldiers' Mothers organizations provide good examples.

Despite a rapid growth in the number of independent social organizations in Russia's regions since 1991, civil society groups have very limited influence on national level policies (Weigle 2000: 338). This study indicates that political influence on local and regional levels is marginal too. There are relatively frequent contacts between local authorities and civil society groups, but we have no indications that this has resulted in any significant civil society influence on the state. Weigle (2000: 377) has argued that '[t]he major problem in the democratization of public life throughout Russian history has not been the absence of independent activism but rather the absence of a link between organized activism and state power'. That missing link might in fact be in the process of being established, at least on the local level, in several regions (and the 'Civic Forum' in 2001 might be an example of this tendency on the federal level), but civil society groups still seem too weak to have any real influence on state authorities. Due to the very unequal power relations, state–civil society interaction tends to take the form of co-optation rather than real participation in decision-making. Civil societies in the Baltic states generally face fewer problems and especially in Estonia state–civil society relations seem to be rather harmonious. However, even in this case civil society actors typically have very limited political influence.

The lack of political influence for civil society actors is partly explained by the lack of a strong political society to link up with. Post-Soviet political parties are generally weak and there is strong scepticism towards political parties among civil society elites. Private companies are somewhat more trusted, but most civil society groups have found it difficult or impossible to receive funding from economic society.

To overcome the communist legacy a radical separation of the economic, social, and political realms was needed (Smolar 2002: 55). Paradoxically, however, the study of contemporary post-Soviet civil societies indicates that the distinction between these different social spheres is again being blurred. There are many efforts from state authorities in Russia to co-opt moderate civil society groups and marginalize more critical activists. This process of state-led inclusion takes the form of different arrangements for 'social partnership' involving the state, and civil and economic society in several Russian regions. Many civil society elites themselves also take the initiative to blur the boundaries between the different social spheres, for instance by taking part in election campaigns and engaging in profit-seeking activities. This is a tendency that is criticized by other civil society activists.

It might in fact be useful to distinguish between two very different types of civil societies (although the distinction is blurred in the case of some specific organizations). First, there are groups that strive to establish civil society as a sphere of political freedom and deliberation, often in opposition not only to state actors, but also to corporate interests. Second, there are many NGOs that see civil society as a sphere of private activity, closely related to the market economy. These actors may be involved in profit-seeking activities reminiscent of private companies and they tend to have good relationships with those state actors who promote privatization and other liberal policies. Some oppositional human rights, environmental and feminist organizations represent the first category whereas most NGOs, especially charity organizations, belong to the second category. These two forms of civil society reflect two major discourses on civil society (cf. Keck 2004: 53–4).

Foreign funding agencies direct a large share of their resources to human rights, environmental and feminist organizations, thus potentially strengthening a more oppositional civil society. However, survey data indicate that civil society groups with foreign donors as the main source of funding tend to pay less attention to membership mobilization and tend to be less involved in influencing policy-makers than other civil society groups. Hence, the impact of foreign funding is mixed. It helps some critical NGOs survive, but it also seems to make civil society groups less interested in local mobilization and less willing to try to influence local politicians. Other forms of transnational networking do not seem to have similar negative effects on civil society activities. On the contrary, those civil society groups that are most transnationalized also tend to be most active in other respects. The concept of a transnational civil society is necessary in order to understand contemporary post-Soviet civil societies, especially in the environmental sector.

Qualitative and quantitative indicators of democracy

Whereas most observers agree that the transition to democracy has been relatively successful in Estonia, Latvia and Lithuania (cf. Raun 1997; Plakans 1997; Krickus 1997) – although problems related to the large Russian-speaking minorities in Estonia and Latvia remain, and support for democracy could be stronger among both the public and elites (Ekman and Åström 2003) – the case of Russia is more complicated.[1] While there have been largely free and fair elections, there have also been irregularities, so it is not even clear that Russia is an 'electoral democracy' (White 2000: 280). Public support for democratic values and principles is also more limited than in many other post-communist societies, and to many Russians the term 'democracy' has negative connotations.[2] Brown (2001) insists that labelling the current regime in Russia as 'democratic' devalues the term. There has been a transition from communism, but not yet a transition to democracy (Brown 2001: 568). Rather the current 'hybrid regime' (Shevtsova 2002) in Russia is a 'guided democracy' (Brown 2002), meaning 'a mixture of arbitrariness, kleptocracy, and democracy' (Brown 2002: 211). Sakwa (2002: 470) describes political developments in Russia in the 1990s as 'a complex interaction between democratization and authoritarianism'. Others have argued that the concept 'delegative democracy' (implying that voters express confidence in a ruler and then leave this person to decide what is best for the country) is a useful descriptive model of post-communist Russia. This, according to Weigle (2000: 3) ignores the impact of mass activism and the construction of an independent public sphere. Given the problems of Russian civil society outlined above, I still tend to agree with the label 'delegative democracy'. This concept is applicable not only to the Russian Federation, but also to regional and local levels (Tsygankov 1998).

The media situation, in particular, casts doubts on Russia's process of democratization, and on this aspect the situation has worsened since Putin replaced Yeltsin. Most critical voices in the Russian media have been muted since Putin came to power (Brown 2002: 211; Fish 2002: 250–1). Taken together, however, the effects of political changes introduced under Putin may prove to be mixed and complex. There are clear tendencies to reverse prior democratic gains (especially related to the control of media), but other policies (e.g. the centralization of state power) might advance democratization (Fish 2002). The absence of an effective state has paved the way for local strongmen, based on 'pockets of neofeudal control over local economic resources' (Weigle 2000: 19). Economic liberalization in this context has led to '*nomenklatura* capitalism'. Most abuses of power in Russia occur on the regional and local level (Fish 2002: 248). Hence, a centralization of state power might strengthen democracy and the development of civil society on the local level. But there is also a risk that the whole process leads to a setback for democracy on the federal level. Russia has overall been more democratic at the federal level than in most regions, but as the central authorities are trying to regain control over the regions they are also taking over many undemocratic attitudes and practices from the regional level, including a tight control of the media and political opposition (Brown 2002: 214).

One reason for the democratic problems in Russia is the existence of an 'immature' bourgeoisie, mainly in the commercial-financial sector, which lacks domestic social support and is more in favour of authoritarian than democratic rule. This, according to Gill and Markwick (2000: 225), has more similarities to Latin America than to Western Europe. There is a split between Russian democrats aiming at building political institutions and strengthening civil society and liberals who are ready to support authoritarianism for the sake of economic reform (Shevtsova 2002: 242). In this situation Russia would need a strong and vivid pro-democratic civil society that could put pressure on the political and economic elite, but civil society elites, with few exceptions, are unable or unwilling to play this democratizing role. The weakness of civil society is, thus, a major explanation of the problems of the Russian democratization process.

The arguments above generalize the situation in the Russian Federation as a whole. Throughout this study, however, I have argued that regional differences are significant. The process of democratization has been more successful in some regions (and more of a failure in others). We therefore need some indicators of democracy in Russia's regions. McMann and Petrov (2000) offer an index based on a survey of Russian and foreign scholars, and representatives from the Russian presidential administration and Federation Council. Twenty-six out of forty 'experts' responded and gave an evaluation of the state of democracy based on Dahl's definition. A ranking was made according to the percentage of respondents selecting each region as one of the ten most democratic minus the percentage of respondents selecting it as one of the 10 least democratic. According to this ranking, St Petersburg was seen as most democratic. Sverdlovsk came in second place. Kaliningrad (6) and Novgorod (9) were also among the top ten. Pskov is the only region included in my study which was selected as one of the ten least democratic regions by more experts than those considering it one of the most democratic. It should, however be noted that Pskov was one of few regions where the level of democracy was disputed by the experts. While being an interesting attempt to measure regional variations in the degree of democracy in Russia, there are obvious problems with this approach. Expert evaluations are necessarily subjective and depend on individual evaluators' values and limited knowledge about different regions.

Another attempt to measure the degree of democracy in Russia's regions has been made by Marsh (2000a; 2000b). Following Vanhanen (1997) he uses two indicators: turnout rates for parliamentary and presidential elections and competition measured as the percentage of votes not given to the winner. The result is counter-intuitive, with regions generally considered to be most democratic (like St Petersburg and Novgorod) scoring among the worst.[3] There is need for more reliable and accurate measurements of democracy in Russia's regions, but the problem, of course, is the lack of suitable data. I will not be able to offer any new and more reliable index of democracy in Russia, but based on survey data I can present a picture of satisfaction with democracy among local elites in a few regions and democratic values held by these elites. While not being an indicator of the actual state of democracy, elite attitudes and values are very important for the functioning of democracy and should, thus, be of great interest when we compare democracy across regions in Russia and the Baltic states.[4]

A country-specific pattern can be seen when considering the question of satisfaction with democracy on the national level (see Table 7.1). Estonian respondents are most satisfied, followed by respondents in Lithuania and Latvia. Russian respondents are least satisfied. When we look at satisfaction with local/regional democracy we find approximately the same level of satisfaction (in most cases slightly more satisfaction than on the national level). However, there are two interesting deviant

Table 7.1 Local elite satisfaction with democracy per region (index from 0 to 100)

Region	Satisfaction with local/regional democracy	Satisfaction with national democracy	Satisfaction with local/regional democracy (Civil society elites only)
Tartu	60	55	57
Pölva	56	53	54
Valmiera	54	40	43
Harju	48	53	50
Novgorod	48	34	44
Vilnius	48	43	46
Riga	47	42	44
Kaunas	46	44	41
Ida-Viru	46	50	44
Pskov	33	35	34
Sverdlovsk	33	29	35
Kaliningrad	30	32	23
St Petersburg	29	27	23
Mean	**44**	**41**	**41**

Source: Democratization: Local and Transnational Perspectives Survey (DLTPS) 1999–2000.

Note: The questions were: 'On the whole, are you very satisfied, fairly satisfied, not very satisfied or not at all satisfied with the way local/regional democracy is developing in your community?' 'On the whole, are you very satisfied, fairly satisfied, not very satisfied or not at all satisfied with the way democracy is developing in your country?' The number of respondents selecting 'very satisfied' was multiplied by 100. The number of respondents selecting 'fairly satisfied' was multiplied by 67. The number of respondents selecting 'not very satisfied' was multiplied by 33, and the number of respondents selecting 'not at all satisfied' was multiplied by 0. The results were summed up and divided by the number of respondents (total 1447 and 1448 respectively). Thus we arrived at a measurement of satisfaction with democracy. 0 would mean complete dissatisfaction and 100 complete satisfaction. An index of satisfaction with local/regional democracy is also given for civil society elites only (N = 364).

cases. Satisfaction with local/regional democracy is significantly higher than with national democracy in the regions of Valmiera and Novgorod. Satisfaction with local/regional democracy is highest away from the national capital. Tartu and Pölva in Estonia and Valmiera in Latvia are the regions where local elites are most satisfied. Satisfaction with local/regional democracy is significantly lower in the Russian regions, with the important exception of Novgorod where satisfaction is on the same level as in the Baltic regions (except for the 'good cases' of Tartu, Pölva and Valmiera). Satisfaction with local/regional democracy is marginally lower among civil society elites than among other local elites in most regions. Valmiera is an interesting exception because civil society elites seem to have a significantly more negative evaluation of local/regional democracy than have other local elites.

It is also interesting to compare support for democratic values and principles among local elites in the different regions. The right to organize opposition, protection of minority rights, and support for popular participation instead of elite rule are central elements in the form of more substantial democracy discussed in Chapter 2. The first two principles are also necessary within a more narrow and formal model of democracy. I will use these three principles as indicators of the degree of support for democratic values. As can be seen in Table 7.2, local elites in this post-Soviet context tend to give relatively strong support to important democratic principles like minority rights and the tolerance of opposition. They score substantially lower on the question of participation. This indicates that the form of democracy that finds support among local elites in Russia, Estonia, Latvia and Lithuania is a rather narrow elite democracy, with little popular participation (cf. Ekman and Åström 2003). Regional variation is relatively small, but there is an interesting pattern with less support for democratic values in the Russian regions of Novgorod and Pskov and more support in Riga and most of Estonia. It is also worth noting that St Petersburg scores much better here than on the satisfaction with democracy index (as well as most indicators of political opportunities of civil society activities as analysed in Chapter 5). This might be an indication that local elites in St Petersburg have rather strong support for democratic values and, hence, are more demanding and critical when it comes to evaluating actual democratic qualities of their political system. The more supportive of democratic ideas you are, the more dissatisfied with democratic shortcomings you are likely to be. Therefore, local elites in St Petersburg might perhaps be labelled 'doubting democrats' (cf. Linde 2004).[5]

The elitist views among local elites, particularly in Russia, become even clearer when we examine two other questions related to elite rule versus popular participation (Table 7.3). Most respondents agree with the statements that most decisions should be left to the judgement of experts and that it will always be necessary to have a few strong, able people actually running everything. Elitist views are particularly strong in the Russian regions. Russian respondents are significantly

Table 7.2 Support for democratic values among local elites per region (index from 0 to 100)

Region	Support for democratic values	Right to organize opposition	Minority rights	Political participation
Riga	79	88	86	62
Harju	74	81	85	56
Ida-Viru	74	81	90	51
Tartu	73	77	87	56
St Petersburg	72	83	90	44
Kaliningrad	71	72	84	56
Kaunas	71	80	88	44
Pölva	70	80	85	44
Sverdlovsk	70	76	85	48
Valmiera	70	81	83	47
Vilnius	70	80	85	44
Novgorod	67	78	86	37
Pskov	65	67	82	47
Total	**71**	**78**	**88**	**49**

Source: Democratization: Local and Transnational Perspectives Survey (DLTPS) 1999–2000.

Note: The question was: 'Below are some questions faced in the daily life of political leaders. Please examine the list closely and check the extent to which you agree or disagree with them.' The statements were: 'Any individual or organization has the right to organize opposition', 'The government has the responsibility to see to it that rights of all minorities are protected', 'Widespread participation in decision-making often leads to undesirable conflicts'. Alternatives given were 'Strongly agree', 'Agree', 'Disagree', and 'Strongly disagree'. For the first two statements the number of respondents selecting 'Strongly agree' was multiplied by 100, 'Agree' by 80, 'Disagree' by 20 and 'Strongly disagree' by 0. For the last question the number of respondents selecting 'Strongly agree' was multiplied by 0, 'Agree' by 20, 'Disagree' by 80 and 'Strongly disagree' by 100. The results were summed up and divided by the number of respondents (total 1451, 1453 and 1438 respectively). Thus we arrived at a measurement of the degree of support for the different central democratic values. 0 would mean a complete lack of support for democratic values and 100 would mean full support. Measurements of the three statements on democracy are combined to produce an index of support for democratic values (by adding the three indicators and dividing by three).

more inclined to agree with the statement that it will always be necessary to have a few strong, able people actually running everything, than are local elites in the Baltic states. Survey research has discovered a fairly solid and widespread support for many aspects of democracy among the Russian public. However, support for minority rights and the tolerance of political opponents are much weaker (e.g. Gibson 1995). By contrast, local elites seem to be quite supportive of minority rights and the right to organize opposition, but very negative about popular participation and generally quite elitist in their orientation. Our findings indicate that local elites in Russia might be equally supportive of democratic values and principles as are the general public, but they tend to support other democratic principles than do people in general.

Table 7.3 Views on elite rule among local elites per region (index from 0 to 100)

Region	Support for political participation	Against expert rule	Against strong man rule
Harju	42	41	44
Tartu	40	44	35
Vilnius	38	32	43
Kaunas	34	27	40
Pölva	30	26	35
Riga	30	42	19
Valmiera	30	37	23
Ida-Viru	28	28	28
S Petersburg	26	35	17
Novgorod	23	32	14
Kaliningrad	21	29	13
Sverdlovsk	19	25	13
Pskov	18	25	11
Total	**28**	**33**	**24**

Source: Democratization: Local and Transnational Perspectives Survey (DLTPS) 1999–2000.

Note: The question was: 'Please examine the statements below and check the extent to which you agree or disagree with them.' Statements were: 'Most decisions should be left to the judgement of experts' and 'It will always be necessary to have a few strong, able people actually running everything'. Alternatives given were 'Strongly agree', 'Agree', 'Disagree', and 'Strongly disagree'. The number of respondents selecting 'Strongly agree' was multiplied by 0, 'Agree' by 20, 'Disagree' by 80 and 'Strongly disagree' by 100. The results were summed up and divided by the number of respondents (total 1451 and 1453 respectively). Thus we arrived at a measurement of the degree of support for the principle of popular participation. 0 would mean a complete lack of support for popular participation and complete support for elite rule and 100 would mean full support for participation and no support at all for elitist ideas. The two indicators were combined to produce an index of support for political participation (by adding the two indicators and dividing by two).

In sum, both qualitative and quantitative indicators point at democratic problems in Russia. The Baltic states (and especially Estonia) seem to be better off (although not unproblematic). Local elites' satisfaction with democracy is significantly lower in the Russian regions (with the exception of the Novgorod region) and elite support for democratic values and principles is lower in the Russian regions (not least in Novgorod) than in the Baltic states.

Civil society and democratization

Let us now revisit the findings of this study in light of the possible relationships between civil society and democracy discussed in Chapter 2. This analysis will not be structured according to different levels. Rather we should conceive of a complex web of processes that are simultaneously local, regional, national and transnational.

The first democratic function of an emerging civil society – forming a parallel society by ignoring or bypassing the authoritarian/post-totalitarian regime – was hard to achieve in the pre-Gorbachev Soviet Union. Political opportunities were too limited, in comparison with some Central and East European satellite states. The second function, however – mobilizing resistance against the authoritarian regime – was performed well by the emergent civil society during *perestroika* and *glasnost*. The new independent movements and groups – supported by transnational civil society actors – were important in the process leading to the breakdown of the communist regime and break-up of the Soviet Union. In the Baltic states civil society also performed the third democratic function – producing political actors for new democracies. The new political leadership was, to a large extent, recruited from the various pro-democracy and independence movements. By contrast, the pro-democracy movement in Russia was not prepared to gain power, and most civil society activists were marginalized when strong political and economic leaders took over the process. Nevertheless, some prominent civil society activists took the step into the state realm.

The fourth pro-democratic function of civil society – being a check against the abuse of state power, thus making the state less dominant – has hardly been performed to any significant extent by post-Soviet civil societies. Most civil society actors included in this study are not interested in being a check against the abuse of state power. They are more oriented towards performing certain social welfare functions, often in cooperation with state authorities. Those critical civil society groups that do try to be a countervailing force against the state in certain areas are typically too weak to have any real political influence. They are dependent on foreign donors, and this dependency seems to limit their local mobilization and potential to influence local politics. Transnational civil society networking in general, however, seems to strengthen the activities of local civil society groups and there are several examples of post-Soviet civil society groups making use of transnational opportunities in situations where local political opportunities are perceived as limited. The emergence of transnational civil societies is in itself also a process that might make states less dominant. The significance of territorial state boundaries is increasingly being questioned by civil society actors creating transnational public spaces, and post-Soviet civil society activists take part in this process. To what extent this might give rise to transnational forms of democracy is, however, too early to say.

The fifth democratic function of civil society – aggregating, articulating and representing interests – is also relatively poorly performed by post-Soviet civil society groups. The low level of membership in most civil society groups is an indication of the failure to aggregate interests, and most indicators show a lack of real influence on state policies.

The sixth proposed democratic function – assisting the state in the design and implementation of various public policies – is more frequently performed by post-

Soviet NGOs, but it is highly questionable to what extent this really strengthens democracy. There is a strong tendency in several Russian regions to include moderate civil society groups in 'partnerships' with local authorities and businesses. This form of inclusion does not meet the criteria of being good for democracy put forward by Dryzek (1996) (see Chapter 2). There is no indication that the main concerns of civil society groups can be assimilated to a state imperative. On the contrary, there seems to be little support for most civil society agendas among the local, regional and national/federal state leadership. Hence, civil society as an independent sphere where critical and oppositional groups can act is weakened by the process of state-led inclusion.

The seventh democratic function of civil society – increasing political participation – is in a way performed just by the existence of multiple groups working in different areas. However, all these civil society groups are not pro-democratic. Many are more or less apolitical and some might be anti-democratic. Even among civil society groups with explicitly pro-democratic goals, internal democracy might be a problem. Previous research has found that leaders of the organizations often govern more or less unilaterally (Berthusen Gottlick 1999: 255), thus leaving little space for political participation. Most NGOs included in this study have a steering committee elected for five years and claim to have regular meetings. In practice, however, decision-making and activities seem to be less formalized. Asked about decision-making procedures in his organization, one informant replied 'On paper or in reality?' (Interview O4). We do not have sufficient data on the internal democracy of civil society groups, but there are reasons to believe that there are democratic problems. Furthermore, civil society groups must reach out to the general public in order to increase political participation and strengthen democracy. As shown in Chapter 4, mobilization of new members and public education are common activities for many post-Soviet civil society groups, indicating at least a potential for supporting democracy by increasing public participation in politics. If we return to Table 5.9 we find that 38 per cent would seek support from the general public, another indication of a limited but still significant public outreach among post-Soviet civil society groups. Hence, the evaluation of post-Soviet civil societies' impact on political participation is mixed. Participatory forms of decision-making are probably relatively rare within most civil society groups and a majority of civil society organizations are not explicitly political and/or lack substantial links to the general public, but at least a significant number of civil society groups try to reach out to the public, thus having a potential to broaden popular political participation.

The final hypothesis about civil society and democracy – that civil society strengthens collective trust and tolerance among citizens, hence strengthening democracy – deserves some more elaborate analysis. We have some survey data that enables us to tentatively test this hypothesis in the post-Soviet context. Table 7.4 shows that civil society elites have somewhat more general trust in people than have

Table 7.4 Different local elites' general trust in people (%)

Elite type	Most people can be trusted
Civil society	80 (284)
Administrative	79 (122)
Media	78 (56)
Political	78 (399)
Economic	67 (216)
Total	**76 (1077)**

Source: Democratization: Local and Transnational Perspectives Survey (DLTPS) 1999–2000.

Note: The question was: 'Generally speaking, would you say that most people can be trusted or that you can't be too careful dealing with people?' Alternatives given were: 'Most people can be trusted' and 'Most people cannot be trusted'. The former answer is shown. N = 1413 (absolute numbers within brackets).

other local elites. Differences between elite types are, however, rather small, although the economic elite has significantly lower trust.[6] Hence, we cannot say that the proposition that activities in civil society generate trust (and social capital) has found any firm support in our data.

As an indicator of social tolerance, respondents were asked to tell which categories of people they would not like to have as neighbours (see Table 7.5). The pattern is that civil society elites are slightly more tolerant than other local elites in most respects (except towards left-wing and right-wing extremists), but differences are small. Again, our survey data has given, at best, very limited support for the argument on civil society's capacity to generate tolerance (and social capital). We should, however, not overstate the importance of this finding. Most respondents have been active in civil society groups for less than a decade so it might be too early to evaluate civil society's capacity to generate social capital.[7]

In sum, this study indicates that post-Soviet civil society elites do not have significantly more general trust in people and they are not significantly more tolerant than are post-Soviet local elites in general. There is a tendency that this elite type scores somewhat better than average on these indicators, but differences are typically marginal. Hence, we have not found any strong evidence of civil society's capacity to strengthen collective trust and social tolerance (although we should remember that most civil society groups are relatively new so it might be too early to evaluate this). A strong civil society is a key aspect of more participatory forms of democracy, but it is questionable to what extent post-Soviet civil society contributes to popular participation in politics. Many civil society groups have an apolitical orientation, their internal democracy is often questionable, and only about half of the groups included in this study try to reach out to the general public on a more regular basis. Most post-Soviet civil society groups seem to be unwilling or unable to influence political decision-making. Their pro-democratic function is

Table 7.5 Social tolerance among local elites (% not wanting certain people as neighbours)

Would not like as neighbours	Civil society elite	Local elites, average
Drug addicts	80 (290)	83 (1208)
Heavy drinkers	79 (287)	85 (1234)
People with a criminal record	69 (252)	72 (1053)
Emotionally unstable people	54 (196)	55 (803)
Left-wing extremists	53 (195)	53 (768)
Right-wing extremists	51 (185)	49 (712)
Homosexuals	44 (162)	47 (694)
People who have AIDS	36 (133)	40 (587)
Gypsies	24 (88)	28 (413)
Muslims	13 (47)	16 (231)
Immigrants/foreign workers	8 (30)	10 (147)
Hindus	7 (24)	8 (119)
People of different race	6 (21)	6 (95)
People with large families	6 (20)	6 (85)
Jews	4 (16)	5 (79)

Source: Democratization: Local and Transnational Perspectives Survey (DLTPS) 1999–2000.

Note: The question was: 'On this list are various groups of people. Could you please sort out any that you would not like to have as neighbours?' N ranges from 1451 to 1454. (Absolute numbers within brackets.)

thus limited. Many civil society groups do indeed try to assist the state in carrying out its functions, but 'partnerships' between civil society, state institutions and businesses are typically a form of co-optation that does not significantly improve democracy. Post-Soviet civil society is not a strong check against state power. Most civil society groups included in this study are not interested in this function and those who are, typically fail to have any significant political impact, although transnational civil society links offer some new opportunities for certain civil society activists. Post-transition civil society in general has failed to play an important role in strengthening democracy (whether formal or societal) in Russia and the Baltic states, although many specific civil society groups do work to improve the state of democracy. During the transition, however, emerging civil society groups played an important role as the main pro-democratic actors. Popular movements were instrumental in the struggle for independence and democracy in Estonia, Latvia and Lithuania, and the Russian pro-democracy movement played an important role during *perestroika* and *glasnost*. To some extent civil society provided the new more democratic regimes with leaders, but this process also weakened post-communist civil society.

Three models of civil society and democracy

In this section I will conclude the regional comparison made throughout the study and arrive at a typology of three models of civil society and democracy (Table 7.6). The three Russian regions that were selected for more in-depth research provide examples of quite different conditions for civil society and democracy. Conventional political opportunities for civil society are perceived to be good in Novgorod, average in Pskov and relatively bad in St Petersburg. This must be interpreted as a sign of a relatively hostile political climate for civil society activities in St Petersburg and a much more open situation in Novgorod. However, it is likely that the existence of more critical and confrontational civil society groups in St Petersburg is a reason behind the more negative evaluation of political opportunities there. There is no indication that conditions for oppositional civil society activities should be better in Novgorod than in St Petersburg, but non-confrontational groups find the political system in Novgorod relatively open and supportive.

An important aspect that is not covered by the conventional indicators of political opportunities is the existence of elite conflicts. Within the transition literature, conflicts within the ruling elite are seen as a triggering factor for regime transitions (O'Donnell and Schmitter 1986). Elite conflicts on the local and regional level may also create political space for pro-democratic civil society initiatives in a post-transition context. In both St Petersburg and Pskov, conflicts between local and federal – or local and regional – authorities provide some opportunities for civil society elites to seek allies on one side or try to play out the conflicting elite groups against each other. In Novgorod, by contrast, no such elite conflicts exist. The governor seems to be in full control and there is no strong opposition. This situation gives little political space for oppositional civil society groups and makes it hard to find any elite allies.

The media situation also indicates very limited opportunities for oppositional civil society activities in Novgorod. There are no independent media in the region. The situation in Pskov is similar, but in this region there is at least competition between newspapers controlled by the local and regional authorities and this has created some opportunities for civil society activists. St Petersburg has some independent media, but with very limited distribution. The lack of independent media is an obstacle to the development of civil society in all three regions (and in Russia in general).

Differences in political opportunities and media situations have led to the development of civil societies with partly different characters. All regions have 'NGO societies'. It is difficult to give any precise number of active NGOs, as estimations vary considerably between different actors. A rough estimation suggests that St Petersburg has the largest and most vivid civil society with approximately 2,500 active NGOs. This is what should be expected from a metropolitan centre. Pskov, being a poorer and more peripheral region, has a smaller civil society, with about

Table 7.6 Three models of civil society and democracy

	Model 1	Model 2	Model 3
	Privately funded, transnationalized, relatively autonomous and oppositional civil society groups. Limited formal democracy, with little societal legitimacy.	Local, state-dependent and mainly moderate civil society groups. Democratic shortcomings, but some space for oppositional activities.	Privately funded, politically supported, moderate civil society groups. Openness and democratic forms, but elitist rule in reality.
Region	St Petersburg	Pskov	Novgorod
Conventional political opportunities	Relatively bad	Average	Good
Elite conflicts	Elite conflicts provide some political space.	Elite conflicts provide some political space.	No elite conflicts. Governor in full control.
Media situation	Some independent media	No independent media, but competition.	No independent media. No competition.
Number of NGOs	Approximately 2,500 active	Approximately 100–200 active	Approximately 400–500 active
Type of NGOs	Relatively many political and oppositional.	Mixed	Many charity organizations
Sources of funding	Private donations and foreign funds.	Public subsidies.	Private donations and some foreign funds.

Transnational links	Extensive	Few	Some
Civil society relations with state	Cooperation, but some significant opposition	Cooperation, but some limited opposition	Cooperation. Little opposition.
Civil society relations with political society	Distrust, but some cooperation	Distrust, but some cooperation	Political parties extremely weak or non-existent
Civil society relations with economic society	Limited cooperation	Very limited cooperation	Cooperation and unclear boundaries
Degree of democracy according to experts	High	Average. (Contradictory interpretations.)	Relatively high
Local elites' satisfaction with democracy	Very dissatisfied	Dissatisfied	Relatively satisfied

100–200 active NGOs. Novgorod, with a similar number of inhabitants as Pskov, but with better opportunities for (moderate) civil society activities has approximately 400–500 active NGOs. Charity organizations and other moderate and politically relatively uncontroversial groups dominate in Novgorod, whereas St Petersburg has considerably more oppositional groups. The types of NGOs in Pskov are more mixed, although politically uncontroversial groups tend to dominate, as in Novgorod.

Civil society groups in Novgorod and St Petersburg rely on private donations and foreign funds as their main source of funding, (although relatively few NGOs in Novgorod have foreign donors as their main source of funding). By contrast, public subsidies seem to be the main source of funding for civil society groups in Pskov. Foreign funding agencies have not paid much attention to civil society in Pskov and the harsh economic situation there does not make local businessmen inclined to sponsor civil society activities. Transnational links in general are relatively rare among civil society groups in Pskov. Such links are more common in Novgorod, and civil society in St Petersburg is to a large extent transnationalized.

The different characters of civil society in the three regions are linked to different patterns of civil society relations with the state. In all three regions there are many NGOs that seek to cooperate with state authorities and accept inclusion through various 'partnership' arrangements. A significant number of actors on the St Petersburg civil society arena, however, have an oppositional and confrontational orientation. To a lesser extent we can also find such oppositional civil society groups in Pskov, but they seem to be very rare in Novgorod. This might be interpreted as an indication of harmonious state–civil society relations in Novgorod, but the situation is problematic from a democratic perspective, as civil society actors do not serve as a check against the dominant state.

Relations between civil and political society are constrained in the post-Soviet context in general because of the weakness of both spheres and the mutual distrust of civil society elites and political parties. Nevertheless there is some cooperation, especially in election campaigns, in St Petersburg and Pskov. In Novgorod, political parties are extremely weak or even non-existent, so linking up with political parties is not even an option for most civil society elites there.

Also, when comparing civil society relations to economic society, Novgorod is different. There is some limited cooperation between local enterprises and civil society groups in St Petersburg and (to a lesser extent) in Pskov, whereas civil and economic society seem to be much more integrated in Novgorod. In the Novgorod region there are more local businessmen willing to give financial support to certain civil society activities, and many civil society groups seem to be engaged in profit-making activities too. The boundaries between the two social spheres are particularly blurred in Novgorod.

The degree of democracy, according to expert evaluations, varies between the three regions. St Petersburg is considered to be most democratic (actually the most democratic region in the whole Russian federation) and Novgorod also receives a positive evaluation, whereas Pskov is considered to be less democratic. Drawing on survey data and qualitative interviews with civil society activists, there are reasons to question the very positive evaluation of democracy in St Petersburg. St Petersburg actually scores among the worst on most indictors related to political opportunities, and local elites themselves tend to be very dissatisfied with the way democracy is developing in the city. Local elites in Pskov are also dissatisfied (although not to the same extent), whereas local elites in Novgorod are relatively satisfied (or very satisfied by Russian standards). A thorough qualitative study of democratization in St Petersburg (Orttung 1995) also gives a more complex picture of the city's democratic achievements and shortcomings in the early 1990s. The pro-democracy movement was strong in St Petersburg and anti-democratic communist and nationalist parties have been weak in the city, but voter turnout has been very low, indicating a lack of public legitimacy for the new political system. Public opinion polls have also shown that leading politicians are extremely unpopular (Orttung 1995: 263–4).

Novgorod stands out as a region with a relatively open political system and comparatively homogenous local elite, which is satisfied with the way democracy is developing. In this respect the findings presented here support the very positive evaluation of democratic developments in Novgorod made by Petro (1999; 2002) although my overall assessment is more complex and less positive. There is indeed a large civil society in Novgorod, but most NGOs are not politically active. The peculiarities of civil society and democracy in Novgorod might be partly explained by the historical experiences of the region. Unlike most regions in Russia, Novgorod has a long history of more or less democratic ways of organizing politics. In the twelfth century political life in the independent city state of Novgorod centred on a popular assembly – *veche* – in which in principle all free men of Novgorod could participate (Badersten 2002: 290). Even lower classes of workmen seem to have been represented. From the mid-twelfth century all administrative leaders, including the *posadnik* – a kind of mayor – were elected by the *veche*. This historical experience of democratic institutions can be seen as a significant legacy that might have some implications for contemporary politics. Despite the democratic forms, however, political life in medieval Novgorod was in practice dominated by a small aristocratic elite (Badersten 2002: 293). Nevertheless, Novgorod had a level of political participation that was unique in Russia. The only other region that has a somewhat similar history is Pskov (Badersten 2002: 306), but there this historical legacy does not seem to have been used in the same way as in Novgorod, where reform-oriented leaders tend to refer to the historical context.

In sum, St Petersburg, Pskov, and Novgorod provide examples of quite different models of civil society and democracy. The first model (St Petersburg) is one of a privately funded, transnationalized, relatively autonomous and oppositional civil society linked to a formal democracy with little societal legitimacy. The second model (Pskov) is a local, state-dependent and mainly moderate civil society associated with a political system with democratic shortcomings but offering some space for oppositional activities. The third model (Novgorod) is a privately funded, politically supported, moderate civil society operating in a wider political system characterized by openness and democratic forms, but with elitist rule in practice.

Conclusion

Michail Gorbachev's reform policies of *perestroika* and *glasnost* opened up political opportunities for the emergence of a civil society in the Soviet Union. What first developed was a 'movement society' in which popular movements for democracy and independence in the Baltic republics played an instrumental role in transition politics. New independent groups and movements in Russia were weaker, but they still took the initiative away from the communist reform leadership and, thus, paved the way for the breakdown of the communist regime.

The decline in mobilization following the breakdown of communist rule led to the 'NGOization' of post-Soviet civil society. There are plenty of NGOs in contemporary Russia, Estonia, Latvia and Lithuania. They typically operate within a broad range of issue areas, including human rights, women's rights, labour, environmentalism, ethnic and nationalist issues, and social welfare. This study indicates that leading activists are extremely well educated. Women seem to be relatively well represented among the post-Soviet civil society elites, but mainly within women's and social welfare organizations. Most NGOs have few members (especially women's organizations) whereas many trade unions have been able to keep a rather large membership, although the degree of organization has decreased substantially. Previous research has depicted post-Soviet civil society as poorly rooted in local society and very weak on membership. The findings in this study suggest a slightly less pessimistic view. While typically having relatively few members, most civil society groups included in the study claim to give priority to the mobilization of new members and a large majority claim to have found local sources of funding, including membership fees, private donations and public subsidies. We should be careful when interpreting this result, as claims by respondents cannot be taken at face value, but it is still an indication that local resource mobilization might be less difficult at the turn of the century than it was during most of the 1990s. Furthermore, public education seems to be a common activity among post-Soviet civil society groups, indicating an ambition to reach out to the public. According to survey results, the main activities in post-Soviet civil society are non-confrontational. Information gathering and networking are common everyday activities, whereas conscious efforts to influence political decision-makers, for example through lobbying and petition writing, are more rare and more confrontational activities like demonstrations, boycotts and strikes are very uncommon. Given the selection of civil society groups for this study, which gave priority to groups in politically sensitive areas like human rights, women, labour, the environment, and ethnic and nationalist issues, the lack of interest in explicitly political activities among respondents is striking. This study confirms the picture of a largely moderate and non-confrontational post-Soviet civil society, although there are obvious cases of politically active and oppositional NGOs too.

A legal framework for civil society has developed in Russia, Estonia, Latvia and Lithuania in the 1990s. The state tries to control and co-opt civil society in different ways (and with significant national and regional variation), but state repression is not common anymore. Political opportunities, conventionally measured as the degree of openness of the political system, the existence of elite allies, and the lack of harassment and repression, are perceived as reasonably good in most regions and by most categories of civil society groups included in this study. The lack of independent media, however, is a severe obstacle to civil society activities in the Russian regions. The situation in the Baltic states is much better in this respect. Civil society elites' trust in state institutions is rather high in Estonia, but very low in the Russian regions. Elite conflicts (between local, regional and national level power-holders) paradoxically create some political space in Russian regions where critical civil society activities are otherwise relatively constrained. Overall, however, post-Soviet civil society elites seem to have little influence on state institutions.

The theoretical implication of this analysis is that the concept of political opportunities needs to be further elaborated. In addition to the conventional components of openness of the political system, the existence of elite allies and the lack of harassment and repression, we also need to pay attention to the media situation. Access to independent media is vital for many civil society activists. Furthermore, we could find more specific indicators of the openness of the political system. The general pattern of contacts between state authorities and civil society actors, and especially how effective civil society activists believe such contacts to be, is important in this respect. The general trust civil society actors have in state authorities is another indicator of political openness. One aspect of the existence of elite allies is the personal overlapping between civil society and power-holders in the formal political sphere. Another important dimension is the existence of elite conflicts which might provide some political space for civil society activists, enabling them to play out one power faction against the other. This might be a reason behind the emergence of certain elite allies. Last, but not least, a power perspective must be introduced. The existence of good political opportunities for civil society activities does not automatically mean that civil society groups have any political influence. The analysis of political opportunities needs to take a step further and also inquire into the actual political influence of civil society groups.

Post-Soviet political parties are very weak, and hence there are few democracy-supporting links between civil and political society. Actors within economic society are not so overwhelmingly distrusted by civil society elites as are political parties, but there is no indication that links between civil and economic society – in the form of funding or participation in state initiated 'partnerships' – contribute to strengthening democracy.

A main conclusion about the relationship between civil society and other arenas is that boundaries tend to be blurred. State–civil society cooperation, often also involving local businesses, is common in the Russian regions. State authorities also create quasi-NGOs and some state institutions perform functions similar to civil society activities. Many civil society activists take an active part in election campaigns, thus linking up with the (weak) political society. Profit-making activities of NGOs are not uncommon and, hence, the boundary between civil and economic society is also blurred. The theoretical implication of this is that we should not be too concerned about how to draw clear-cut conceptual boundaries between different social spheres or arenas. Rather we should examine and theorize the intersection between, and overlapping of, different arenas.

Territorial boundaries of the state are also becoming less relevant for civil society activities. Increasingly, civil society activists from different countries link up to share information and experiences, and in some cases cooperate in specific campaigns. Foreign funding is another aspect of the transnationalization of local civil society. Foreign aid to post-Soviet NGOs has become very common, but its importance should not be overstated. Survey data presented here indicate that many civil society groups in Russia and the Baltic states have been able to mobilize local resources. By contrast, some human rights, environmental and feminist NGOs have to rely on foreign funding. While sustaining important civil society activism that would not have been possible without foreign support, international funding agencies tend to strengthen civil society groups that have comparatively little public support and relatively limited political influence. Transnational networking in general, however, seems to make local civil society groups more active in most respects. Transnational links have provided local post-Soviet civil society groups with important political opportunities that they lacked on the local level. About three-quarters of the groups included in this study claim to have some transnational contacts, but regional variation is significant. Civil societies in metropolitan areas tend to be largely transnationalized, whereas transnational civil society links in more peripheral regions are relatively rare. The role of the internet in transnational networking should not be overstated. More respondents mention personal contacts and surface mail as important means of communication for transnational civil society contacts. It should be evident that a theory of civil society would be inadequate without a thorough examination of the transnational dimensions.

The development of civil society has implications for democracy on all levels, and a multi-level approach is most fruitful when analysing civil society and democratization. A combination of local and transnational civil society initiatives was important in the transition from communist rule in the Soviet Union. In post-transition Russia, Estonia, Latvia and Lithuania civil society has not been able to strengthen democracy in the same way. Most post-Soviet civil society groups seem to be either unwilling or unable to be a countervailing force against state power. Transnational funding has provided support for some NGOs with such ambitions, but mostly foreign funding tends to make NGOs less inclined to mobilize members and influence local politics. Furthermore, there is little support in survey data for the view that activities in civil society generate social capital.

The weakness of post-Soviet civil society helps explain the difficulties experienced in the democratization process in Russia. Civil society seems to be somewhat better developed in the Baltic states (and especially in Estonia) and the process of democratization has also been more successful there. However, even in the most positive case – Estonia – civil society groups have hardly been able to play a significant democracy-strengthening role after the transition. Regional variation within (and across) countries is significant. Differences between centre and periphery within a country are often more significant than difference between countries. The Russian regions of St Petersburg, Pskov and Novgorod, for instance, provide examples of quite different models of civil society and democracy. Such differences can to some extent be explained by different historical experiences. History matters for the development of civil society and democracy, something that is also demonstrated by the less problematic developments in the Baltic states compared to Russia.

Finally, it should be stressed that the generalizations resulting in a rather negative view of post-Soviet civil society and its role in strengthening democracy should not make us ignore the struggle for democracy that many civil society activists are involved in, on local as well as transnational levels. There are many activists in different regions of Russia, Estonia, Latvia and Lithuania who are engaged in important struggles for human rights in general or the specific rights of women, workers and ethnic minorities, etc. and against environmental destruction. Many people also rely on civil society groups for their social welfare. These struggles should not be forgotten although civil society in general has not been able to contribute to the consolidation of democracy in the former Soviet Union.

Notes

1 Introduction

1 This study draws mainly on previous research on civil society in the former Soviet Union. Important findings from comparative studies of civil society in other post-communist contexts are also taken into account, but the specific status of the Soviet Union as the dominant power in relation to Eastern Europe makes this an adequate focus.

2 For a brief critical review of Russian literature on civil society see Bron Jr 2001.

3 Much research on regions in Russia (and to a much lesser extent in the Baltic states) has indicated substantial differences across regions. For analyses of regional and local politics in the post-Soviet context see e.g. Campbell 1995; Friedgut and Hahn 1994; Slider 1997; Stoner-Weiss 1997; Kirkow 1998.

4 The last fieldwork for this study was carried out in October 2001 and the analysis does not cover developments after the Russian Civic Forum in November 2001.

5 Including republics, *oblasts*, *krai*, autonomous *krai* and metropolitan areas.

6 Kaliningrad, Novgorod, Pskov and Sverdlovsk are *oblasts*, whereas St Petersburg is a metropolitan area. Nevertheless they all have the same constitutional status.

7 The survey is referred to as the Democratization: Local and Transnational Perspectives Survey (DLTPS).

8 One of the most ambitious attempts to provide a directory of post-Soviet NGOs (Ruffin *et al.* 1999) focuses mainly on groups with transnational contacts, and is too incomplete to provide a starting point for this project. The website of Civil Society International – the organization responsible for this directory (http://www.civilsoc. org//) – contains brief presentations of several of the internationally more well known organizations included in the present study. When revisited in October 2003, however, this information had not been updated since early 1999.

9 Similar lists were provided for other categories of local elites, including political, administrative, economic, media and church elites. We define local elites as persons who, through their organizational positions, are able to affect local politics in a much more regular and substantial way than are ordinary citizens (cf. Burton *et al.* 1992: 8). In the case of political elites, all elected members of the local parliament were included. Administrative elites representing different key sectors were selected. Economic elites were randomly selected, but guaranteeing that we included both new firms and older state-owned companies as well as enterprises from different sectors. Representatives from what was considered the most important local media were also selected. See Åström (2005) for a detailed description of the other types of local elites.

10 I use the concepts 'civil society elites' and 'civil society activists' interchangeably. The use of the term 'elite' only refers to respondents' leading positions within their respective organizations and does not say anything about their actual political influence (which is an open empirical question). In theory, civil society should be the realm of ordinary citizens' activities whereas political society and economic society are made up of elite actors in pursuit of power and profit (Howard 2003: 35). In practice, however, civil society may be quite elitist too, as will be shown in this study (cf. Henderson 2003: 10). For recent interesting elite studies in Russia see Steen (2003) which excludes civil society elites and Åström (2005) which includes civil society elites. See also Szücs 1998; Petersson 2001; Gelman 2002.

11 Russian language questionnaires were used for some respondents in Estonia and Latvia too.

12 In regions where senior researchers were responsible for the interviews (St Petersburg and Sverdlovsk) the response rate is higher than in the other regions, where students were responsible. This may not only reflect the senior researchers more advanced skills, but also their more extensive social networks and easier access to respondents.

13 A few respondents did not answer all questions or answered 'do not know' to some questions. Missing data and the answer 'do not know' are typically very small (usually less than 2 per cent) and therefore excluded from the analysis. The total number of interviews (N) excluding missing data and the reply 'do not know' is given for each question in the tables throughout the book.

14 When referring to the interviews in the text I use a code with one or two letters indicating to which category the respondent belongs, and a number to distinguish between respondents. E = environmental, HR = human rights, L = labour, O = other, S = state, SW = social welfare, W = women.

2 Democratization and civil society: a framework for analysis

1 It goes beyond the scope of this study to elaborate on very precise meanings of these terms. The idea is merely to demonstrate the usefulness of not limiting the analysis to a rather narrow version of formal democracy – as is common in most democratization research – but also include the broader societal and more substantial aspects of democracy. I contend that the two broad perspectives are not mutually exclusive, but should be treated as complementary.

2 A narrow, market-oriented process of democratization may, for instance, provide powerful elites with new devices of control whereas more radical demands for societal democracy are marginalized (cf. Hippler 1995). It is not uncommon that societal democratization has to be left to the uncertain future in order to secure the acceptance of a limited version of formal democracy by old authoritarian elites. Such compromises between pro-democratic reformers and soft-liners within the authoritarian regime might have been beneficial for the consolidation of formal democracy in many cases, but at the expense of more substantial aspects of societal democracy.

3 For a different perspective, understanding civil society as a sphere of social networks, see Gibson 2001.

3 Civil society and the fall of communist rule

1 For an excellent analysis of what it meant to be a citizen in the Soviet Baltic Republics, see Danjoux 2002: ch 4.

2 For criticism against state centred approaches to the analysis of new societal organizations in the Soviet Union see Fish 1995: 9–15.

3 It should, however, be noted that groups that called themselves political parties did not function as such. The only organization that at least vaguely resembled a political party was Democratic Russia, which defined itself as a 'movement organization' instead of a party (Fish 1995: 81).

4 The Moscow based Memorial organization formed around high profile dissident Andrei Sakharov. In 1989 branches were registered in several regions.

5 Transnational links within the USSR were also limited. Linguistic barriers between the Baltic republics and the rest of the USSR prevented the spread of subversive ideas and 'transnational' cooperation among dissidents. Similar linguistic barriers existed between the three Baltic republics too (Danjoux 2002: 203).

4 Actors and activities in post-Soviet civil society

1 Estonia, Latvia and Lithuania have different historical experiences and there are significant variations between civil societies in the three states. Nevertheless there are some homogenizing historical factors, which have influenced the development of civil society in similar directions (Ruutsoo 2002: 56). First, the westernization experienced under the first period of national independence (1920–1940). Second, the common experience of forceful inclusion into the Soviet Union. Third, the adaptation to European standards following independence from the Soviet Union, and the impact of the EU accession process in particular.

2 Women are in the majority among respondents from Novgorod, Harju, Pölva, Riga and Valmiera. In Kaliningrad and Vilnius women are significantly underrepresented. There is no obvious reason (such as the share of women's and social welfare organizations) for this regional variation.

3 When looking at the regional variation we find younger respondents in Tartu, Kaliningrad and Novgorod, and older respondents in Harju, Ida-Viru and Valmiera. The number of respondents in several regions, however, is so small that we should not try to draw any conclusions concerning this regional variation.

4 Regional variation shows the highest level of education in Harju, Vilnius and (somewhat surprisingly) Pskov. The lowest level of education is found outside the capital regions in the three Baltic states.

5 As will be shown later (Table 4.8) this results in a relatively high score of 68 for mobilization of new members on the activity index ranging from 0 to 100.

6 For further discussion on foreign funding of post-Soviet civil society groups see Chapter 6.

7 Novgorod also stands out as a region with more isolated civil society groups as there is less networking with similar organizations both within the country and abroad. Twenty-one per cent of respondents in Novgorod say there is no networking nationally compared to 6 per cent on average. Forty-seven per cent of the civil society groups in Novgorod claim to often network within the country. The average percentage is 68. The same pattern appears when we look at transnational networking. This, however, can probably to a large extent be explained by the relatively large share of respondents in peripheral municipalities in the Novgorod region. National as well as transnational networking is much more common in the regional centre than in the periphery.

8 The federal umbrella organization claims 33 million members (Interview O7). These numbers, however, seem to be highly exaggerated.

5   Civil society, the state, and other arenas: conflict, cooperation, and unclear boundaries

1 Labour unions had some limited success in lobbying against the worst aspects of the new labour code, but it is still considered repressive against the labour movement (Crowley 2002: 237).
2 For example, human rights activists in the Pskov-based NGO *Veche* had great hopes in Yeltsin and supported his election campaign in 1996 in order to prevent the communists from regaining power. However, they became increasingly disappointed with Yeltsin. They are very sceptical towards Putin, who they claim uses the old communist way of ruling (Interview HR2).
3 The Central Election Commission, however, judged only 1,873,000 signatures to be authentic, thus making the campaign fail to get the two million signatures required for a referendum. Putin signed the nuclear waste importation into law in July 2001 (Henry 2001: 28–9; Henry 2002: 200–1; Tysiachniouk and Reisman 2002).
4 There are not enough respondents to make it meaningful to compare different cities, towns and villages within each region.
5 Variation across civil society sectors is not very pronounced, but trade union and labour activists seem to have somewhat more trust in regional newspapers and television, and ethnic and nationalist groups have somewhat less trust in these types of media.
6 Women's groups and organizations belonging to the category 'other' have the most optimistic view of the effectiveness of using media, whereas ethnic and nationalist groups are more pessimistic.
7 Comparing different categories of civil society groups, we find that representatives of civil society groups belonging to our category 'other', including NGO resource centres and youth groups, think they have more clout over local authorities than do other sectors of civil society. Nationalist and ethnic groups in particular see themselves as relatively powerless.
8 Other regions in Russia have similar policies.
9 Similar measures to guarantee political openness should, according to the law, exist in all Russian regions, but they seem to be more consistently implemented in Novgorod.
10 Variation across civil society sectors is less pronounced. Social welfare organizations have least trust in political parties (only 9 per cent) and groups belonging to the category 'other' have most trust (34 per cent).
11 Trade union and labour activists are (not surprisingly) most sceptical towards private companies (32 per cent have some or a lot of trust). Representatives of social welfare organizations (more surprisingly) have a similarly low trust in private companies (33 per cent). As expected, we find most trust in private companies among respondents belonging to the category 'other' (58 per cent having some or a lot of trust).

6   The transnationalization of local civil society

1 However, Shineleva (2002), ch. 7, is an exception.
2 Concerning demonstrations and boycotts or strikes, the tendency becomes clearer when looking at the answer 'sometimes' and 'never' too. Fourteen per cent of groups not having foreign donors as their main source of funding sometimes organize demonstrations. The similar figure for groups with foreign donors as their main source of funding is only 6 per cent. Seventy-eight per cent of mainly foreign-funded groups claim that they never organize demonstrations compared to 63 per cent among other

civil society groups. Seven per cent of groups not relying on foreign donors as their main source of funding claim to sometimes organize boycotts or strikes whereas only 1 per cent of mainly foreign-funded groups make the same claim. Ninety-four per cent of groups with foreign donors as their main source of funding never organize boycotts or strikes compared to 81 per cent of other civil society groups. Hence, the pattern clearly indicates that civil society groups mainly dependent on foreign funding are less confrontational than other groups.

3 Published by St Petersburg Government and infoDev St Petersburg Project Organization.

4 The question asked was: 'With approximately how many organizations (or individual representatives of organizations) of different character and on different levels does the organization/group have contact? (Give approximate number for each category.)' Respondents were asked to give a number for both state institutions and civil society organizations on local, regional (within country), national, former Soviet Union, European and global levels respectively. The numbers given above are the absolute numbers of respondents claiming to have any contact at all with civil society organizations in the former Soviet Union, Europe and on a global level. Only 27–39 per cent of all respondents answered these questions, so the results must be interpreted with great caution. It is however, reasonable to assume that most of those who did not respond to the question did not have any transnational contacts at all.

7 Civil society and democratization: a multilevel analysis

1 Freedom House classified Estonia, Latvia and Lithuania as free in 1999, while Russia was classified as partly free (White 2000: 286).

2 A recent innovative study on democracy discourses in post-communist countries indicates that democracy is a negative symbol for many Russians (Dryzek and Holmes 2002).

3 The competition component is later taken out of the index, thus leaving only voter turnout as an indicator of the level of democracy (Marsh 2000a: 87–8), making the index even more dubious.

4 For a critical discussion of the 'satisfaction with democracy' indicator, see Linde and Ekman 2003.

5 Following this way of reasoning and observing that Novgorod scores much worse on support for democratic values (especially on the political participation indicator where Novgorod is far below any other region) than on satisfaction with local and regional democracy (as well as most indicators of political opportunities), one might ask if local elites there tend to be 'satisfied nondemocrats'.

6 Within the civil society category, environmental and human rights and democracy activists have more trust (88 and 84 per cent respectively), whereas women's rights activists and those working on ethnic and nationalist issues have less trust (76 per cent).

7 Furthermore, the causal effects assumed by the argument on the positive effects of civil society activity are not obvious. It might also be the case that people who have more trust and are more tolerant in the first place tend to join civil society groups.

References

Ahrne, G. (1998) 'Civil society and uncivil organizations', in Jeffrey C. Alexander (ed.) *Real Civil Societies: Dilemmas of Institutionalization*, London: Sage.

Anheier, H., Glasius, M. and Kaldor, M. (eds) (2001) *Global Civil Society 2001*, Oxford: Oxford University Press.

Arato, A. (1991) 'Social movements and civil society in the Soviet Union', in J. B. Sedaitis and J. Butterfield (eds) *Perestroika from Below: Social Movements in the Soviet Union*, Boulder, CO: Westview Press.

Åström, L. (2005) *Gatekeepers of Democracy? A Study of Elite Support for Democracy in Russia*, (manuscript).

Aves, J. (1992) 'The Russian labour movement, 1989–91: the mirage of a Russian Solidarnosc', in G. A. Hosking, J. Aves and P. J. S. Duncan (eds) *The Road to Post-Communism: Independent Political Movements in the Soviet Union 1985–1991*, London: Pinter Publishers.

Badersten, B. (2002) *Medborgardygd: Den europeiska staden och det offentliga rummets etos* (Civic Virtue: The European city and the ethos of public space) Stockholm: Natur och Kultur.

Baltic Data House (1998a) *Latvian Omnibus Survey: Non-governmental organizations*, Riga: Baltic Data House.

—— (1998b) *The Programme for Studies and Activities 'Towards a Civic Society', the Results of 1st and 2nd Stages*, Riga: Baltic Data House.

—— (1998c) *Survey of Latvian Inhabitants: Towards a Civic Society*, Riga: Baltic Data House.

Beckman, B. (1997) 'Explaining Democratization: Notes on the concept of civil society', in E. Özdalga and S. Persson (eds) *Civil Society, Democracy and the Muslim World*, Swedish Research Institute in Istanbul, Transactions vol. 7.

—— (1998) 'The liberation of civil society: Neo-liberal ideology and political theory in an African context', in M. Mohanty, P. N. Mukherji and O. Törnquist (eds) *People's Rights: Social Movements and the State in the Third World*, New Delhi: Sage.

—— (2001) 'Civil society and alliance politics', in B. Beckman, E. Hansson and A. Sjögren (eds) *Civil Society and Authoritarianism in the Third World*, Stockholm: PODSU.

Beckman, B. and Sjögren, A. (2001) 'Civil society and authoritarianism: Debates and issues – an introduction', in B. Beckman, E. Hansson and A. Sjögren (eds) *Civil Society and Authoritarianism in the Third World*, Stockholm: PODSU.

Beetham, D. (1993) 'Liberal democracy and the limits of democratization', in D. Held (ed.) *Prospects for Democracy: North, South, East, West*, Cambridge: Polity Press.

Belokurova, E. (1999) *Russian Political Science on Regional Politics: An Overview*, Södertörns högskola, Working Paper.

Benda, V., Simecka, M., Jirous, I. M., Dienstbier, J., Havel, V., Hejdanek, L. and Simsa, J. (1988) 'Parallel polis, or an independent society in Central and Eastern Europe: an inquiry', *Social Research* 55, 1–2: 211–46.

Berglund, S., Hellén, T. and Aarebrot, F. H. (eds) (1998) *The Handbook of Political Change in Eastern Europe*, Cheltenham: Edward Elgar.

Berglund, S., Aarebrot, F. H., Vogt, H. and Karasimeonov, G. (2001) *Challenges to Democracy: Eastern Europe Ten Years after the Collapse of Communism*, Cheltenham: Edward Elgar.

Bermeo, N. (2000) 'Civil society after democracy: some conclusions', in N. Bermeo and P. Nord (eds) *Civil Society before Democracy: Lessons from Nineteenth Century Europe*, Lanham, MD: Rowman & Littlefield.

Bernhard, M. (1993) 'Civil society and democratic transition in East Central Europe', *Political Science Quarterly* 108, 2: 307–26.

Berthusen Gottlick, J. F. (1999) 'From the ground up: Women's organizations and democratization in Russia', in J. M. Bystydzienski and J. Sekhon (eds) *Democratization and Women's Grassroots Movements*, Bloomington, IN: Indiana University Press.

Boussard, C. (2003) *Crafting Democracy: Civil Society in Post-transition Honduras*, Lund University, Department of Political Science.

Bova, R. (1991) 'Worker activism: the role of the state', in J. B. Sedaitis and J. Butterfield (eds) *Perestroika from Below. Social Movements in the Soviet Union*, Boulder, CO: Westview Press.

Braman, S. (1996) 'Interpenetrated globalization: scaling, power and the public sphere', in S. Braman and A. Sreberny-Mohammadi (eds) *Globalization, Communication and Transnational Civil Society*, Cresskill, NJ: Hampton Press.

Bridges, O. and Bridges, J. (1996) *Losing Hope: The Environment and Health in Russia*, Aldershot: Avebury.

Bron Jr., M. (2001) 'Civil society in Russia. A non-existent phenomenon?', in M. Schemmann and M. Bron Jr. (eds) *Adult Education and Democratic Citizenship IV*, Krakow: Impuls Publisher.

Brown, A. (2001) 'Evaluating Russia's democratization', in A. Brown (ed.) *Contemporary Russian Politics. A Reader*, Oxford: Oxford University Press.

—— (2002) 'From democratization to "guided democracy"', in L. Diamond and M. F. Plattner (eds) *Democracy after Communism*, Baltimore, MD: The Johns Hopkins University Press.

Bunce, V. (2000) 'The historical origins of the East-West divide: Civil society, political society, and democracy in Europe', in N. Bermeo and P. Nord (eds) *Civil Society before Democracy. Lessons from Nineteenth Century Europe*, Lanham, MD: Rowman & Littlefield.

—— (2002) 'Comparing East and South', in L. Diamond and M. F. Plattner (eds) *Democracy after Communism*, Baltimore, MD: The Johns Hopkins University Press.

Burton, M., Gunther, R. and Higley, J. (1992) 'Introduction: Elite transformations and democratic regimes', in J. Higley and R. Burton (eds), *Elites and Democratic Consolidation in Latin America and Southern Europe*, Cambridge: Cambridge University Press.

Butterfield, J. and Sedaitis, J. B. (1991) 'The emergence of social movements in the Soviet

Union', in J. B. Sedaitis and J. Butterfield (eds) *Perestroika from Below: Social Movements in the Soviet Union*, Boulder, CO: Westview Press.

Caiazza, A. (2002) *Mothers and Soldiers: Gender, citizenship, and civil society in contemporary Russia*, London: Routledge.

Camilleri, J. A. and Falk, J. (1992) *The End of Sovereignty? The politics of a shrinking and fragmenting world*, Aldershot: Edward Elgar.

Campbell, A. (1995) 'Regional power in the Russian Federation', in A. Coulson (ed.) *Local Government in Eastern Europe: Establishing Democracy at the Grassroots*, Aldershot: Edward Elgar.

Centre for Non-Governmental Organizations (2002) *NGO Sector in Latvia 2000/2001*, Riga.

Chilton, P. (1994) 'Mechanics of change: Social movements, transnational coalitions, and the transformation process in Eastern Europe', *Democratisation* 1, 1: 151–81.

Civil Society International, http://www.civilsoc.org//.

Clarke, G. (1998) *The Politics of NGOs in South-East Asia: Participation and protest in the Philippines*, London: Routledge.

Cohen, J. L. and Arato, A. (1992) *Civil Society and Political Theory*, Cambridge, MA: The MIT Press.

Cortright, D. (1993) *Peace Works: The Citizen's Role in Ending the Cold War*, Boulder, CO: Westview Press.

Crotty, J. (2003) 'Managing civil society: Democratisation and the environmental movement in a Russian region', *Communist and Post-Communist Studies* 36: 489–508.

Crowley, S. (2002) 'Comprehending the weakness of Russia's unions', *Demokratizatsiya* 10, 2: 230–55.

Danjoux, O. (2002) *L'Etat, C'est Pas Moi. Reframing Citizenship(s) in the Baltic Republics.* Lund University, Department of Political Science.

Dawn Hemment, J. (2000) *Gender, NGOs and the Third Sector in Russia: An Ethnography of Post-socialist Civil Society*, PhD dissertation, Cornell University.

della Porta, D. and Kriesi, H. (1999) 'Social movements in a globalizing world: An introduction', in D. della Porta and H. Kriesi (eds) *Social Movements in a Globalizing World*, London: Macmillan.

Devlin, J. (1995) *The Rise of Russian Democrats: The Causes and Consequences of the Elite Revolution*, Aldershot: Edward Elgar.

Diamond, L. (1994) 'Toward democratic consolidation', *Journal of Democracy* 5, 3: 4–17.

Diamond, L., Linz, J. J. and Lipset, S. M. (1990) 'Introduction: comparing experiences with democracy', in L. Diamond, J. J. Linz and S. M. Lipset (eds) *Politics in Developing Countries*, Boulder, CO: Lynne Rienner.

Dryzek, J. S. (1996) 'Political inclusion and the dynamics of democratization', *American Political Science Review* 90, 1: 475–87.

Dryzek, J. S. and Holmes, L. T. (2002) *Post-Communist Democratization: Political Discourses across Thirteen Countries*, Cambridge: Cambridge University Press.

Duka, A., Kornev, N., Voronkov, V. and Zdravomyslova, E. (1995) 'Round table of Russian sociology, the protest cycle of perestroika: the case of Leningrad', *International Sociology* 10, 1: 83–99.

Duncan, P. J. S. (1992) 'The return of St Petersburg', in G. A. Hosking, J. Aves and

P. J. S. Duncan (eds) *The Road to Post-Communism: Independent Political Movements in the Soviet Union 1985–1991*, London: Pinter Publishers.

Ehrenberg, J. (1999) *Civil Society: The Critical History of an Idea*, New York: New York University Press.

Ekman, J. and Åström, L. (2003) 'Demokratins vägvisare? Demokratiattityder på elitnivå och massnivå i Estland, Lettland och Litauen' (Guides of democracy? Attitudes towards democracy on elite and mass level in Estonia, Latvia and Lithuania), paper presented at the Annual Meeting of the Swedish Political Science Association, Umeå, 16–18 October 2003.

Elofsson, K. and T. Rindefjäll (1998) Flernivådemokrati – En teoretisk såväl som praktisk utmaning (Multilevel democracy – A theoretical as well as practical challenge), Lund University, Department of Political Science.

Engelstein, L. (2000) 'The dream of civil society in Tsarist Russia: Law, state, and religion', in N. Bermeo and P. Nord (eds) *Civil Society before Democracy: Lessons from Nineteenth Century Europe*, Lanham, MD: Rowman & Littlefield.

Essig, L. and Mamonova, T. (1991) 'Perestroika for women', in J. B. Sedaitis and J. Butterfield (eds) *Perestroika from Below: Social Movements in the Soviet Union*, Boulder, CO: Westview Press.

Evangelista, M. (1999) *Unarmed Forces: The transnational movement to end the Cold War*, Ithaca, NY: Cornell University Press.

Evans Jr., A. B. (2002) 'Recent assessments of social organizations in Russia', *Demokratizatsiya* 10, 3: 322–42.

Ferree, M. M. and Risman, B (2001) 'Constructing global feminism: Transnational advocacy networks and Russian women's activism', *Signs: Journal of Women in Culture & Society* 26, 4.

Fish, M. S. (1995) *Democracy from Scratch: Opposition and Regime in the New Russian Revolution*, Princeton, NJ: Princeton University Press.

—— (2002) 'Putin's path', in L. Diamond and M. F. Plattner (eds) *Democracy after Communism*, Baltimore, MD: The Johns Hopkins University Press.

Fisher, W. F. (1997) 'Doing good? The politics and antipolitics of NGO practices', *Annual Review of Anthropology* 26: 439–64.

Foley, M. W. and Edwards, B. (1996) 'The paradox of civil society', *Journal of Democracy* 7, 3: 38–52.

Friedgut, T. H. and Hahn, J. W. (eds) (1994) *Local Power and Post-Soviet Politics*, Armonk, NY: M. E. Sharpe.

Gelman, V. (2002) 'Russia's elites in search of consensus: What kind of consolidation?' *Demokratizatsiya* 10, 3: 343–61.

Gibbon, P. (1996) 'Some reflections on "civil society" and political change', in L. Rudebeck and O. Törnquist (eds) *Democratisation in the Third World: Concrete Cases in Comparative and Theoretical Perspective*, The Seminar for Development Studies, Uppsala University.

Gibson, J. L. (1995) 'The resilience of mass support for democratic institutions and processes in the nascent Russian and Ukrainian democracies', in V. Tismaneanu (ed.) *Political Culture and Civil Society in Russia and the New States of Eurasia*, Armonk, NY: M.E. Sharpe.

—— (2001) 'Social networks, civil society, and the prospects for consolidating Russia's democratic transition', *American Journal of Political Science*, 45, 1: 51–69.

Gill, G. (2002) *Democracy and Post-Communism: Political Change in the Post-communist World*, London: Routledge.

Gill, G. and Markwick, R. D. (2000) *Russia's Stillborn Democracy? From Gorbachev to Yeltsin*, Oxford: Oxford University Press.

Golenkova, Z. T. (1999) 'Civil society in Russia', *Russian Social Science Review* January/February.

Gordenker, L. and Weiss, T. G. (1996) 'Pluralizing global governance: Analytical approaches and dimensions', in L. Gordenker and T. G. Weiss (eds) *NGOs, the UN, and Global Governance*, Boulder, CO: Lynne Rienner.

Gorodetskaya, I. E. (1998) 'Stanovlenie "tretyego sektora" i dobrovolchestva' (The establishment of a 'Third Sector' and voluntary service), in K. G. Kholodkovsky (ed.) *Grazhdanskoe Obshchestvo v Rossii: Struktury i Soznanie* (Civil Society in Russia: Structures and Conscience), Moscow: Nauka.

Grugel, J. (1999) 'Contextualizing democratisation: the changing significance of transnational factors and non-state actors', in J. Grugel (ed.) *Democracy Without Borders: Transnationalization and Conditionality in New Democracies*, London: Routledge.

—— (2002) *Democratization: A Critical Introduction*, Basingstoke: Palgrave.

Hadenius, A. (1992) *Democracy and Development*, Cambridge: Cambridge University Press.

Hadenius, A. and Uggla, F. (1995) *Making Civil Society Work: Promoting Democratic Development: What Can States and Donors Do?* Department of Government, Uppsala University (Uppsala Studies in Democracy No. 9).

Hale, H. A. (2002) 'Civil society from above? Statist and liberal models of state-building in Russia', *Demokratizatsiya* 10, 3: 306–21.

Henderson, S. (2000) 'Importing civil society: Foreign aid and the women's movement in Russia', *Demokratizatsiya* 8, 1: 65–82.

—— (2003) *Building Democracy in Contemporary Russia: Western Support for Grassroots Organizations*, Ithaca, NY: Cornell University Press.

Henry, L. (2001) 'Sponsored democratization: Environmentalists as bearers of civil society in Russia', Paper presented at the 2001 Annual Meeting of the American Political Science Association, San Francisco, August 30 – September 2.

—— (2002) 'Two paths to a greener future: Environmentalism and civil society development in Russia', *Demokratizatsiya* 10, 2: 184–206.

Hewison, K. and Rodan, G. (1996) 'The ebb and flow of civil society and the decline of the left in Southeast Asia', in G. Rodan (ed.) *Political Oppositions in Industrialising Asia*, London: Routledge.

Higgott, R. A., Underhill, G. R. D. and Bieler, A. (2000) 'Introduction: Globalisation and non-state actors', in R. A. Higgot, G. R. D. Underhill and A. Bieler (eds) *Non-State Actors and Authority in the Global System*, London: Routledge.

Higley, J., Kullberg, J. and Pakulski, J. (2002) 'The persistence of postcommunist elites', in L. Diamond and M. F. Plattner (eds) *Democracy after Communism*, Baltimore, MD: The Johns Hopkins University Press.

Hippler, J. (ed.) (1995) *The Democratisation of Disempowerment: The Problem of Democracy in the Third World*, London: Pluto Press.

Hosking, G. A. (1992) 'Popular movements in Estonia', in G. A. Hosking, J. Aves and P. J. S. Duncan (eds) *The Road to Post-Communism: Independent Political Movements in the Soviet Union 1985–1991*, London: Pinter Publishers.

Hosking, G. A., Aves, J. and Duncan, P. J. S. (eds) (1992) *The Road to Post-Communism: Independent Political Movements in the Soviet Union 1985–1991*, London: Pinter Publishers.

Howard, M. M. (2002) 'The weakness of postcommunist civil society', *Journal of Democracy* 13, 1: 157–69.

—— (2003) *The Weakness of Civil Society in Post-Communist Europe*, New York: Cambridge University Press.

Hudock, A. C. (1999) *NGOs and Civil Society: Democracy by Proxy?* Cambridge: Polity Press.

Hydén, G. (1995) *Assisting the Growth of Civil Society: How Might it be Improved?* Department of Government, Uppsala University (Uppsala Studies in Democracy No. 10).

—— (1997a) 'Building civil society at the turn of the millennium', in J. Burbidge (ed.) *Beyond Prince and Merchant: Citizen Participation and the Rise of Civil Society*, New York: Pact Publications.

—— (1997b) 'Civil society, social capital, and development: Dissection of a complex discourse', *Studies in Comparative International Development* 32, 1: 3–30.

Jubulis, M. A. (2001) *Nationalism and Democratic Transition: The Politics of Citizenship and Language in Post-Soviet Latvia*, Lanham, MD: University Press of America.

Kaldor, M. (1999) 'Transnational civil society', in T. Dunne and N. J. Wheeler (eds) *Human Rights in Global Politics*, Cambridge: Cambridge University Press.

—— (2000) '"Civilising" globalisation? The implications of the "battle in Seattle"', *Millennium: Journal of International Studies* 29, 1: 105–14.

—— (2003) *Global Civil Society: An Answer to War*, Cambridge: Polity Press.

Kaldor, M. and Vejvoda, I. (1997) 'Democratization in Central and East European countries', *International Affairs* 73, 1: 59–82.

Karatnycky, A., Motyl, A. and Shor, B. (eds) (1997) *Nations in Transit 1997: Civil Society, Democracy and Markets in East Central Europe and the Newly Independent States*, New Brunswick, NJ: Transaction Publishers.

Karklins, R. (1994) *Ethnopolitics and Transition to Democracy: The Collapse of the USSR and Latvia*, Washington, DC: The Woodrow Wilson Center Press, and Baltimore, MD: The Johns Hopkins University Press.

Karklins, R. and Zepa, B. (2001) 'Political participation in Latvia 1987–2001', *Journal of Baltic Studies* 32, 4: 334–46.

Karl, T. L. (1990) 'Dilemmas of democratisation in Latin America', *Comparative Politics* 23, 1: 1–21.

Karlsson, M. (2002) 'The significance of security considerations to transnational actors: Three puzzles from an ongoing research project', in Olav F. Knudsen (ed.) *Cooperation or Competition? A Juxtaposition of Research Problems Regarding Security in the Baltic Sea Region*, Stockholm: The Swedish Institute of International Affairs and Södertörns Högskola.

Keane, J. (1988) 'Despotism and democracy: The origins and development of the distinction between civil society and the state 1750–1850', in J. Keane (ed.) *Civil Society and the State: New European Perspectives*. London: Verso.

—— (2003) *Global Civil Society?*, Cambridge: Cambridge University Press.

Keck, M. E. (2004) 'Governance regimes and the politics of discursive representation', in N. Piper and A. Uhlin (eds) *Transnational Activism in Asia: Problems of Power and Democracy*, London: Routledge.

Keck, M. E. and Sikkink, K. (1998) *Activists Beyond Borders: Advocacy Networks in International Politics*, Ithaca, NY: Cornell University Press.

Kholodkovsky, K. G. (ed.) (1998) *Grazhdanskoe Obshchestvo v Rossii: Struktury i Soznanie* (Civil Society in Russia: Structures and Conscience), Moscow: Nauka.

Kirkow, P. (1998) *Russia's Provinces: Authoritarian Transformation versus Local Autonomy?*, Basingstoke: Macmillan.

Kisovskaya, N. K. (1998) 'Gruppy interesov i partii' (Interest groups and parties), in K. G. Kholodkovsky (ed.) *Grazhdanskoe Obshchestvo v Rossii: Struktury i Soznanie* (Civil Society in Russia: Structures and Conscience), Moscow: Nauka.

Kopecky, P. and Mudde, C. (eds) (2003) *Uncivil Society? Contentious Politics in Post-communist Europe*, London: Routledge.

Krickus, R. J. (1997) 'Democratization in Lithuania', in K. Dawisha and B. Parrott (eds) *The Consolidation of Democracy in East-Central Europe*, Cambridge: Cambridge University Press.

Kubicek, P. (2002) 'Civil society, trade unions and post-Soviet democratisation: Evidence from Russia and Ukraine', *Europe–Asia Studies* 54, 4: 603–624.

Kumar, K. (1993) 'Civil society: An inquiry into the usefulness of an historical term', *The British Journal of Sociology* 44, 3: 375–95.

Kurilla, I. (2002) 'Civil activism without NGOs: The communist party as a civil society substitute', *Demokratizatsiya* 10, 3: 392–400.

Lagerspetz, M. and Vogt, H. (1998) 'Estonia', in S. Berglund, T. Hellén and F. H. Aarebrot (eds) *The Handbook of Political Change in Eastern Europe*, Cheltenham: Edward Elgar.

Latvia Human Development Report 1999, Riga: UNDP.

Latvia Human Development Report 2000/2001, Riga: UNDP.

Leech, B. L. (2002) 'Asking questions: Techniques for semistructured interviews', *PS: Political Science and Politics* 35, 4: 665–68.

Levi, M. (1996) 'Social and unsocial capital: A review essay of Robert Putnam's Making Democracy Work', *Politics & Society* 24, 1: 45–55.

Li, X. (1999) 'Democracy and uncivil societies: A critique of civil society determinism', in R. K. Fullinwider (ed.) *Civil Society, Democracy, and Civic Renewal*, Lanham, MD: Rowman & Littlefield.

Lieven, A. (1994) *The Baltic Revolution: Estonia, Latvia, Lithuania and the Path to Independence*, 2nd edn, New Haven: Yale University Press.

Linde, J. (2004) *Doubting Democrats? A Comparative Analysis of Support for Democracy in Central and Eastern Europe*, Örebro University (Örebro Studies in Political Science 10).

Linde, J. and Ekman, J. (2003) 'Satisfaction with democracy: A note on a frequently used indicator in comparative politics', *European Journal of Political Research* 27, 2: 391–408.

Linz, J. J. and Stepan, A. (1996) *Problems of Democratic Transition and Consolidation: Southern Europe, South America, and Post-communist Europe*, Baltimore, MD: The Johns Hopkins University Press.

Lipset, S. M. (1959) 'Some social requisites of democracy: Economic development and political legitimacy', *American Political Science Review* 53, 1: 69–105.

McAdam, D. (1996) 'Conceptual origins, current problems, future directions', in D. McAdam, J. D. McCarthy and M. N. Zald (eds) *Comparative Perspectives on Social Movements: Political Opportunities, Mobilizing Structures, and Cultural Framings*, Cambridge: Cambridge University Press.

—— (1998) 'On the international origins of domestic political opportunities', in A. N. Costain and A. S. McFarland (eds) *Social Movements and American Political Institutions*, Lanham, MD: Rowman & Littlefield.

McAdam, D., McCarthy, J. D. and Zald, M. N. (1996) 'Introduction: opportunities, mobilizing structures, and framing processes – toward a synthetic, comparative perspective on social movements', in D. McAdam, J. D. McCarthy and M. N. Zald (eds) *Comparative Perspectives on Social Movements: Political Opportunities, Mobilizing Structures, and Cultural Framings*, Cambridge: Cambridge University Press.

Macdonald, L. (1997) *Supporting Civil Society: The Political Role of Non-governmental Organizations in Central America*, London: Macmillan and New York: St Martin's Press.

McFaul, M. A. (2002) 'Introduction' (to special issue on civil society), *Demokratizatsiya* 10, 2: 109–16.

McIntosh Sundstrom, L. (2001) 'Transnational norms in domestic contexts: The cases of women's and soldiers' rights NGOs in Russia', Paper presented at the 2001 Annual Meeting of the American Political Science Association, San Francisco, August 30–September 2.

—— (2002) 'Women's NGOs in Russia: Struggling from the margins', *Demokratizatsiya* 10, 2: 207–29.

McMann, K. M. and Petrov, N. V. (2000) 'A survey of democracy in Russia's regions', *Post-Soviet Geography and Economics* 41, 3: 155–82.

Marsh, C. (2000a) *Making Russian Democracy Work: Social Capital, Economic Development, and Democratization*, Lewiston, NY: The Edwin Mellen Press.

—— (2000b) 'Social capital and democracy in Russia', *Communist and Post-Communist Studies* 33: 183–99.

Memorial, http://www.memo.ru/eng/index.htm

Mendelson, S. E. and Glenn, J. K. (eds) (2002) *The Power and Limits of NGOs: A Critical Look at Building Democracy in Eastern Europe and Eurasia*, New York: Columbia University Press.

Meyer, D. S. and Marullo, S. (1992) 'Grassroots mobilization and international politics: Peace protest and the end of the Cold War', in L. Kriesberg and D. Segal (eds) *The Transformation of European Communist Societies*, Greenwich, CT: JAI Press (Research in Social Movements, Conflicts and Change vol. 14).

Miller, R. F. (ed.) (1992) *The Development of Civil Society in Communist Systems*, Sydney: Allen & Unwin.

Mishler, W. and Rose, R. (1997) 'Trust, distrust and skepticism: Popular evaluations of civil and political institutions in post-communist societies', *The Journal of Politics* 59, 2: 418–51.

Moore, B. (1966) *The Social Origins of Dictatorship and Democracy*, Boston, MA: Beacon Press.

Muiznieks, N. R. (1995) 'The influence of the Baltic popular movements on the process of Soviet disintegration', *Europe-Asia Studies* 47, 1.

Nechemias, C. (1991) 'The prospects for a Soviet women's movement: Opportunities and obstacles', in J. B. Sedaitis and J. Butterfield (eds) *Perestroika from Below: Social Movements in the Soviet Union*, Boulder, CO: Westview Press.

Neidhardt, F. and Rucht, D. (1991) 'The analysis of social movements: The state of the art and some perspectives for further research', in D. Rucht (ed.) *Research on Social Movements: the State of the Art in Western Europe and the USA*, Frankfurt: Campus Verlag and Boulder, CO: Westview Press.

Nikitin, A. and Buchanan, J. (2002) 'The Kremlin's civic forum: Cooperation or co-optation for civil society in Russia?' *Demokratizatsiya* 10, 2: 147–65.

Nodia, G. (2002) 'How different are postcommunist transitions?', in L. Diamond and M. F. Plattner (eds) *Democracy after Communism*, Baltimore, MD: The Johns Hopkins University Press.

O'Brien, R., Williams, M., Goetz, A. M. and Scholte, J. A. (2000) *Contesting Global Governance: Multilateral Economic Institutions and Global Social Movements*, Cambridge: Cambridge University Press.

O'Donnell, G. and Schmitter, P.C. (1986) *Transitions from Authoritarian Rule: Tentative Conclusions about Uncertain Democracies*, Baltimore, MD: Johns Hopkins University Press.

Orttung, R. W. (1995) *From Leningrad to St Petersburg: Democratization in a Russian City*, New York: St Martin's Press.

Ostrowska, I. (1997) 'The developing civil society: Peculiarities in Latvia', in R. Hjerppe, T. Kanninen, H. Patomäki and K. Sehm (eds) *Democracy, Economy and Civil Society in Transition: The Cases of Russia and the Baltic States*, Helsinki: The Finnish Institute of International Affairs, UPI, and the National Research and Development Center of Welfare and Health, STAKES.

Owens, B. (2002) 'The independent press in Russia: Integrity and the economics of survival', in C. Marsh and N. K. Gvosdev (eds) *Civil Society and the Search for Justice in Russia*, Lanham, MD: Lexington Books.

Ozolina, I. (2003) 'Associational voluntarism and social capital in the Baltic states', in E. Loftsson and Y. Choe (eds) *Political Representation and Participation in Transitional Democracies: Estonia, Latvia and Lithuania*, Huddinge: Södertörns högskola (Södertörn Academic Studies 10).

Pabriks, A. and Purs, A. (2002) *Latvia: The Challenges of Change*, London: Routledge.

Pagnucco, R. (1995) 'The comparative study of social movements and democratization: Political interaction and political process approaches', *Research on Social Movements, Conflict and Change* 18: 145–83.

Pateman, C. (1970) *Participation and Democratic Theory*, Cambridge: Cambridge University Press.

Patomäki, H. and Pursiainen, C. (1998) *Against the State, With(in) the State, or a Transnational Creation: Russian Civil Society in the Making?* The Finnish Institute of International Affairs, Working Papers 4.

—— (1999) 'Western models and "Russian idea": Beyond "inside/outside" in discourses on civil society', *Millennium: Journal of International Studies* 28, 1: 53–77.

Pearce, J. (2000) 'Development, NGOs, and civil society: The debate and its future', in D. Eade (ed.) *Development, NGOs, and Civil Society*, London: Oxfam.

Petersson, B. (2001) *National Self-Images and Regional Identities in Russia*, Aldershot: Ashgate.

Petro, N. (1991) 'Perestroika from below: Voluntary sociopolitical associations in the RSFSR', in A. J. Rieber and A. Z. Rubinstein (eds) *Perestroika at the Crossroads*, Armonk, NY: M. E. Sharpe.

—— (1999) 'The Novgorod region: A Russian success story', *Post-Soviet Affairs* 15, 3: 235–61.

—— (2002) 'A Russian model of development: What Novgorod can teach the west', in C. Marsh and N. K. Gvosdev (eds) *Civil Society and the Search for Justice in Russia*, Lanham, MD: Lexington Books.

Piper, N. and Uhlin, A. (2004) 'New perspectives on transnational activism', in N. Piper and A. Uhlin (eds) *Transnational Activism in Asia: Problems of Power and Democracy*, London: Routledge.

Plakans, A. (1997) 'Democratization and political participation in postcommunist societies: The case of Latvia', in K. Dawisha and B. Parrott (eds) *The Consolidation of Democracy in East-Central Europe*, Cambridge: Cambridge University Press.

Porter, T. E. (1991) *The Zemstvo and the Emergence of Civil Society in Late Imperial Russia 1864–1917*, San Francisco, CA: Mellen Research University Press.

Powell, L. (2002) 'Western and Russian environmental NGOs: A greener Russia?' in S. E. Mendelson and J. K. Glenn (eds) *The Power and Limits of NGOs: A Critical Look at Building Democracy in Eastern Europe and Eurasia*, New York: Columbia University Press.

Przeworski, A. (1991) *Democracy and the Market: Political and Economic Reforms in Eastern Europe and Latin America*, New York: Cambridge University Press.

Putnam, R. D. (1993) *Making Democracy Work: Civic Traditions in Modern Italy*, Princeton, NJ: Princeton University Press.

—— (2000) *Bowling Alone: The Collapse and Revival of American Community*, London: Simon & Schuster.

Racioppi, L. and O'Sullivan See, K. (1997) *Women's Activism in Contemporary Russia*, Philadelphia, PA: Temple University Press.

Rau, Z. (ed.) (1991) *The Reemergence of Civil Society in Eastern Europe and the Soviet Union*, Boulder, CO: Westview Press.

Raun, T. U. (1997) 'Democratization and political development in Estonia, 1987–96', in K. Dawisha and B. Parrott (eds) *The Consolidation of Democracy in East-Central Europe*, Cambridge: Cambridge University Press.

Richter, J. (2002) 'Evaluating Western assistance to Russian women's organizations' in S. E. Mendelson and J. K. Glenn (eds) *The Power and Limits of NGOs: A Critical Look at Building Democracy in Eastern Europe and Eurasia*, New York: Columbia University Press.

Rodan, G. (1997) 'Civil society and other political possibilities in Southeast Asia', *Journal of Contemporary Asia* 27, 2: 156–78.

Rucht, D. (1999) 'The transnationalization of social movements: Trends, causes, problems', in D. della Porta and H. Kriesi (eds) *Social Movements in a Globalizing World*, London: Macmillan.

Rueschemeyer, D., Stephens, E. H. and Stephens, J. D. (1992) *Capitalist Development and Democracy*, Cambridge: Polity Press.

Ruffin, M. H., Deutschler, A., Logan, C. and Upjohn, R. (1999) *The Post-Soviet Handbook: A Guide to Grassroots Organizations and Internet Resources in the Newly Independent States*, (Revised edn), Seattle, WA: Center for Civil Society International in association with University of Washington Press.

Ruutsoo, R. (2002) *Civil Society and Nation Building in Estonia and the Baltic States: Impact of Traditions on Mobilization and Transition 1986–2000 – Historical and Sociological Study*, Rovaniemi: Lapin Yliopisto, Acta Universitatis Lapponiensis 49.

Sakwa, R. (1998) *Soviet Politics in Perspective*, (2nd edn), London: Routledge.

—— (2002) *Russian Politics and Society*, (3rd edn), London: Routledge.

Scholte, J. A. (1999) *Global Civil Society: Changing the World?* University of Warwick, Coventry: Centre for the Study of Globalisation and Regionalisation Working Paper No. 31/99.

—— (2004) 'Civil society and democratically accountable global governance', *Government and Opposition* 39, 2: 211–33.

Schumpeter, J. (1976) *Capitalism, Socialism and Democracy*, London: George Allen & Unwin.

Sedaitis, J. B. (1991) 'Worker activism: Politics at the grass roots', in J. B. Sedaitis and J. Butterfield (eds) *Perestroika from Below: Social Movements in the Soviet Union*, Boulder, CO: Westview Press.

Sedaitis, J. B. and Butterfield, J. (eds) (1991) *Perestroika from Below: Social Movements in the Soviet Union*, Boulder, CO: Westview Press.

Shevtsova, L. (2002) 'Russia's hybrid regime', in L. Diamond and M. F. Plattner (eds) *Democracy after Communism*, Baltimore, MD: The Johns Hopkins University Press.

Shineleva, L. T. (2002) *Obschchestvennye Nepravitelstvennye Organizatsii i Vlast* (Non-governmental organizations and power), Moscow: Dashkov.

Skilling, H. G. (1971) 'Interest groups and communist politics: An introduction', in G. Skilling and F. Griffiths (eds) *Interest Groups in Soviet Politics*, Princeton, NJ: Princeton University Press.

Slider, D. (1997) 'Regional and local politics', in S. White, A. Pravda and Z. Gitelman (eds) *Developments in Russian Politics 4*, Basingstoke: Macmillan.

Smith, J. and Johnston, H. (eds) (2002) *Globalization and Resistance: Transnational dimensions of social movements*, Lanham, MD: Rowman & Littlefield.

Smith, J., Chatfield, C. and Pagnucco, R. (eds) (1997) *Transnational Social Movements and Global Politics: Solidarity Beyond the State*, New York: Syracuse University Press.

Smith-Sivertsen, H. (1998) 'Latvia', in S. Berglund, T. Hellén and F. H. Aarebrot (eds) *The Handbook of Political Change in Eastern Europe*, Cheltenham: Edward Elgar.

Smolar, A. (2002) 'Civil society after communism', in L. Diamond and M. F. Plattner (eds) *Democracy after Communism*, Baltimore, MD: The Johns Hopkins University Press.

Soldiers' Mothers of St Petersburg (1999) 'Non-Governmental Presentation', (Paper)

Sperling, V. (1999) *Organizing Women in Contemporary Russia: Engendering Transition*, Cambridge: Cambridge University Press.

Squier, J. (2002) 'Civil society and the challenge of Russian *gosudarstvennost*', *Demokratizatsiya* 10, 2: 166–82.

St Petersburg Government and infoDev St Petersburg Project Organization (1999) 'The Baltic Sea information society project – Start up: Information society strategy for St Petersburg', Washington, DC: infoDev/The World Bank.

Steen, A. (2003) *Political Elites and the New Russia: The Power Basis of Yeltsin's and Putin's Regimes*, London: RoutledgeCurzon.

Stiles, K. W. (2000) 'Grassroots empowerment: States, non-state actors and global policy formulation', in R. A. Higgot, G. R. D. Underhill and A. Bieler (eds) *Non-State Actors and Authority in the Global System*, London: Routledge.

Stoner-Weiss, K. (1997) *Local Heroes: The Political Economy of Russian Regional Governance*, Princeton, NJ: Princeton University Press.

Stubbergaard, Y. (1998) 'Civilt samhälle och demokrati' (Civil society and democracy), *Statsvetenskaplig tidskrift* 101, 1: 3–14.

Sundstrom, L. (2003) 'Limits to global civil society: Gaps between Western donors and Russian NGOs', in G. Laxer and S. Halperin (eds) *Global Civil Society and its Limits*, Basingstoke: Palgrave Macmillan.

Szücs, S. (1998) *Democracy in the Head: A Comparative Analysis of Democratic Leadership Orientations among Local Elites in Three Phases of Democratization*, Department of Political Science, Göteborg University, Göteborg Studies in Politics No. 52.

Tarrow, S. (1998) *Power in Movement: Social Movements and Contentious Politics* (2nd edn), Cambridge: Cambridge University Press.

Temkina, A. (1997) *Russia in Transition: The Cases of New Collective Actors and New Collective Actions*, Jyväskylä: Kikimora Publications.

Thomas, D. C. (1999) 'The Helsinki accords and political change in Eastern Europe', in T. Risse, S. C. Ropp and K. Sikkink (eds) *The Power of Human Rights: International Norms and Domestic Change*, Cambridge: Cambridge University Press.

Tsygankov, A. (1998) 'Manifestations of delegative democracy in Russian local politics: What does it mean for the future of Russia?', *Communist and Post-Communist Studies* 31, 4: 329–44.

Tysiachniouk, M. and Reisman, J. (2002) 'Civil society and global security: Russia's decision to import spent nuclear fuel', *Journal of Eurasian Research* 1, 2.

Uhlin, A. (1997) *Indonesia and the 'Third Wave' of Democratization: The Indonesian Pro-democracy Movement in a Changing World*, Richmond: Curzon Press.

—— (2002) 'Globalization, democratization and civil society in Southeast Asia: Observations from Malaysia and Thailand', in C. Kinnvall and K. Jönsson (eds) *Globalization and Democratization in Asia*, London: Routledge.

Umland, A. (2002) 'Toward an uncivil society? Contextualizing the decline of post-Soviet Russian parties of the extreme right wing', *Demokratizatsiya* 10, 3: 362–91.

Urban, M. (with Igrunov, V. and Mitrokhin, S.) (1997) *The Rebirth of Politics in Russia*, Cambridge: Cambridge University Press.

Van Rooy, A. and Robinson, M. (1998) 'Out of the ivory tower: Civil society and the aid system', in A. Van Rooy (ed.) *Civil Society and the Aid Industry: The Politics and Promise*, London: Earthscan.

Vanhanen, T. (1997) *Prospects of Democracy: A Study of 172 Countries*, London: Routledge.

Volodin, A. G. (ed.) (1998) *Grazhdanskoe Obshchestvo: Mirovoy Opyt i Problemy Rossii* (Civil society: World Experience and Russia's Problems), Moscow: Editorial URSS.

Walzer, M. (1992) 'The civil society argument', in C. Mouffe (ed.) *Dimensions of Radical Democracy: Pluralism, Citizenship, Community*, London: Verso.

Warren, M. E. (2001) *Democracy and Association*, Princeton, NJ: Princeton University Press.

Wartenweiler, D. (1999) *Civil Society and Academic Debate in Russia 1905–1914*, Oxford: Clarendon Press.

Waylen, G. (1994) 'Women and democratization: Conceptualizing gender relations in transition politics' *World Politics* 46, 3: 327–54.

Weigle, M. A. (2000) *Russia's Liberal Project: State–society relations in the transition from communism*, University Park, PA: The Pennsylvania State University Press.

—— (2002) 'On the road to the civic forum: State and civil society from Yeltsin to Putin', *Demokratizatsiya* 10, 2: 117–46.

Weigle, M. A. and Butterfield, J. (1992) 'Civil society in reforming communist regimes: The logic of emergence', *Comparative Politics* 25: 1–23.

Weiler, J. D. (2002) 'Human rights in post-Soviet Russia', *Demokratizatsiya* 10, 2: 257–76.

Werning Rivera, S., Kozyreva, P. M. and Sarovskii, E. G. (2002) 'Interviewing political elites: Lessons from Russia', *PS: Political Science and Politics* 35, 4: 683–88.

White, A. (1999) *Democratization in Russia under Gorbachev, 1985–91: The Birth of a Voluntary Sector*, New York: St Martin's Press.

White, G. (1994) 'Civil society, democratization and development (I): Clearing the analytical ground', *Democratisation* 1, 3: 375–90.

White, S. (2000) *Russia's New Politics: The Management of a Postcommunist Society*, Cambridge: Cambridge University Press.

White, S. and McAllister, I. (2004) 'Dimensions of disengagement in post-communist Russia', *Journal of Communist Studies and Transition Politics* 20, 1: 81–97.

Wolfson, Z. and Butenko, V. (1992) 'The green movement in the USSR and Eastern Europe', in M. Finger (ed.) *The Green Movement Worldwide* (Research in Social Movements, Conflicts and Change, Supplement 2), Greenwich, CT: JAI Press.

Zaleski, P. (2001) 'The nongovernmental elite', in M. Schemmann and M. Bron Jr. (eds) *Adult Education and Democratic Citizenship IV*, Krakow: Impuls.

Zdravomyslova, E. (1996) 'Opportunities and framing in the transition to democracy: The case of Russia', in D. McAdam, J. D. McCarthy and M. N. Zald (eds) *Comparative Perspectives on Social Movements: Political Opportunities, Mobilizing Structures, and Cultural Framings*, Cambridge: Cambridge University Press.

Zepa, B. (ed.) (1999) *Conditions of Enhancement of Civic Participation*, Riga: Baltic Data House.

Zeruolis, D. (1998) 'Lithuania', in S. Berglund, T. Hellén and F. H. Aarebrot (eds) *The Handbook of Political Change in Eastern Europe*, Cheltenham: Edward Elgar.

Ziegler, C. E. (1991) 'Environmental politics and policy under *perestroika*', in J. B. Sedaitis and J. Butterfield (eds) *Perestroika from Below: Social Movements in the Soviet Union*, Boulder, CO: Westview Press.

Interviews

I use a code with one or two letters indicating to which category the respondent belongs, and a number to distinguish between respondents. E = environmental, HR = human rights, L = labour, O = other, S = state, SW = social welfare, W = women.

Novgorod

Interview E1: Ecology Club 'Ekologija', Inessa Antonovna Pochotova, Novgorod, 23 April 2001.

Interview E2: Borovichy's Ecology Club, Leonid Ivanovich Bykov, Borovichy, 20 October 2001.

Interview E3: *Nos 4* (ecological organisation), Marina Alekseyeva, Borovichy, 20 October 2001.

Interview HR1: United Democratic Centre, Igor Borisovich Alexandrov, Novgorod, 23 April 2001.

Interview O1: North-Western Community Development Centre, Roman Zolin, Novgorod, 23 April 2001.

Interview O2: Resource Centre, Galina Mikhailovna Masley, Starya Russa, 24 April 2001.

Interview O3: Consumer Rights, Nina Lvovna Zhigulyova, Starya Russa, 24 April 2001.

Interview S1: Vice-Mayor and Vice-Chairman of Novgorod City Duma, Sergei A. Bessonov, Novgorod, 19 October 2001.

Interview S2: Novgorod City Administration, Head of Department for Media and Public Relations, Alexander Strekin, Novgorod, 19 October 2001.

Interview W1: Centre for Support for Women Entrepreneurs – 'Happiness', Irina Yurevna Shulga, Starya Russa, 24 April 2001.

Pskov

Interview HR2: *Veche*, Venedikt Ivanovich and Nadezhda Pavlovna, Pskov, 20 April 2001.

Interview HR3: Soldiers' Mothers of Pskov, Valentina Afanaseva, Pskov, 20 April 2001.

Interview L1: Construction Workers Union, Vyacheslav Polupanov, Pskov, 18 October 2001.

Interview O4: Recreation, (Vozrozhdenie), Viktor Ostrenko, Pskov, 19 April 2001.

Interview O5: Regional Centre for People's Creativity, Larisa Fyodorova, Pskov, 18 October 2001.

Interview S3: Pskov City Administration, specialist on NGOs, Sofia Belyakova, Pskov, 17 October 2001.

Interview W2: Union of Women, (regional organisation), Elena Vasilevna Pokkas, Pskov, 19 April 2001.

Interview W3: Union of Women's and Youth Initiatives, Tatyana Ryzhova, Pskov, 19 April 2001.

St Petersburg

Interview E4: Greenhipp, Anton Lustberg, St Petersburg, 26 April 2001.

Interview E5: Green World, Sosnovy Bor, Oleg Bodrov, St Petersburg, 27 April 2001.

Interview HR4: Memorial, Venyamin Yofe, St Petersburg, 26 April 2001.

Interview HR5: Soldiers' Mothers of St Petersburg, Elena Y. Vilenskaya, St Petersburg, 26 April 2001.

Interview HR6: St Petersburg Public Foundation for Galina Starovoitova, Olga Starovoitova, St Petersburg, 27 April 2001.

Interview L2: Council of Labour Unions 'Unity', Vadim A. Sukach, St Petersburg, 22 October 2001.

Interview O6: Regional Political Party 'Free St Petersburg', Sergei Balnev, St Petersburg, 25 April 2001.

Interview O7: Council of Veterans of St Petersburg and Leningrad Oblast, Ivan Ivanovich Korobov, St Petersburg, 24 October 2001.

Interview S4: St Petersburg City Administration, Department for International Relations, Elena Nikandrova, St Petersburg, 22 October 2001.

Interview S5: St Petersburg City Administration, Department for Public Relations, Andrei Vetrov, St Petersburg, 23 October 2001.

Interview S6: Walking Together, Terenti Aleshcheryakov, St Petersburg, 23 October 2001.

Interview SW1: Shelter, Valeri Sokolov, St Petersburg, 28 April 2001.

Seminar

Evgeniya Machonina, St Petersburg NGO Development Centre, 8 March 2001, Stockholm, Forum Syd.

Personal communications

Elena Belokurova, European University, St Petersburg, 25 April 2001, 22 October 2001, 23 October 2001.

Elena Zdravomyslova and Anna Temkina, European University, St Petersburg, 5 October 1999.

Index

For Product Safety Concerns and Information please contact our EU
representative GPSR@taylorandfrancis.com
Taylor & Francis Verlag GmbH, Kaufingerstraße 24, 80331 München, Germany

www.ingramcontent.com/pod-product-compliance
Lightning Source LLC
Chambersburg PA
CBHW050435280326
41932CB00013BA/2119

* 9 7 8 0 4 1 5 4 4 4 0 5 7 *